The Complete Copywriter

The Complete Copywriter

The definitive guide to marketing with words

Alan Barker

KoganPage

Publisher's note

Every possible effort has been made to ensure that the information contained in this book is accurate at the time of going to press, and the publishers and authors cannot accept responsibility for any errors or omissions, however caused. No responsibility for loss or damage occasioned to any person acting, or refraining from action, as a result of the material in this publication can be accepted by the editor, the publisher or the author.

First published in Great Britain and the United States in 2025 by Kogan Page Limited

Apart from any fair dealing for the purposes of research or private study, or criticism or review, as permitted under the Copyright, Designs and Patents Act 1988, this publication may only be reproduced, stored or transmitted, in any form or by any means, with the prior permission in writing of the publishers, or in the case of reprographic reproduction in accordance with the terms and licences issued by the CLA. Enquiries concerning reproduction outside these terms should be sent to the publishers at the undermentioned addresses:

2nd Floor, 45 Gee Street
London
EC1V 3RS
United Kingdom

8 W 38th Street, Suite 902
New York, NY 10018
USA

www.koganpage.com

Kogan Page books are printed on paper from sustainable forests.

© Alan Barker, 2025

The right of Alan Barker to be identified as the author of this work has been asserted by him in accordance with the Copyright, Designs and Patents Act 1988.

All trademarks, service marks, and company names are the property of their respective owners.

ISBNs

Hardback	978 1 3986 1355 3
Paperback	978 1 3986 1353 9
Ebook	978 1 3986 1354 6

British Library Cataloguing-in-Publication Data

A CIP record for this book is available from the British Library.

Library of Congress Control Number

2024950244

Typeset by Integra Software Services, Pondicherry
Print production managed by Jellyfish
Printed and bound by CPI Group (UK) Ltd, Croydon, CR0 4YY

CONTENTS

INTERLUDE 5

What about AI?

PART SIX

Surviving and thriving

Introduction

Can I justify the title of this book? What, after all, is a Complete Copywriter?

Well, I've written the book in part as a response to the books that currently exist on copywriting. Most of them, in my experience, focus almost exclusively on sales copy. But the copywriters I work with regularly write much more, and much more varied, copy. Marketing is no longer just about advertising – if indeed it ever was – and copy is no longer just about selling. If you want evidence, look at the growth of content writing, which demands the skills of journalism as much as the skills of marketing. *The Complete Copywriter* will help you to produce both great copy and great content.

Another change is in the range of organizations using copywriters. More than ever before, we're hired or employed by national and local government, in international agencies and in not-for-profits. If we're not marketing products or services, we're promoting ideas or helping people contribute to change. I wanted to help every copywriter, wherever they work.

The existing books also strangely tend to bypass the idea of copywriting *as writing*. I wanted to celebrate our craft, and how we apply that craft in our work.

The Complete Copywriter presents a method. It's assembled into six sections that take you from where you are – at your desk, trying to find the right words – outwards into the workplace where, with luck, you make your money.

Part 1: You and the copy starts with your core skills as a writer and how copy works.

Part 2: Planning the copy looks at the three essential elements of planning: understanding your reader, articulating your argument or proposition, and finding an appropriate voice.

Part 3: Shaping the copy covers ways of structuring the copy and how we choose between those structures – or, sometimes, combine them.

Part 4: Bringing your copy to life talks about how to use sentences and words – especially verbs and nouns – to energize your writing and avoid the perils of zombie copy.

Part 5: Content planning puts our skills into a strategic context and applies them to various types of copy and content.

Part 6: Surviving and thriving: copywriting as a career, finally, explores your working relationships with other creatives and with clients, and how you can make a successful career.

There's no need to work through the book from start to finish. *The Complete Copywriter* is a guide – as with any guide, you can use it wherever you happen to be in the copywriting landscape. I also show you how to take productive and enjoyable journeys around that landscape: look out for 'Find out more' boxes that point you in different directions. Choose the journeys that offer you the most benefit.

You'll also find plenty of exercises here. Look for the white boxes in each chapter. A few are one-off tests with correct answers (supplied at the end of the relevant chapter). Most are not tests at all; you can repeat them, and I strongly recommend that you do so. You can do them in any order and as often as you like. I may be offering you a method, but it's not a curriculum and you're not going to be examined. You are completely in charge of the route you take. I hope that, eventually, you'll explore the whole landscape of copywriting and emerge as something close to that ideal, the Complete Copywriter.

I've taken inspiration from many people. First and foremost, I've learned a huge amount from the hundreds of copywriters I've worked with on the Copywriting Masterclass run by the Chartered Institute of Marketing. They showed me why I needed to write this book. To all of them, my heartfelt thanks.

I'm also grateful to thinkers and writers, past and present, whose ideas have informed my own. Some of them I mention at an appropriate point, others I refer to in Chapter 19, which lists resources to inspire you further. Those people include Linda Anderson, Aristotle, David Abbott, Tom Albrighton, Kim Arnold, Walter Benjamin, Nerissa Bentley, John Bevins, Edward de Bono, Claudia Bourna, Dorothea Brande, Kenneth Burke, Kristin Byron, Julia Cameron, John Caples, Robert Cialdini, Roy Peter Clark, MaryLou Costa, Mihály Csíkszentmihályi, Angela Denly, Dusty DiMercurio, Yellowlees Douglas, Peter Elbow, Harold Evans, Estelle Fallon, Susan Fournier, Joe Friedlein, Seth Godin, Remy Gieling, Joe Griffin, Brian

Halligan, Steve Harrison, Sam Hayakawa, Bob Hoffman, Tom Hollihan, Wendy Ann Jones, Beth Kempton, Peter Koechley, Justin Kruger, Michael Lanning, Lara Lee, Bob Levenson, George Loewenstein, Clare Lynch, Ed McCabe, Steve McCornish, Larry McEnerney, Andy Maslen, Michael Masterson, Tim Mellors, Edward Michaels, Jamie Michaels, Donald Miller, Barbara Minto, Alan Monroe, Joe Moran, David Ogilvy, Randy Olson, Alexander Osterwalder, Nick Parker, David Perkins, Lauren Plug, Gary Provost, Rosser Reeves, Tim Riley, Joe Rospars, Bruce Ross, Erica Santiago, Eddy Shleyner, Eugene Schwartz, Ellen Sluder, Matthew Stafford, John Stingley, Lyndall Talbot, Rashidi Tayabali, Ivan Tyrell, Louise Willder, Henry Williams, Joseph M Williams and Maryanne Wolf.

Finally, my thanks to my wife, Gillian, and my daughter, Imogen. They both read through the manuscript several times and kept me – in all sorts of ways – on the straight and narrow.

PART ONE

You and the copy

In this first part of the book, we look at the relationship between you and your work.

- Chapter 1 looks at what it means to be a writer. What skills do you need? What habits can you cultivate?
- Chapter 2 looks at copy. What is it? How does it work? How does it create a relationship between you and your reader? And how does copywriting fit into the broader strategies of marketing?

1

Being a writer

This chapter is all about you.

You're a copywriter. Whatever your situation – working in a marketing team, or for a copywriting agency, or as a freelancer – one thing's for certain.

You're a writer.

And I assume that you're reading this book because you want to become a better writer.

So: where to start?

ASSESSING COPY

Find a piece of copy that you think is well written – or, maybe, *quite* well written. It could be anywhere: on a website, on a food packet, in an email, on the street.

Copy it out. Take the time to copy the copy, word for word, into a Word file. Print it off. Read it carefully.

- What do you like about this copy? Why do you think it works well? Make some notes.
- Now ask: what's wrong with this copy? How could you improve it?

Rewrite the copy. That might mean changing no more than a word or two. It might mean rewriting it wholesale. Try to keep to the original word count: no more and no less.

Is your new version better than the original? How would you judge?

Get into the habit

Writing well is not a gift. It's a habit.

The best way to become a better writer is to write. You need to keep at it. If you're earning money as a writer, your client won't wait for you to be inspired; you'll need to be able to hit the word count and the deadline.

Which means you need to practise. And the best kind of practise – as with running or anything else – is little and often. When do you work most productively? For me, drafting is morning work and the afternoons are for editing. You might be different. Don't ignore the times when inspiration might strike: late at night, first thing in the morning, when you're relaxing or doing something else. Be ready for those moments. But don't rely on them.

CREATING A RITUAL

Writing demands a space off to the side of real life. We need to quieten the noise and bring our full attention to the work.

If you're working in a hectic, open-plan office, finding that space might be tricky. If you're a lonely freelancer working out of your spare room, life might keep tempting you outside.

Create a ritual. It could be making a pot of tea, or going for a short walk, or simply sitting and concentrating on your breathing. Whatever you choose to do, do it every single time to prepare to write. The ritual will let your brain know that you're about to begin and that you're coaxing it to be creative.

Exercise your writing muscles

Writing calls on unusual muscles. In 1934, Dorothea Brande published *Becoming a Writer*, in which she suggested a method for giving those muscles a gentle warm-up. 'The best way to do this,' she wrote, 'is to rise half an hour, or a full hour, earlier than you customarily rise. Just as soon as you can – and without talking, without reading the morning's paper, without picking up the book you laid aside the night before – begin to write. Write anything that comes into your head... Write any sort of early morning reverie, rapidly and uncritically.' The aim of the exercise is to write something that's not pure nonsense.

Julia Cameron popularized this exercise in her book, *The Artist's Way*, published in 1992, and called it Morning Pages. Cameron sets three rules for creating these pages:

- Do it first thing in the morning.
- Write in longhand.
- Complete three sides of A4.

That last rule is important. It's difficult to write about *nothing* for three whole pages. Something interesting is likely to appear. And you must stop after three pages.

Morning Pages, like an early morning jog, can have all sorts of benefits. It can calm your fears and provoke new ideas. It's also completely private – which can be helpful if your professional writing is under constant scrutiny.

Give it a go. All you need to start is an alarm clock, a pen and a notebook. And a little determination.

START A NOTEBOOK

Good writing feeds on ideas. Everything that happens to you – what you see, hear, think and feel – can contribute to your work.

Start a notebook. Jot down:

- observations while you're working, from meetings, or out and about
- your rants and raves
- writing exercises (like the ones in this book)
- memories
- inspirational ideas for copy, blog posts, headlines…

Your notebook is personal and private. Nobody else should ever read it. Keep project-specific work in separate files.

Don't forget to read

Now, I don't want to come on all heavy about the improving benefits of reading. Many of us were put off reading at school or college. If that's you, then I strongly urge you to rekindle (sorry) your love of reading. Reading should be pleasurable. But, for copywriters, reading brings other benefits too.

To begin with, the more you read, the more *efficiently* you read. The more efficiently you can read, the better you'll do all that market research.

Reading will also help you broaden your horizons. The better we can understand different points of view, the more creative our work will be.

Most importantly, reading will help you write. Of course, it helps to read stuff that's well written, but that doesn't mean you should restrict yourself to serious literature. Or even books.

- **Read what you enjoy reading.** Be guided by your taste. Check out interesting magazines and blogs. Read reviews and suggestions from readers on social media or blogs. But discriminate: seek out good writing. Find good writers and follow them.

- **Browse bookshops and libraries.** Let yourself be tempted.

- **Read widely. Read more than one book at a time.** (Yes, you can!) If a book bores you, don't hesitate to put it down and try something else.

- **Keep a reading journal.** It might be no more than a list of the books you read, with dates. But you can also add notes about them, or quotations from them, or thoughts inspired by them.

- **Join a reading circle.** Or a book club. That way, you can make reading a sociable activity. Discussing your reading with others also helps you develop your critical skills.

Here's the bottom line: reading feeds writing. They go together.

WRITE A BLURB

Pick a book that you read recently or that means a lot to you: maybe a book that you loved as a child.

Write a blurb that would go on the back cover of a new edition. What is the book about? What makes it different? This blurb will be read by someone browsing in a bookshop, or online. How can you entice them to buy the book?

Maximum word count: 200 words.

Four core competences of copywriting

These skills sit at the heart of your work:

- curiosity;
- mental mobility'

- design thinking;
- objectivity.

And we can understand these skills as sitting within the process of writing: a process that has two stages.

1 At Stage One, we look at the brief – or the product, or the task of the day – and explore it or play around with it. Curiosity helps us discover new information. Mental mobility helps us discover new ideas.

2 At Stage Two, we create copy with what we've discovered. Design thinking helps us craft copy that fits together well and looks good. Objectivity helps us judge whether our copy fits the brief and does what it's supposed to do.

The great danger is that we might ignore Stage One. In the high-pressure environment of marketing, we might feel driven to Stage Two: we leap into solution mode and fail to allow first-stage thinking to do its work. But the quality of our work at Stage Two depends directly on the quality of our work at Stage One. Starve your curiosity or your ability to play around and the resulting copy will be formulaic and uninspiring.

DEVELOPING YOUR CORE COMPETENCES

As you work through the rest of this chapter, think about where you already use these four skills and which ones you could begin to develop further.

Make some notes and draw up an action plan. Work on one skill at a time.

Curiosity

Copywriters sometimes ask me, 'How can I write about something that's boring?'

I think the answer is to be curious. Ask lots of questions. Research your products, your organization and your readers. (Who finds this subject fascinating? Ask *them*.) The more questions you ask, the more interesting the subject will become – and the more interesting your copy will be.

EXPLORING A WORD

Pick a word. It might be a word that you are using in a current copywriting project. It could be a word that figures largely in your company or industry. Alternatively, pick a word using a random word generator: you'll find one online. Ideally, choose a word that has more than one meaning.

Research the word. Use books, online resources and your own experience. You could also ask friends and colleagues what the word means to them.

- List the meanings of the word in your own language.

- What's the equivalent word in another language? If you have colleagues who speak different languages, ask them. Explore how words translate between languages: one-to-one equivalences are rare. The subtle differences in meaning can be exciting and revealing.

- What's the etymology of the word? Where are its roots in other or older languages? How has the meaning of the word changed over time?

- Do people use the word in different ways? How does the word change its meaning in different circumstances or situations?

- Do people have misconceptions about the word or emotional responses that differ from person to person?

- Are there any controversies about the word? Perhaps people argue about the way to use it. Does the word challenge any assumptions or values? Are there any ways in which people might feel uncomfortable using the word?

Now write a 500-word article for a blog called *Interesting Words*. If the word is commonly used in your company or industry, this article could be great copy for a newsletter or blog post.

Mental mobility

Copywriters need to be able to think about the same thing in different ways. You will be producing many different kinds of copy and content. If you're working for multiple clients, you'll need to switch voices and topics instantly. Versatility is the name of the game.

Change your point of view

The most obvious kind of mental mobility is changing your point of view. Look at the topic as someone else might look at it: your reader or customer, especially.

I think of copywriting as being rather like acting. You need to be able to take on another person's thoughts, feelings and values.

INVENTING A PERSON

Find an old photograph of someone, maybe in a junk shop. Or Google 'vintage photograph'. Give this person a name and imagine their life. Write some notes about them: their age, their family, their work, their dreams and desires and fears. Write about the world they inhabit and how they made their way through it. Fast forward a few decades (or back, if they're elderly) and write about what happened to them or how they came to be where they are now.

Now write 500 words *in the voice of the person you've invented*. Let them speak to you.

To find out more about constructing reader personas, go to Chapter 3.

Make new connections

We can also become more mentally mobile by making new connections between ideas.

Mostly, we make mental connections that we've made before. The more frequently we make the connection, the stronger it becomes. So, if we want to make *new* connections, we may have to trick our mind away from its usual habits. One way to do that is to allow the mind to relax – and let intuition do its work. Another way is to juxtapose ideas deliberately and see what connections arise: a technique sometimes called 'force-fitting'. (Google 'force-fitting idea generation' to find out more.)

WORD CLUSTERS

Words come surrounded by clouds of associations. When we're producing copy, these networks of associations can help us see our topic in new ways.

Pick a word that sits at the heart of a current copywriting project. Write the word in the centre of a page or a large piece of paper. Draw a circle around it.

Now, write down all the words and phrases that connect to that word in your mind. Let them fan out around the central word, as a mind map. (Google the phrase 'mind map' for more.) If you find that one of the new words sets off a new set of associations, add them to the map.

Explore the ways in which words connect. If you want to put a bit of structure on this exercise, think about making three types of associations:

- What things are similar to this word? The word *shoe*, for instance, might trigger words like *sandal*, *boot* or *horseshoe*.

- What things are close to the word? The word *clock* might trigger the words *timetable*, *tower* or *anxiety*. You might assemble closely related words into categories: the word *apple* might take you to *fruit* or *trees* – or *computers*.

- What things are the opposite of your chosen word? What's the opposite of *walking*, or *paper*, or *a blizzard*?

Now write three pieces of short copy based on any of these associations: 100–200 words each. They don't need to link to each other. See what ideas emerge.

Start a swipe file

You can increase your mental mobility by exploring what others have written. In an interview in 1996, Steve Jobs quoted Pablo Picasso. 'He said, "Good artists copy, great artists steal." And we have always been shameless about stealing great ideas.'

Actually, it might not have been Picasso. It might have been Igor Stravinsky, William Faulkner or T S Eliot. Nobody seems to know. The point remains: if you understand how a master has created their work, you can apply the lesson to your own work. Call it stealing, if you will. Call it sampling. Marketers often call it swiping. And they use a swipe file to do it.

A swipe file is a place where you store inspiration. Use it to jog your memory and find new ideas. You might use an old-style box file; you might create a digital swipe file. You can find apps and websites that will provide you with one.

WHAT TO INCLUDE?

You could include whole blog posts or parts of blog posts. You could include copy that's well structured or that tells a great story. You could collect content that demonstrates the canny use of words. You could include examples of clever graphics, ingenious combinations of text and image, or instances of tight and punchy social messaging.

If it excites you – swipe it.

A word of warning. Avoid plagiarism. To truly steal an idea, you have to take ownership of it. Rather than just copying the words, you discover the secret principle or the hidden technique behind the words, and then you apply the principle or use the technique in your own copy.

USING YOUR SWIPE FILE

Find a piece of copy that you think is worth swiping. Before you file it away, ask these questions:

- Why does this work?
- What methods or techniques is it using?
- What words is it using?
- How are the sentences constructed?
- How does the copy capture my attention and hold it to the end?
- How is the copy structured?
- Is every part of the copy equally good?
- What makes this copy different?

Now apply some of these techniques to a piece of copy that you're working on. Make it as different as possible from the copy that inspired you.

Design thinking

Design thinking is Stage Two thinking. We do design thinking to organize our ideas into copy that is elegant, neat and beautiful.

'You do not write copy,' wrote Eugene Schwartz, hailed as one of the best copywriters ever. 'You assemble it. You are working with a series of building blocks, you are putting the building blocks together, and then you are putting them in certain structures, you are building a little city of desire for your person to come and live in.'

WRITING A HAIKU

A haiku is a short, Japanese poetic form. Traditionally, it depicts a moment in time: a moment of awareness, insight, surprise or delight. A haiku usually depicts something in nature. It contains no reference to your feelings; indeed, it might not refer to you at all.

Writing a haiku shows us how words can work together, especially in very tight or limited forms. It also helps us evoke feelings without using emotional language – an essential copywriting skill, as we'll see later.

Here are some basic rules about how to write a haiku:

- It includes a reference to a season.
- It's written in the present tense.
- It includes a kireji or 'cutting word' ('kigo' in Japanese). In Japanese, a kireji is a grammatical category of words that create a pause or sense of closure. There is no direct equivalent to kireji in English; you might use punctuation like a dash or an ellipsis (three dots). But the haiku will usually juxtapose two things around this point.
- It's written in three lines. The first and third lines have five syllables, the second line has seven syllables. The lines never rhyme.

You'll find plenty of haiku online, many of which don't follow these guidelines rigorously.

Here's a haiku by Bashō, who is said to have invented the form of the haiku:

stillness.
sinking into the rocks –
the cicada's voice.

And here's one I wrote recently while staying at a house in the country:

Cockerel, pecking
scratching in dry leaves. Eyes me –
refuses to crow.

To discover how copy should evoke emotion, go to Chapter 5.

Objectivity

Objectivity means testing your work in the real world. Without objectivity, you might write copy that doesn't meet the brief or address your reader's needs.

Objectivity also means understanding the way language works. Without a solid grasp of grammar, punctuation and stylistics – how word choice affects your copy's voice – you could make embarrassing errors.

But this technical understanding of language should never inhibit your creativity. It's all too easy to become hung up on notions of correctness. Language doesn't operate by rules; it operates by conventions. And true objectivity understands that conventions change, from place to place and over time.

To learn more about the technicalities of language, go to Chapter 10 and Chapter 11.

You can develop your sense of objectivity in three ways. You could take a break before editing. You could read the copy aloud. (I strongly recommend doing this as a matter of habit.) Or you could ask someone else to read it for you and give you their honest opinion. Choose someone whose opinion you trust. Ask them to read the copy aloud without reading it first. Make a note wherever they stumble – it's a good sign that you could improve the copy at that point.

CULTIVATING OBJECTIVITY

Find a piece of copy that you wrote in the past. Go as far back into the past as you can.

How could you improve it?

Rewrite the copy, keeping as much as possible to the original brief (if you can remember it).

What about creativity?

Have I left out the most important skill of all?

In the marketing world, copywriters, along with graphic designers and video makers, are often labelled 'creatives'. But do you see yourself as creative? Angela Denly, a copywriter working out of Sydney, Australia, answered that question in a recent post on her blog.

'I don't see myself as a creative person. At least not in the way that is typically meant. You see, I don't do creative writing. I'm not working on my novel, I don't write poems for fun, I don't paint or make music or do any of the things that the general public will typically think of when you hear the word "creative". And neither do many of my copywriting mates.'

Angela asked some of those mates on a Facebook group, 'Do you need to be creative to be a copywriter?'

Some denied that creativity was part of the role. 'After copywriting for some years,' replied Rashidi Tayabali, 'I've understood how formulaic it is. The real skill is in writing simple and clear messages, not how creative one is with the words.' And Estelle Fallon commented, 'I haven't got a creative bone in my body, nor ever had a creative idea for writing. What I can do is take other people's ideas and make them sound good.'

Intriguingly, however, some colleagues highlighted the skills we've explored in this chapter. Lyndall Talbot, for instance, talked about curiosity. 'What I love about copywriting is that I get to play detective at my desk. I dig up information, assemble it so that everyone can understand it and then release my findings. It's the perfect job for a generalist who loves to learn and the writer who loves to communicate.'

And Nerissa Bentley described mental mobility. 'I add a bit of creativity by including elements such as interesting research studies or case studies. The words themselves might not be creative, but I'd argue that to make your writing stand out from the other boring, bland copy, you need to do something different and that's where the creativity comes in for me.'

Design thinking? 'To me,' said Claudia Bourna, 'copywriting is like making a jigsaw puzzle and you just have to figure out how to put the pieces together.'

Angela herself acknowledges the need for objectivity in her work. 'A lot of copywriting is actually very logical and an analytical process,' she says. 'Before I write a single word, there's a lot of time put into researching my client's point of difference, analysing customer needs, reading reviews to understand customer pain points and the language that they use.'

Maybe we need to change our idea of what it means to be creative. Creativity, like athletics or cookery, is a *set* of skills. And copywriting is applied creativity. It relates to creative writing in the same way that design relates to fine art: we're applying our creative skills to the demands of a client or a brief.

The rest of this book is all about how to do just that.

SUMMARY

Try any or all of the exercises in this chapter. Try them more than once.

   Get into the habit of writing – and reading.

   Regularly assess copy that you haven't written and rewrite it.

   Regularly assess copy you have written and rewrite it.

   Create a ritual for starting to write.

   Do Morning Pages to exercise your writing muscles.

   Start a notebook.

   Identify which of the four core writing skills you want to develop:

- Curiosity

- Mental mobility

- Design thinking

- Objectivity

Start a swipe file.

2

How copy works

You already know how copy works. You've been learning all your life.

Copy is everywhere. It's on the packaging in your food cupboard. It's on the brochures and leaflets that crowd out your post. It's in the leaflet from the local takeaway. It's on posters and public notices as you walk down the street. It's in magazines and newspapers: not just the ads, but the articles too.

And, of course, there's copy on the screens you use: paid search ads on search engines; banner ads; social media ads; headlines on your browser; sponsored tweets. It's on every page of every website you use. It's in every blog you read and every email newsletter you subscribe to.

You almost certainly write a wide range of copy, too.

WHAT DO YOU WRITE?

Take a look at this list and mark the types of copy that you produce, either regularly or occasionally.

Advertisements	Email newsletters
Advertorials	Emails
Banner ads	Facebook posts
Blog posts	Facebook ppc ads
Brochures	Flyers
Campaign briefs	Guides
Direct mail (emails)	Inserts
Direct mail (letters by post)	Instagram memes
Editorials	Instagram stories

Instructions	Press releases
Leaflets	Product copy (website or catalogue)
Letters to stakeholders	Product specifications
LinkedIn articles	Reports
LinkedIn posts	Speeches
Newsletters	Thought leadership articles
Packaging copy	Tweets
Podcast scripts	Video scripts
Policy schedules	Web copy
Posters	White papers

Sort the types of copy you've chosen into a list with the most formal at the top and the most informal at the bottom. What distinguishes formal from informal? List all the factors you can think of.

In that last exercise, you probably listed lots of different factors to distinguish formal from informal copy: subject matter, purpose, the medium or channel where they appear, and, of course, the readership.

Here's another way of thinking about it.

Browsing and searching

Copy works by managing its reader's attention.

In 2012, the broadcaster Terry Wogan talked about his work as a DJ on the BBC. 'We're not talking to an audience,' he said. 'We're talking to one person, and they're only half listening anyway.'

Copywriting is rather like that. Think of yourself as talking – not writing – to one person, who may or may not be paying attention.

Your reader's attention works in two modes. I'll call the first mode **browsing**: scanning the copy for something potentially interesting. I'll call the second mode **searching**: focusing on the copy, looking for something that will answer a question or solve a problem.

Good copy works by responding to the kind of attention the reader is paying *when they first see the copy*.

The browsing reader

Imagine sitting in the dentist's waiting room. Or at the hairdresser's, if that's more comfortable. Perhaps you're leafing through a copy of a magazine, glancing at pictures and headlines, lighting on captions or margin text – perhaps, even, noticing an advertisement. Or maybe you're scrolling through pages on your smartphone. Or flicking through your feeds on social media.

You're browsing. If you're online, you might be using a browser: so named because it helps you find something that will capture your attention.

The searching reader

Now imagine a different situation. You have a specific goal, a question that needs an answer or a problem that you must solve. Maybe you need to choose a new car. Or you're wondering where to go on holiday. Or gathering material for a report.

You're searching. Your search is guided by certain words and phrases. Online, you might be using a search engine, which looks for matches between your search terms and information on the internet. SEO is the algorithm that does just that.

Copy and content

Copywriters respond to browsing and searching readers differently.

We capture the attention of a browsing reader by writing copy. It seeks to capture their attention and hold it long enough to persuade them to do something: to buy something, or donate; to click on a button, or turn the page, or enter a website.

We capture the attention of a searching reader by producing content. It seeks to inform or persuade them by discussing a topic in enough depth to answer their question or solve their problem.

COPY OR CONTENT?

These summary points don't tell the whole story, but they serve to distinguish copy from content reasonably well.

- Copy sells. Content informs.
- Copy seeks to convert. Content generates traffic.

- Copy seeks to convince the reader to act *now*. Content guides the reader towards future action.
- Copy tends to be shorter. Content tends to be longer.
- Copy usually addresses the reader directly. Content usually talks about a topic.

In reality, the dividing line between copy and content is fuzzy. A leaflet, for instance, might have copy on the front cover and content on the inside pages. An advertorial might be predominantly content but include some important copy-like features, like calls to action. But the distinction between copy and content remains useful. After all, you'll probably be writing both.

COPY OR CONTENT?

Here's the list we looked at just now. I've reorganized it so that copy tends towards the bottom right and content tends towards the top left. My listing is by no means definitive. Where do your copywriting tasks sit?

Reports	Facebook posts
Campaign briefs	Web copy
White papers	Newsletters
Thought leadership articles	Email newsletters
Editorials	Letters to stakeholders
Advertorials	Emails
Press releases	Direct mail (emails)
Policy schedules	Direct mail (letters by post)
Product specifications	Podcast scripts
Instructions	Speeches
Guides	Video scripts
Blog posts	Brochures
LinkedIn articles	Leaflets
LinkedIn posts	Flyers

Inserts	Banner ads
Product copy (website or catalogue)	Facebook ppc ads
Packaging copy	Instagram stories
Advertisements	Instagram memes
Posters	Tweets

How to capture your reader's attention

Whether your reader is browsing or searching, you'll need to attract their attention. How do you do that?

Let me introduce you to John Caples. Caples is a legend in the world of direct marketing. He cut his copywriting teeth writing ads for hair-growers, fat-reducers and dandruff-removers. He wrote books on mental healing and personal magnetism, applying the novel insights of psychology to business. And in 1932, Caples wrote *Tested Advertising Methods*, which has been in print ever since.

Caples was fascinated by headlines. He thought that a headline will capture the reader's attention if it does at least one of three things.

1 It arouses the reader's curiosity.

2 It offers the reader something new.

3 It addresses a need in the reader.

We can apply these principles to any type of copy – not just to headlines.

Arouse curiosity

Curiosity helps us survive. It helps us learn, and learn more effectively. Curiosity improves our memory, too.

In 1994, behavioural economist George Loewenstein published a paper entitled 'The Psychology of Curiosity'. 'Curiosity will arise spontaneously,' he writes, 'when situational factors alert an individual to the existence of an information gap in a particular domain.'

The key phrase there is *information gap*. To stimulate your reader's curiosity, you have to create a gap in their knowledge that they'll want to fill.

STIMULATING CURIOSITY

Loewenstein suggests five ways to create an information gap.

Pick a product or service that you're working with or know well. Write five headlines. (I've created some examples to guide you.)

1   Ask a curiosity-inducing question.
    How many types of burger can you name?

2   Start a sequence of events, but don't finish.
    This chef tried to invent a new type of burger. What happened next changed his life.

3   Violate the reader's expectations about something.
    Why burgers are much healthier than you think.

4   Imply that you have the information that the reader doesn't have.
    Five facts about fast-food burgers you need to know now.

5   Imply that the reader used to know something that they've since forgotten.
    How to rediscover the magic burger of your childhood.

Now write 50 words of copy to support each of your headlines.

Offer something new

We're attracted to new information because it might be useful – or dangerous. And so we assume that any product labelled 'new' must be better: that it must offer us some kind of advantage and must, therefore, be worth buying.

Address a need in your reader

You can appeal to the reader's curiosity; you can offer something new or groundbreaking; but the most effective approach is to appeal to the reader's self-interest. The best marketing copy aims at a specific audience and offers them something that they badly need.

Hence the mantra beloved of all marketers.

Focus on benefits, not features.

So, when you're arousing your reader's curiosity or offering them something new, think about the ultimate advantage. What need are you aiming to meet?

Caples' three principles apply both to browsing readers and to searching readers. The difference between the two? A browsing reader *doesn't know* that they need something when they see your copy; a searching reader *knows* what problem they need to solve.

How to hold your reader's attention

Having captured your reader's attention, you must now hold it.

If your reader is browsing, you'll need to take them from where they are to where you want them to be: clicking on a link, buying a product, donating to your cause. You'll need to structure your copy as a journey.

If your reader is searching, you'll need to show them immediately that they've found what they're looking for. Then you'll need to explain it in more detail. You'll need to make your point and then support it. You'll need to organize your material as a kind of pyramid.

JOURNEYS AND PYRAMIDS

Pick a product or service that you're working with or know well. Write 60–70 words of copy promoting this product or service to your reader. Start by saying something that will capture their attention by making them curious, offering something new or talking about a need that the reader has. Then take them on a journey towards a call to action.

Now write a single paragraph explaining what the product or service does: about 60 or 70 words. When you've written a first draft, check out the paragraph's opening sentence. It should summarize what you're saying in the paragraph. Make your point and then support it.

Compare your two pieces of copy. Are you writing in roughly the same voice? How does the tone of each piece differ?

Everything in *The Complete Copywriter* is based on this principle of capturing your reader's attention and then holding it. We'll look at different ways of shaping the copy or content and different styles of copy, responding to these two modes of attention: browsing and searching.

The important point to grasp right now is that your reader's attention is on a spectrum. It can shift between browsing and searching, sometimes very quickly. We might capture a browsing reader's attention so well that they begin to search for what our copy is promising. Alternatively, we might fail to hold a searching reader's attention by making reading difficult or giving them irrelevant information. In a moment, they'll switch to browsing – and we'll have lost them.

From interruption marketing to permission marketing

In the late 1990s, Seth Godin invented the term 'interruption marketing'. Interruption marketing assumes that every reader is browsing. It tries to capture your attention. A commercial interrupts an enthralling soap opera on television; a billboard interrupts a beautiful view from the road; a pop-up ad interrupts your exploration of a website.

In recent decades, says Godin, interruption marketing has approached a crisis point. Advertising spaces – both in the real world and online – have become ever more cluttered. And consumers have found more and more ways to ignore all these interruptions. The same media channels that carried mass advertising now offer premium ad-free services. We can actively block advertising by using ad blockers or skipping ahead during our favourite podcast. Research suggests that the average click rate for banner ads is less than 10 in 10,000.

According to Seth Godin, the antidote to interruption marketing is permission marketing. Permission marketing replaces the instant hit with long-term, interactive marketing, in which customers are rewarded in some way for focusing on increasingly relevant messages. Permission marketing tends to prioritize content over copy.

Godin explains this idea using the brilliant metaphor of getting married. 'Walking into the singles bar,' he writes, 'the Interruption Marketer marches up to the nearest person and proposes marriage. If turned down, the Marketer repeats this process on every person in the bar. A Permission Marketer goes on a date. If it goes well, the two of them go on another date. And then another… Finally, after three or four months of dating, the Permission Marketer proposes marriage.'

Many of the rules of dating, suggests Godin, apply to marketing. And so do many of the benefits.

Copywriting as a conversation

Permission copy seeks to create a conversation with its reader: to *hold* the reader's attention, rather than just capture it.

That doesn't mean you can ignore interruption marketing. Far from it. Most of the time, though, you need to interrupt the reader with a message that will encourage them to give you their permission to hold a conversation.

One way to do that is to make them an offer. That offer should seek to meet a need or to solve a problem, *at no cost to the reader*. Your offer should be a gift. 'The less you ask of the consumer,' says Godin, 'and the bigger the "bribe", the more likely the consumer will give you permission. The permission won't be broad or deep. But it will guarantee that your next interaction will be significantly more impactful.' A typical 'bribe' might be a regular email newsletter in return for an email address.

Then, at step two – once the reader has given you their permission to hold a conversation – you need to make good use of it. Like going on a date, you're seeking to build trust by finding common ground. By gradually offering more and better rewards, you can keep them interested.

This is copywriting as conversation. A good conversation has three elements: two people, speaking and listening; a subject, an argument or a proposition; and a shared language. Effective copy – and content – replicates these three features of conversation.

In the next section, we'll look at ways of making our copy more conversational.

SUMMARY

Conduct an audit on all the different types of copy and content you produce.

Sort the types of copy you've chosen into a list, with the most formal at the top and the most informal at the bottom.

Some readers browse. Some readers search.

Copywriters respond to browsing and searching readers differently.

We capture the attention of a browsing reader by writing copy.

We capture the attention of a searching reader by producing content.

- Copy sells. Content informs.
- Copy seeks to convert. Content generates traffic.
- Copy seeks to convince the reader to act *now*. Content guides the reader towards future action.

- Copy tends to be shorter. Content tends to be longer.
- Copy usually addresses the reader directly. Content usually talks about a topic.

In reality, the dividing line between copy and content is fuzzy.

Copy or content will capture the reader's attention if it:

- arouses curiosity
- offers something new
- addresses a need in the reader

Five ways to arouse curiosity:

- Ask a curiosity-inducing question.
- Start a sequence of events but don't finish.
- Violate the reader's expectations about something.
- Imply that you have the information that the reader doesn't have.
- Imply that the reader used to know something that they've since forgotten.

Focus on benefits, not features.

For browsing readers, structure your copy as a journey.

For searching readers, structure your copy as a pyramid.

Interruption marketing is giving way to permission marketing.

Permission copy seeks, in all sorts of ways, to create a conversation with its reader.

You will need to create interruption copy *and* permission copy.

A very brief history of copy

The word 'copy' has its origins in the Latin word *copia*, meaning 'abundance, riches'.

In 1512, the great humanist Erasmus published *De Copia*, a textbook on how to speak and write persuasively. The book was a bestseller – and is still in print. Copywriters continue to use many of the techniques discussed by Erasmus: examples, comparisons, metaphors, three-part lists. Erasmus also reminds us that good copy is nearly always founded on a clear argument. Marketers might call that argument a value proposition.

Fast forward to the late nineteenth century and another technological revolution.

The telegraph was invented in 1837. Samuel Morse developed his famous code in 1838. In 1876, Alexander Graham Bell patented the telephone. By 1880, journalists were using these new electronic technologies to dictate text down the line to newspaper offices, where editors would copy it. By 1889, the playwright George Bernard Shaw was referring to 'what the newspapers call "good copy"'.

Very quickly, this meaning of the word 'copy' transferred from journalism to advertising. The word 'copy' meaning the text of an ad first appeared in 1905. But the first full-time copywriter is usually said to have been John Emory Powers, who was writing advertising copy for a department store in the 1870s and went freelance in 1886 (thus establishing a career path that many copywriters have since followed).

Copywriters have inherited this double history. Advertising copy still draws on the traditions of the ad men and Mad Men; content draws on the traditions of journalism. As digital media proliferate, these two great traditions of copywriting are converging and cross-fertilizing still further.

PART TWO

Planning the copy

Great copy is like a conversation.

- The best copy sounds like an individual speaking to another individual. So, we need to create a **customer persona.**

- It addresses a subject that the reader can immediately recognize and relate to. If the copy is seeking to persuade or influence, it should present an argument. In marketing, this argument is often called the **value proposition.**

- And the copy uses a **voice** that the reader can understand easily. The copy *speaks* – the reader will feel that they can hear a voice when they are reading.

These three elements are at the heart of good copywriting. In the next section, we'll look at each one in detail.

- In Chapter 3, we look at how to create a reader persona. We'll use some of the skills of mental mobility that we explored back in Chapter 1.

- In Chapter 4, we explore different ways of constructing an argument, whether a value proposition or any other kind of argument that we might use to persuade our reader to act.

- In Chapter 5, we look at how to create an effective voice for our copy.

- And in Chapter 6, we consider writing enticing headlines and subject lines.

3

Profiling your reader

The only person your copy needs to please is your reader.

That might seem obvious. But businesses – like writers – often put themselves first. And too much copy talks about the company rather than focusing on the needs of the customer or user.

As a result, you may find yourself having to act as a customer advocate for your client.

WHO ARE THEY TALKING TO?

Find three home pages from three companies or organizations – as varied as you can.

Which pieces of copy directly address the reader and promise to solve a problem for them? Which pieces of copy explain only what the company or organization does?

Pick one piece of copy that you think you could improve. Try to rewrite it so that it directly addresses the reader and offers practical benefits.

Review your rewrite. How much research did you need to do to improve the quality of the copy?

To become an effective customer advocate, you need to develop empathy for the customer. Empathy means understanding another person's situation, their thoughts and feelings (unlike sympathy, which means feeling those same feelings). Developing empathy is a core skill for any copywriter.

Three reasonable assumptions about your reader

To build real empathy, you need to gain a sense of your reader as a living individual. So, let's start with three reasonable assumptions about them.

THEY ARE NOT AN IDIOT

Ok. Some people are idiots. But not many. And it's wise to assume that anyone you meet is not an idiot and then adjust your impression as the conversation proceeds. Making this assumption will allow you to navigate the next key assumption.

THEY'RE ALMOST CERTAINLY NOT INTERESTED IN WHAT YOU WANT TO TALK ABOUT

Of course, they might be interested because they might have found your copy while searching for some piece of information that's of urgent, vital concern to them. In which case, you're in a great opening position. But it's more likely that you're interrupting them while they're browsing. They're not interested in your proposition. They're interested in something far more important. Specifically:

THEY'RE INTERESTED IN THEMSELVES

No, your reader is not a self-obsessed narcissist. (Probably.) But they *are* interested in anything that affects them directly: some problem that needs solving; some aching concern that keeps them awake at night.

You need to create copy that meets the reader where they are. You need to create copy that's personal.

How do we create personal copy?

No, I'm not talking about personalizing your copy. Personalizing is relatively easy: substitute <Ms Smith> for <name> in your email's salutation, and – hey presto! – you've personalized it. Writing personal copy is quite different. Personal copy pays the reader the respect of treating them like a person.

To do that, begin by thinking like your reader. Draw on your imagination. Draw on the skills of your inner novelist or playwright. Create a three-dimensional, believable, living person. Put yourself into their situation and find their voice.

It's time to invent a reader.

Creating a persona

Charles Dickens claimed that he never invented anything; he merely wrote down what he heard his characters saying. Apparently, his children could always tell when he was writing because they could hear him through the study door.

You did something very similar back in Chapter 1 when you did the exercise called 'Inventing a person'. Now we'll take that exercise one step further.

Imagine a fictional, typical customer or user of your products or services. You might call them a customer persona or a user persona. Imagine meeting this person. Ask them about themselves. What's their name? Where do they live? What are they willing to tell you about their background or personal life? Listen to their answers. And write them down. In their voice.

You're inventing this persona for a specific purpose. You will want to persuade them to do something: to buy something, join something or donate to a good cause. So, as you listen to your persona, listen for the information that will be most useful to you. You'll need to imagine, as it were, 'double': listening as openly as possible to what your persona is telling you *and* keeping in mind your purpose in listening to them.

The work they do

Ask your persona about the work they do. We can distinguish three types of work.

FUNCTIONAL WORK
Ask:

- Do you have a job?
- What are your domestic tasks?
- Do you work in your community?
- What does a typical day look like?

SOCIAL WORK
Ask:

- How do you see yourself at work?
- How do others view you?
- How would you like others to view you?

EMOTIONAL WORK
Ask:

- How do you feel at work?
- What do you do to relax?
- Are you concerned about your wellbeing?
- What keeps you awake at night?

The problems they face

Problems include anything that annoys or worries your persona when they're working: obstacles, undesired outcomes and risks. Explore each in turn.

OBSTACLES
Ask:

- What stops you from getting a job done?
- What prevents you from removing an obstacle in your path?
- What do you need?

UNDESIRED OUTCOMES
Ask:

- What tends to go wrong when you're working?
- What always annoys you when you're doing this job?
- Does this task have unpleasant consequences?

RISKS
Ask:

- What could go wrong?
- How likely is it to go wrong?
- How serious would the consequence be of this going wrong?
- How bothered are you about this risk?

The goals they're pursuing

Finally, ask your persona about their goals. Goals include targets, ambitions and dreams. They include the outcomes and benefits that your persona wants or needs.

REQUIRED GOALS
Ask:

- What do you have to achieve to get a job done?
- What do you need to do your work properly?
- What counts as failure?

EXPECTED GOALS
Ask:

- What do you assume you can do at work?
- What do you expect from the products or services you use?
- What would disappoint you?

DESIRED GOALS
Ask:

- What's your biggest dream?
- What are your ambitions for the future?
- What would an ideal world look like to you?

CREATING A PERSONA

Use the lists above to develop a profile of your chosen persona. Now write a short introductory statement for your chosen persona. Write *as the person themselves*, in the first person. (You'll find some examples at the end of this chapter.)

You might write anything between 200 and 400 words. Print off your profile and put it to one side.

Your persona's needs

Your reader is a human being. Which means that just like you, me and everyone else, they have needs. Somewhere in your persona's statement will be clues about those needs.

We all have physical needs. We need breathable air, clean water, nutritious food and sleep. If these needs aren't met, we'll quickly die. We also need to be able to stimulate our senses and exercise our muscles, and we need secure shelter. If these physical needs aren't met, we may not die but we will surely become unwell.

We also have emotional needs. If you can help your persona meet one of these emotional needs, then you'll be more likely to engage them. We can map out this network of needs under three headings. You can remember them by using the mnemonic CAR.

Competence

We need to feel that we're good at what we do, at work, in our relationships, as parents or members of a team. We also need to feel that our skills can be stretched: that we can learn and develop.

Autonomy

We need to feel that we're in control of our lives and that we can choose what to do. We also need privacy: the opportunity to be alone to reflect on our experiences and make sense of them.

Relatedness

We need to feel that at least one person accepts us for who we are. We need to feel that we have a secure place in a community that allows us to live and develop fully. We need to feel that we have status in our relationships and that our status is recognized by others. We also want to feel that we're connected to the wider world: to nature, to our environment, or to a system of ideas or beliefs. We need to feel that our lives have meaning and purpose.

Good copy addresses these needs. The benefits of a product or service always help to meet these emotional needs in some way.

EMOTIONAL NEEDS

The Human Givens Institute has created an Emotional Needs Audit. It's freely available online. You might find it useful to explore your persona's needs – and, maybe, your own.

Using your reader persona

Writing a vivid persona in this way can be revelatory. Suddenly, you have a person in your mind's eye that you can hold a conversation with.

What is your persona talking about? Are they focused on work or home life? What have they chosen to tell you? What have they chosen *not* to tell you?

Look, also, at the way your persona speaks. Do they use long sentences or short ones? Simple or complicated ones? How do they connect their sentences together? Do they gather their thoughts into neat paragraphs or let them emerge in a stream of consciousness? What sorts of words do they use? Are they speaking carefully or spontaneously?

Analysing these two aspects of your persona's statement – the content and the voice they use – will help you to produce copy that speaks to them. Will your argument interest them? Do you want to mirror their voice? Or maybe use a voice that responds to their voice? If they sound agitated, for instance, could you create a voice that reassures them?

IDENTIFY YOUR READER PERSONA'S PROBLEMS

Review your reader persona and list some of the problems they talk about. Write down each problem as a single statement. It might be a statement of something that's wrong; it might be a statement about how to do something.

Focus on one problem; don't try to solve all the problems you've discovered. How could your copy – your product, service or idea – address that problem? Identify also one need that you can help to fulfil.

- Competence: how could your product help them do a job better?

- Autonomy: how could it give them more control over their life?

- Relatedness: how could it help them connect to the outside world?

Write 100 words of copy explaining how your product or service could solve the problem and meet the need. As you write, imagine speaking directly to your reader. Argue the case for your product or service in concrete terms: how it can change your persona's life.

Try writing your copy in two different ways:

1   First, start with the solution (the product or service and the benefit it offers) and explain how it solves the reader's problem.

2   Second, start with the persona's problem and don't mention the solution until the very end.

Compare your two pieces of copy. Which do you think works better? Why?

If your market has multiple segments, or you're talking to a range of stake-holders, you may want to create a portfolio of personas. And those personas will probably change over time. Review them regularly so that they don't go out of date or become stale.

Three reader personas

Here are three reader personas, produced using the process outlined in this chapter. They'll give you an idea of how writing these personas can generate a wealth of interesting information to support your copywriting.

CUSTOMER PERSONA: CLAIRE

Hi, my name is Claire and I currently live in Birsington. I am a 26-year-old nurse working in Kewborough hospital. Whenever I have free time, I enjoy researching the newest developments in the paediatric nursing field to help further my development. One of the main obstacles I face is booking time off to attend training courses and webinars. I try my best to spend my evenings catching up, but I am exhausted as I work long hours. I need to attend courses and events to keep myself updated with the newest research and practices. I enjoy attending online or physical events to network with peers. Ideally, I would need to know about upcoming online or physical events a few weeks prior so I can organize my schedule.

Claire begins by saying *Hi*. She is undoubtedly friendly and easy to strike up a conversation with. But that second sentence is very revealing: everything she says relates to her work. Claire seems ambitious and single-minded. She's likely to be interested only in products or services that will meet her career goals and help her grow her professional network.

Accordingly, her sentences are almost all grammatically simple: each one expresses just one idea. Exceptions include the very first sentence and the third sentence, which begins with a brief subordinate clause. The fifth sentence – *I try my best to spend my evenings catching up...* – expresses in its three-part structure a clear sense of energy frustrated by hard work.

The voice we use for Claire will need to offer clear benefits with no fuss. It will need to use mostly simple sentences, with as little padding as possible. And it will need to satisfy Claire's need for knowledge and learning.

CUSTOMER PERSONA: LIAM

I am Liam, I am 21 years old and I have been in the Army since I was 18. I have dealt with more stress at this age than most would before reaching 40. I am trusted to make mature decisions even though I have only been in my career for a few years.

In the military I have to fulfil job tasks for combat engineering roles such as breaching, bridging and obstacle creating. It is crucial, for myself and my team, that I can do these tasks quickly and efficiently, using fewer resources and less time.

I want to be seen by my team as effective, brave and strong. A leader that will one day be a sergeant. I do this by voicing my opinions, helping others and undertaking work without errors or complaint.

I want to feel safe and know that the people I spend every day with are going to be safe and return to their families too. I want to have confidence that the equipment I need to do this is reliable and accurate. If I face failures this could create casualties; I could lose a crew member or never see my family again. We cannot afford to witness time wasting, danger or death.

I am on Facebook because I miss my family and friends, even though I am surrounded by a new family that I care about just as much. I go on Instagram to research my interests of cars and motorbikes; I like anything with a big engine. I often find myself on YouTube because I want to research the world I am a part of so that my senior leaders know I am keen to get ahead in my career.

Liam writes mostly in a style that's forthright and assertive. Notice how he introduces himself: simply *I am Liam*. Notice also that second sentence. And how he characterizes his leadership style: *voicing my opinions, helping others and undertaking work without errors or complaint* – in that order.

His voice becomes less assertive in the last paragraph. (Notice, also, the number of short paragraphs here.) Liam reveals a bit more about his private self and his feelings, but only towards the end. And the sentences in that final paragraph are distinctly longer and more complicated.

Liam seems to like two stylistic devices in particular. He has a great fondness for three-part lists: *effective, brave and strong*; *time wasting, danger or death*. He also sometimes structures his sentences to point up a contrast (a technique known as antithesis): *I am trusted to make mature decisions even though I have only been in my career for a few years*; *I miss my family and friends, even though I am surrounded by a new family that I care about just as much*.

The voice we use for Liam will need to have a similar rhythm to the voice he uses here. Three-part lists and contrasts will probably go down well. It will also need to maintain its cool, while acknowledging the emotions below the surface. And it will need to sound technically smart.

CUSTOMER PERSONA: KEITH

I'm Keith Jayson, a 42-year-old male who works in the banking sector. I have a wife and two children currently living on the outskirts of Manchester. My day consists of an early rise, usually around 5am, travelling by train into the city, a full day's work, followed by coming home to be a doting dad whilst maintaining the running of the family home. My wife and I both work full working weeks so the little time we have together is precious, we each have specific responsibilities: mine include the management of bills and the children's sporting activities. Due to this I enjoy the fast pace of the online world and like any purchases I may make to be straightforward and at the tip of my fingers. Companies which carry a strong online presence using chat bots and maintaining short customer wait times I favour when looking for a product or service. I enjoy keeping up with the latest sport and news through platforms like X and Facebook, especially when on a wind-down from a busy day. I appreciate any necessary purchases to be quick and simple, with any relevant documentation sent to me via email for ease.

Keith begins not by greeting us but by defining himself. And as a male – even though his name makes his gender clear. He also puts his profession up front. Being a doting dad sits in the shadows, in the middle of its sentence. This is someone who puts his life and work into categories. He also likes clear routines.

Keith's style strives to be sophisticated. Only the first two of his sentences are less than 12 words long. All his other sentences are 20 words or over; many of them are more than 30 words long. His phrasing is sometimes more complicated than it needs to be: *we each have specific responsibilities*; *companies which carry a strong online presence*; *I appreciate any purchases to be quick and simple*. Is Keith trying to make an impression?

The voice we use for Keith will need to flatter his desire for sophistication without becoming overblown. Anything that can be categorized or put into a procedural list will probably go down well. But it will need to balance these qualities with a steady pace and a cool clarity. Keith will demand copy that's smart: both intelligent and up to date.

SUMMARY

The only person your copy needs to please is your reader.

Developing empathy is a core skill for any copywriter.

Three reasonable assumptions about your reader:

- They are not an idiot.

- They're almost certainly not interested in what you want to talk about.

- They're interested in themselves.

Personal copy pays the reader the respect of treating them like a person.

To do that, begin by starting to think *like* your reader.

Invent a customer persona, reader persona or user persona.

In your imagination, ask them about their work, the obstacles they face and their goals or dreams.

Think about their needs – especially their emotional needs: competence, autonomy and relatedness.

Write a personal statement in the voice of your customer persona.

Study this statement in terms of its content – what is your persona talking about? – and its style – how are they using language?

Analysing these two aspects of your persona's statement will help you to produce copy that speaks to them more effectively.

4

Finding your argument

You've created a persona. Your task is to persuade that persona to do something.

In other words, you need to find an argument. 'Words, for me,' wrote copywriting superstar David Abbott, 'are the servants of the argument. I believe that I'm paid to be an advocate and though I get pleasure from the bon mot, the bon motivator thrills me more.'

So, let's begin by thinking about what an argument is, how it works and how we can make *any* argument more persuasive.

The secret of *because*

In its basic form, an argument consists of three elements:

- a claim (the idea that you're arguing for);
- a reason (a statement that supports the claim);
- the word 'because'.

Your claim and your reason sit on either side of that word:

[claim] *because* [reason]

If *because* binds the claim and the reason convincingly for your reader, then the argument will persuade them. But the word *because* harbours a secret. Unlock that secret and you'll construct arguments that are truly persuasive.

Let's take a simple example. Suppose you're writing copy for a leaflet giving advice on healthy eating. One of your core arguments might be:

Eat more vegetables because they're good for you.

How persuasive is that argument? It depends on your reader. If they assume that they should do what's good for them, then your argument will persuade them. But suppose your reader is a child. Are they likely to assume that they should do what's good for them? Maybe not. To persuade *them*, you'd need to find a reason based on a different assumption.

> Eat your vegetables because it's fun to eat vegetables.
>
> Eat your vegetables because then you can eat ice cream.
>
> Eat your vegetables because Spiderman always eats his vegetables.

Here's the secret. Every argument is based on assumptions. And it's these assumptions that tie the reason to the claim, through that magic word *because*. If your reader shares the assumption underlying your reason, you have a good chance of persuading them. But if they don't share that assumption, then your argument is likely to fail, however logical it is.

So, how do you identify the assumptions underlying your reader's thinking? You must show how your product, your service or your idea benefits your reader. That benefit must align with the assumptions your reader holds about the world: their attitudes, values and beliefs. That's why we worked so hard on creating a reader persona in the previous chapter.

Know your product

The product you're promoting might be a physical product or a service. In a commercial context, your product is likely to be one of four types:

- a business-to-consumer product like orange juice or a dishwasher;
- a business-to-consumer service like car insurance or house cleaning;
- a business-to-business product like a photocopier or a forklift truck; or
- a business-to-business service like accountancy or secure document disposal.

But we can think of products, also, in non-commercial settings. For a charity or not-for-profit organization, the product might be a donation or a subscription. For a local authority, the product might be a service like fostering or recycling. If you're writing a blog post, your product might be an idea.

You must know what you're talking about. 'In the absence of such knowledge,' writes Bob Levenson, 'you will be doomed to rely more and more on adjectives; always a mistake.'

To find out more about adjectives and how to use them, go to Chapter 5.

Start with simple questions about the product itself.

- What is it? What does it do? How does it work?
- Who uses the product? How do they use it? When and where?
- What's unusual, or unique, about this product? Is it the only one of its type? What does it do that its rivals *don't* do?
- What is the product's position in the market? Is it basic, regular or premium? Is it newly launched or well established?

Now think about who's producing the product.

- How does the product reflect the history and culture of the company or organization? Are you dealing with an established market leader or an ambitious, disruptive start-up?
- What about the people who are handling, selling and delivering the product? Talk to salespeople, retailers, franchisees, brokers. If you're in the public sector, think about the people in local offices, on helplines or in drop-in centres. What do they think about this product or service?

Now think about customers or users.

- Why do people buy or use this product? Where do they buy or use it?
- Is buying the product quick and easy or long and complicated? Is the product an impulse buy (like a chocolate brownie) or a planned purchase (like a house)? If it's planned, how do people go about researching and deciding?
- How does the customer receive the product? Who delivers or sells it?
- What about your product's reputation? What reviews is it getting? Where? Is the product being covered in the media? Are you getting customer reviews?

Now look at the negatives.

- If someone bought or used this product, would they need to stop buying or using something else? Might they resist doing that?

- What alternatives are available? The alternative might not be a competitor's product; your reader might just choose to spend their money on something else. For instance, your reader might choose to go to the cinema rather than visit your restaurant for a meal.

Knowing too much: The dangers of product research

I'm tempted to say that you can't research the product too much. But researching the product does carry two dangers.

The curse of knowledge

The first danger is the curse of knowledge. As you learn more and more about your product, you might find it increasingly difficult to put yourself into your customer's position of *not* knowing about it.

How do you lift the curse of knowledge? By looking at the product from the reader's point of view. If you can, use the product or service yourself. Sometimes that's easy: you can wear a pair of socks or sample a sausage roll. Experiencing a service might be trickier, especially if it's expensive or time-consuming. But if you're writing copy for a hotel, you really should try to stay there; if you're promoting a cruise, you should – if you possibly can – go on a cruise. Alternatively, you can talk to people who have had the experience themselves.

The curse of the client

The second danger in product research we might call the curse of the client. By working with the client, you start to see advantages and benefits solely from the client's point of view, rather than the customer's.

This can be a surprisingly common problem. Some clients are so concerned with their problems that they ignore the problems their customer faces. Maybe sales are down; maybe faulty returns are up; maybe 60 per cent of customers are still not paying by direct debit. These are the problems that keep your client awake at night. They might want you to write copy that solves these problems for them.

Too much copy panders to the client and ignores the customer. Watch out for headlines like *Tomorrow's Technology Today* or *The Best Just Got Better*. Check out press releases that begin *We're delighted to announce the appointment of our new Head of Meaning.* Your client may thank you – and even pay you – for such self-promotional copy. Their customers will probably not even read it.

Take your client to one side and – gently – point out that their customers have their own problems. Your job as copywriter is to show how the client's product can solve *those* problems.

Features, advantages and benefits

A few months ago, I decided to take up cycling again. I went to my local store: the cycles looked very different from the bike I'd ridden around London 15 years before. Somewhat nervously, I approached the sales assistant – young, intimidatingly fit-looking – and told him I was looking for a bicycle for cycling about town and weekend trips out into the country. Nothing sporty.

Now, this story could continue in three ways. Here's the first way.

The sales guy launches into an enthusiastic pitch. He tells me I need a hybrid bike. I've never heard of a hybrid bike, but I don't dare ask. He shows me a model: 24 gears, cantilever brakes, a groupset including top-of-the-range drivetrain and derailleurs…

I feel stupid. (What on earth is a groupset?) He lists feature after feature. He's even looking at the bike rather than at me.

Eventually, I make an excuse and make my escape.

Now, here's the second way.

The sales guy explains *why* he's pointing out these features on the bike. The 24 gears help you cycle up, down and on the flat. The derailleurs help you change gear smoothly. The cantilever brakes are more efficient than cheaper brakes.

This argument is much more persuasive. Superfit Sales Guy is arguing his case, not just by listing features but by pointing out the *advantages* of each feature. I'm certainly feeling less stupid. But, as he keeps listing advantages – the ergonomic saddle, the five-year warranty, the feather-light aluminium frame – my mind starts to wander. Too Much Information.

Now for the third way this conversation might run. And this is the way it did run in reality.

The sales guy asked me a few questions. He identified some of my needs and some of the problems I wanted to avoid. He then carefully linked some of the features on the bike he'd chosen to those needs and problems. I live in a hilly part of town: those 24 gears will help me, even on the toughest gradient. I often need to lift the bike up steps: the frame is as light as they come. The cantilever brakes could save my life when I'm negotiating heavy traffic in wet weather.

Advantages became *benefits*.

I started to see the bike as something that could fit into my life. I was feeling considerably smarter than I had when I walked into the store. Superfit Sales Guy was well on the way to making a sale.

In this third version of the story, the sales guy was doing two things. First, he used curiosity and mental mobility to understand my point of view. Then he used design thinking and objectivity to fit a particular model to my needs. He transformed features into advantages and advantages into benefits. He answered the question that was uppermost in my mind: 'What's in it for me?'

You can do exactly the same thing when you're writing copy. FAB analysis transforms a product's features into benefits.

- **Features** are the bald facts about a product.
- **Advantages** are what makes the product better than its competitors.
- **Benefits** identify how advantages make life better for your customer.

The trick is to express a benefit in terms of what will *happen* if the customer uses the product. Describe the benefit in concrete detail, using verbs to express what the product will *do* to make life better for the reader.

DIY FAB ANALYSIS

Find a small object nearby. Anything will do. Examine the object and list its key features. Then ask how each feature gives this object an advantage over similar objects. Finally, identify the benefit that the advantage gives the user of the object. (You could choose the persona you worked on in the previous chapter. How would this object benefit *them*?)

Express the benefit in terms of *action*. What will happen as a result of this advantage?

Write 100 words.

More about benefits

Here are four ways you can develop your thinking about benefits.

'So what?'

Your reader – your customer – is interested primarily in themselves. What's in it for them? The best way to answer that question is to apply the 'So what?' test.

Imagine you're selling an oven. It includes a fast preheat system. That's a feature: it's one of the things the oven does.

So what?

It's ready to start cooking your pasta bake more quickly than other ovens.

So what?

Your dinner will be on the table sooner.

So what?

You waste less time when you come home from work. And you don't have to worry that you might forget to preheat your oven. Life is less stressful.

Double-check: does your reader want a less stressful life? Does fast food matter to them? If they're a busy commuter, quite probably. If they're into slow food and fine dining, maybe not.

Be specific

Powerful benefits link to specific needs or goals. Your reader might want to save money. If you can persuade them that buying your product will save them a specific amount of money, the benefit will be more convincing.

MAKING BENEFITS SPECIFIC

Take a look at this list of benefits. Try to create a specific version of each one. Thanks to Andy Maslen for this idea. For instance:

Look better → Create a younger looking face and neck in just two weeks.

Look better

Save time

Lose weight

Get the perfect figure

Stay on the right side of the law

Cut down on waste

Sleep peacefully every night

Get my dream home

Find my dream holiday

Make money

Save money

Make my money go further

Stop worrying about debt

Provide for my family

Keep my family safe

Help my children learn

Get promoted

Make friends

Gain respect

Enjoy life more

Be healthy

Be happy

Gain peace of mind

Provide evidence

A FAB analysis will help you argue from the benefit back to the product. Listing benefits alone might persuade in the short term, but most customers will want to see evidence of the benefit.

Some readers will want to see more evidence than others. A casual user of a computer will want to know that it's easy to use, that it won't go wrong and that they can call a helpline whenever they need to. An enthusiast, a professional or a hobbyist will want to see a detailed technical specification.

Don't assume, however, that the evidence-hunters lack emotion. Benefits happen in your reader's head. Their decision to buy or use a product will be guided just as much by their feelings as by their powers of deduction and reasoning.

So:

Identify tangible and intangible benefits

Some benefits are tangible. They're objective and practical facts about the product that readers can use to make a rational buying decision. Tangible benefits include what the product does and how well it does it.

Other benefits are intangible. They address the customer's emotional needs: competence, autonomy and relatedness. The superior functionality of a computer might make the customer feel more competent or more in control; they may now feel that they belong to a privileged élite. L'Oréal's famous tagline offers the intangible benefit of greater self-esteem.

> Because you're worth it.

Intangible benefits might well be more powerful in your reader's mind than tangible ones.

Now that you've discovered a benefit that you think will convince your reader or customer, it's time to formulate a proposition that articulates that benefit persuasively.

MAKING LIFE BETTER FOR YOUR READER

Take a product or service and imagine your reader looking at it with you. They ask: 'How will my life be improved if I buy this/use this/do what you want me to do?'

Imagine answering that question in a real conversation with your reader. Don't try to make it clever copy, don't try to sell the product or service – simply answer the question. How will their life be better if they act as you want them to?

When you've finished, look back over the copy and edit for clarity and length. Aim for no more than 100 words. End with a call to action.

Do you need to change it?

In the beginning was the USP

The Unique Selling Proposition first appeared in a book called *Reality in Advertising*. Its author, Rosser Reeves, was one of the original Mad Men. He more or less invented the television advertisement. Reeves explains that a USP must both differentiate the product from the competition and offer a profound benefit to the customer.

According to Reeves, the USP has three main features.

1 **The ad must make a proposition.** The ad must argue, explicitly: buy this product and you will get this specific benefit.

2 **The proposition must be unique.** It must be something that the competition does not, or cannot, offer. It's not enough to offer a benefit. The USP must differentiate the product from competing products: you get this benefit only with this product.

3 **The proposition must sell.** It must be so strong that it can move large numbers of customers over to your product. So the USP can't be trivial; it must solve a serious problem, or meet a deep need, for the customer.

Once he'd defined the USP of a product, Reeves repeated it, over and over, in his copy.

His most powerful weapon was the slogan: a memorable statement that encapsulated the USP. His most famous example was for M&M's, the first sugar-coated chocolate on the market.

Melts in your mouth, not in your hand.

Enter the value proposition

USPs are still very much in evidence. But they are slowly giving way to value propositions.

The phrase 'value proposition' appeared in a paper for McKinsey by Michael Lanning and Edward Michaels, 'A business is a value delivery system'. Lanning and Michaels define a value proposition as 'a clear, simple statement of the benefits, both tangible and intangible, that the company will provide, along with the approximate price it will charge each customer segment for those benefits'.

How does a value proposition differ from a USP? Principally, by focusing on the customer rather than the product. Where Reeves was interested in selling to his reader – in the true spirit of interruption marketing – Lanning and Michaels focus on creating a relationship with the customer.

Creating a value proposition

We can define value very simply:

$$Value = benefit - cost$$

The greater the benefit or the lower the cost, the greater the value. Benefits and costs might be monetary or numerical, but they don't need to be. Costs, for instance, could include extra work, customer service in case of breakdowns and so on.

Here are some simple sentence models that you could use to create a value proposition.

> Our [product] helps [customer] to [perform a task/solve a problem/meet a need] by doing [beneficial activity].
>
> Our [product] is the only [category] that [delivers a benefit].
>
> Our [product] helps [customer category] [do X] by [delivering benefit].
>
> For [target customer] who [needs or wants X], our [product] is [category] that [offers benefit Y].

Value propositions as strategic tools

Think of the value proposition not just as a statement aimed at your customer but also as an internal statement, for you and your colleagues. Michael Lanning believes that a value proposition can be developed into a strategic document to guide all parts of a business. That document should, he thinks, answer five questions.

1 **Who are the target customers?** What are their demographics? How do they use products or services? What makes them your target?

2 **What is the timeframe?** If a value proposition is specific enough, it will probably be time-limited. Produce a value proposition for a specific timeframe and plan to revise it later.

3 **What do you want your customer to do?** Be clear. (You're going to need to formulate clear calls to action, after all, in your marketing copy.) For example, you might want the customer to:

  o buy your product or service;

  o use your product or service in a particular way;

  o sell your product or service to their customer; or

  o use it to make another product.

4 **What are their competing alternatives?** What is your customer likely to do if they don't do what you want? Perhaps nothing. Perhaps use a direct competitor's product.

5 **What value will the customer enjoy?** Remember: value equals benefit minus cost.

   o If B2C, how will the customer's life improve? Will they have more fun, save money, be better entertained, save time or improve their health? Express these benefits specifically and measurably.

   o If B2B, how will the customer's business improve? Will they increase sales? Reduce cycle times? Cut operating costs? Again: be specific and measurable.

A good value proposition can link product development, marketing and sales into a single strategy, helping everyone in the value chain communicate better with each other and with your customers. Marketing should take the lead in developing the value proposition itself, the branding framework it generates and the marketing campaigns it supports.

And for you, the copywriter, this value proposition is the foundational statement on which all your marketing copy rests.

SUMMARY

In its basic form, an argument has this form:

   [claim] *because* [reason]

Every argument is based on assumptions. If your reader shares the assumption underlying your reason, you have a good chance of persuading them.

You must show how your product, your service or your idea *benefits* your reader.

Know your product. What is it? Who uses it? What are the negatives or potential negatives?

Counter the curse of knowledge by looking at the product from the customer's point of view.

Counter the curse of the client by helping them see the product from the customer's point of view.

Work from features through advantages to benefits.

- **Features** are the bald facts about a product.
- **Advantages** are what makes the product better than its competitors.
- **Benefits** identify how advantages make life better for your customer.

The trick is to express a benefit in terms of what will *happen* if the customer uses the product.

- What's in it for them?
- Make benefits specific.
- Provide evidence.

Identify tangible and intangible benefits.

A Unique Selling Point has three main features:

- The ad must make a proposition.
- The proposition must be unique.
- The proposition must sell.

USPs are slowly giving way to value propositions.

> Value = benefit – cost

Think of the value proposition not just as a statement aimed at your customer but also as an *internal* statement, for you and your colleagues.

A good value proposition can link company departments into a single strategy. The VP is also the foundation for all your copy.

5

Finding your voice

It's called 'voice' for a reason.

When you read good copy, you hear a voice speaking to you. If you notice that you're reading – if, for instance, you have to re-read a sentence – then the voice is failing.

What about 'tone of voice'? Is that different?

Think of your own voice. It's usually recognizable all the time. Your brand's voice, similarly, should be distinctive. We'd find it disconcerting if someone's voice kept changing during a conversation; similarly, your brand's voice should be consistent.

Voice is consistent, but *tone* of voice can vary. It will change in different situations, depending on who you're talking to (a child; a colleague; a member of the royal family), your intention (to persuade, to explain, to tell a story), how you feel (relaxed; angry; apologetic) or how you want the other person to feel (reassured; excited; intrigued). In exactly the same way, the tone of your brand's voice can shift, depending on the situation and your intention.

VARYING YOUR TONE OF VOICE

Think about the voice you would use to market your own services as a copywriter. (We'll think a lot more about that voice as this chapter goes on.)

Write three short pieces of copy. For each piece of copy, ask, 'What do I want this copy to do? How do I want to influence the reader's thoughts and feelings?'

1   Write up to 50 words that will appear on the home page of your website.

2   Now write up to 50 words inviting a customer to subscribe to your newsletter.

3 And finally, write the microcopy that will appear on an error page for your website.

The voice in all three examples should be identifiably the same voice. The tone of voice should differ subtly in each case.

Creating a new voice for a brand or a company can be tricky. Adapting to an existing brand voice can be even trickier. Think about the kind of company you are and what your reader expects from that kind of company. An insurance company should probably not use a voice that wisecracks about disasters. A company hiring out bouncy castles for children's parties should probably not have a voice that sounds like a corporate lawyer.

Make it speakable

To test whether your voice is speakable, simply read your copy aloud.
    Take a look at this copy.

> At Worldfoodsource, we operate alongside farmers, communities and like-minded partners to deliver sustainable food ingredients to our customers. Working globally, a sustainable balance between producers and the environment is promoted by our partnership strategy. By connecting with communities through health initiatives and promoting prosperous farming, our company is uniquely positioned to reconfigure global agricultural and food systems.

Could you imagine someone saying this to you in a normal conversation?
    How could we improve this copy? Imagine speaking to your reader and write down what you would say – word for word.
    Like this, maybe.

> At Worldfoodsource, we work with farmers and communities to deliver food that's sustainable. That means promoting a sustainable balance between food producers and the environment.

We call it a net-positive approach.

We work with communities and like-minded partners globally, running health initiatives and promoting farming that's truly prosperous. As a result, we're uniquely positioned to reimagine a model of agriculture that's balanced, fair and responsible.

Some aspects of this new version are obviously related to speaking rather than writing: the use of contractions (*we're* for *we are*; *that's* for *that is*); starting a sentence with *and*. But the copy remains well structured:

MAKING IT SPEAKABLE

Find a piece of homepage copy that is hard to speak aloud. (It shouldn't be too difficult to find. B2B businesses are a good place to start looking. Legal firms, tech companies or financial institutions are likely candidates.)

Rewrite the copy to make it easier to speak.

Does your copy retain the qualities that you think the original was trying to convey?

The three qualities of an effective voice

Joe Moran, in his superb book *First You Write a Sentence.* (the full stop is part of the title, naturally), spends a few pages discussing copywriting. He identifies three key characteristics that he thinks every effective voice will display.

Sure and steady

When the voice is sure and steady, there are no diversions: 'the prose,' writes Moran, 'must feel as if it's going somewhere.' You need to know what argument you're pursuing.

To find out more about arguments, go to Chapter 4.

Take a look at this copy, from a 1990 ad by David Abbott.

GUESS WHAT SAINSBURY'S NEW CANNED GRAPEFRUIT TASTES LIKE?

In its own little way our new canned grapefruit is something of a milestone.

It's vacuum-packed. (As far as we know, the first on sale in Britain.)

The outcome is grapefruit that tastes uncannily like the fresh fruit.

But taste isn't the only advantage. With vacuum-packing, we're able to put much more grapefruit into the can.

On average, 25% more fruit than with traditional canning methods.

You can buy our new 'flavour seal' grapefruit, unsweetened in pure juice or in a syrup.

Either way, you get more flavour and more fruit.

Good food costs less at Sainsbury's.

'I like headlines that draw the reader into the ad,' writes Abbott. 'A question is the obvious way to do it.' (It's probably best to use a question that can't be answered 'no'.)

The copy answers the question with a clear, two-pronged argument, moving surely and steadily towards its crystal-clear conclusion: more flavour and more fruit. The sentences, too, roll out steadily, with no jolts or jitters. Every sentence is constructed slightly differently – very short and simple sentences are balanced by slightly longer, more complicated ones.

Now read this copy.

DRIED FLOWERS FOR MOTHER'S DAY‽

Our Dried Flower Posies and Wreaths are a great alternative for giving your Mum, this Mother's Day with a vintage and rustic feel. Not only are they cost effective, our dried arrangements will last so she can enjoy them afterwards. They are full of a whole range of dried flowers, grasses and other treats like Oats. These arrangements are bold and hand-arranged in our Farm Floristry to stay looking amazing for a while!

That interrobang in the headline (the combined question mark and exclamation mark) scuppers the argument of the copy before it's even begun. The body copy fails to rescue the argument: what precisely *is* the benefit of dried flowers, for you or for your mother? (And what about those oats? How will mother enjoy those?) The punctuation creates a jolting rhythm that never settles. The promiscuous capital letters, the frankly odd use of adjectives (rustic? vintage?) and the car-crash of the last sentence – with its desperate attempt at emotional energy signalled by the exclamation mark – all create a sense of dithery distractedness.

This voice is the very opposite of sure and steady: it's uncertain and wavering.

WRITE SURE AND STEADY

Rewrite the copy about dried flowers. Aim to be sure and steady.

Hint: clarify the *argument* of the copy. What is your value proposition?

Clear and cool

Clear copy can be understood on first reading. The sentences connect well and the words are easy to understand. Different readers use different vocabularies; plain English in the wrong place might look patronizing or foolish (see 'smart and specific', below).

Cool copy provokes emotion without itself being too emotional. In my experience, trying to inject emotion into copy can backfire: *we're excited to announce…; this sensational offer…; our company is passionate about…*

Read this. Aloud.

NEW YORK'S CROWN JEWEL

Since 1837, Tiffany & Co. has created designs of immense beauty that have captivated the world. Now, a new era begins with the unveiling of The Landmark at the famed corner of 57th Street and Fifth Avenue.

With 10 magnificent floors, you'll discover legendary diamonds, radiant gems and extraordinary art pieces by the world's most acclaimed artists. An icon unlike any other. The Landmark celebrates our House's heritage, innovative spirit and passion for craftsmanship and design.

It's our most beautiful creation yet.

The lack of cool here is mainly in the adjectives: *immense, famed, magnificent, legendary, radiant, extraordinary, acclaimed, beautiful*. They shout emotion, but they fail to *evoke* emotion. Why? Because they're generalized. They're adjectives that don't describe anything. All they do is emphasize.

Now read this.

> **THE WATER KASSA DRINKS COULD KILL HIM, BUT HE HAS NO CHOICE.**
>
> You may have seen Kassa in our recent TV appeal. Your donation to CleanWaterForAll could offer him a new life.
>
> No more drinking filthy river water, teeming with parasites, bacteria and animal waste.
>
> An end to the worry of diarrhoeal diseases, which kill 900 children every day.
>
> A pump or tap in the heart of the community, rather than a daily trek to the river with a heavy jerry can.
>
> Please, choose to bring clean, safe water to families today. Your kindness will be felt for generations to come.

Two emotive words here: *worry* and *kindness*. The copy evokes emotion in the reader by describing things in detail (and offering a single, sober statistic).

Paint a picture; let the reader provide the emotion. That's cool.

Smart and specific

Your copy should make the reader feel smarter for having read it. Listen to this.

> Our conviction is that responsibility is an opportunity to shape and share solutions that serve people, businesses and communities.

This certainly sounds smart. But where are we? What's the copy promoting? More importantly, do you *feel* smarter for having read this copy?

The copy wanders, rootless and untethered, in an interplanetary vacuum of generalizations that relate to nothing at all.

Now listen to this.

> **YOUR GREATEST ALLY IN THE STRUGGLE TO STOP SMOKING.**
> **A BOWL OF CORNFLAKES.**
>
> Instead of your usual early morning cigarette, eat some breakfast.
>
> It'll take your mind off the cravings and keep your blood sugar levels up.
>
> So you'll be less likely to feel tired or grumpy later on and start smoking again.
>
> For information and support call... or visit...

This copy, by Tim Riley for the National Health Service in the UK, addresses a need in the reader and offers a single solution. That solution is surprising – a great way to capture the reader's attention – and the copy argues for the solution in three simple, logical steps.

To be smart, be specific. Make ideas concrete. Avoid generalizations and argue in terms that relate directly to your reader's lived experience. Your reader will feel smarter.

These three pairs of characteristics, it seems to me, will work for any voice.

- Sure and steady
- Clear and cool
- Smart and specific

Apply them to any copy that you produce. They're guaranteed to improve it. Or your money back.

Creating a role

I said just now that your copy's voice should not simply speak; it should perform. Think about the role that your brand voice might perform. Here's an example of a role-based voice profile, taken from the voice guidelines of a consultancy organization.

Hello.

I'm the Facilitator. I make things happen. I spark change and transform the lives of thousands of people. It's rewarding work, but it demands determination, drive and lots of energy.

You'll hear those qualities in my voice.

I like to get to the point. My style is energized and purposeful; a brisk walk rather than a leisurely ramble. I always know where I'm going, and I make sure that I take my reader with me. Sure and steady is my motto.

It's vital that we win the trust of people we meet, so I'm confident and clear. I'm comfortable talking about complicated subjects, but I always want to make people feel smarter for talking to me. I'm inspiring and always talk about new ideas in a way that makes people want to know more, and keen to get involved. In fact, I'm happiest when people think they had the idea themselves. And if they want to get stuck in and take command, I help them do just that.

I often achieve my goals by telling stories: stories about our people and partners, the people who use our innovations, the people whose lives we've changed. We must bring these highly technical issues to life, and stories are a way of doing that.

Creating a role will help your voice speak like a person. Your voice is more likely to remain sure and steady, as well as clear and cool. And by playing a role for your reader, you help the reader to engage more with the copy – which should help to make them feel smarter for having read it.

FINDING A ROLE FOR MY BRAND VOICE

If your brand were a person, how would they relate to customers? Choose one role from this list – or choose your own.

Advisor	Doctor
Artist	Friend
Coach	Geek
Confidant	Guide
Diplomat	Kind relative

Leader	Problem-solver
Mentor	Teacher
Nerd	Therapist
Parent	Troubleshooter

Write a voice profile, speaking in the voice of this role.

Lateral thinking for brand voice

The term 'lateral thinking' was invented by Edward de Bono in the 1960s. It's a mental mobility tool: it allows us to discover new ideas by moving laterally – sideways – from ideas we already know.

Lateral thinking, for de Bono, is the exact opposite of 'vertical thinking'. In vertical thinking, we have to be correct at every stage in order to get a correct answer. Adding up a set of numbers is a good example. Think of vertical thinking as like being on a ladder: we have to stay on the rungs of the ladder. A single move sideways would be disastrous.

In lateral thinking, we don't have to be correct at any stage because we're not looking for a correct answer. We're looking for a new idea and any move might take us towards it. If vertical thinking is like being on a ladder, lateral thinking is like using stepping stones. The aim is to cross the river, but there may be many different routes. Lateral thinking breaks mental conventions or habits. It helps us become more mentally mobile.

We can use lateral thinking to develop a brand voice. Imagine that your brand is in a completely different sector. If you're writing copy for an engineering firm, go to the lingerie sector. If you're writing for a lingerie firm, go into farming. What brand would your brand be in that new sector?

LATERAL THINKING FOR BRAND VOICE

Here's a list of sectors you can use to stimulate some lateral thinking.

If my brand were a...	it would be...
Hotel	
Car	
Restaurant	

Shoe	
Fashion house	
Handbag	
Watch	
Bank	
Department store	
Breakfast food	
Credit card	
Alcoholic drink	
Fragrance	
Camera	
Toy	
Holiday destination	

You can develop this exercise in at least two ways.

1   Go to the website of the brand you've chosen and look at its voice. How does it differ from yours? What ideas could you take away? What are you doing better than them?

2   Link this exercise to your customer or reader persona. What brands in these sectors would your persona choose? Examine the copy for those brands and answer the same questions as in (1) here. How would your brand fit into that portfolio of brands?

Record your discoveries in your swipe file or notebook.

Finally: go back to the very first exercise in this chapter. Try running that exercise again, using one or more of the techniques we've explored in this chapter. Your brand's voice, like any other voice, will only be successful if it stays alive. Renew it regularly and test it with your colleagues and with your readers, customers and users.

SUMMARY

Good copy speaks to its reader.

Its voice should be consistent. Its tone can vary. Think about the kind of company you are and what your reader expects from that kind of company.

To test whether your voice is speakable, read your copy aloud. It must sound like heightened speech.

Any brand voice should be:

- sure and steady
- clear and cool and
- smart and specific

A sure and steady voice pursues its argument with no diversions.

A clear voice can be understood at first reading. Cool copy provokes emotion without itself being too emotional.

A smart and specific voice makes its reader feel smarter for having read it.

Think about the role that your voice might perform.

Use lateral thinking to develop your voice. Imagine that your brand is in a completely different sector. Explore brands in that sector and take ideas for your own voice.

Revisit your brand voice regularly to keep it fresh.

6

Writing headlines and subject lines

Your copy is almost always going to need a headline. Or, if it's an email, a subject line.

A headline needs to do some heavy lifting. It must capture the reader's attention and entice them to read on. A great headline signals your copy's argument – your value proposition – in language that's familiar to your reader and in a voice that's recognizably your brand voice.

David Ogilvy, one of the all-time great copywriters, used to say that once you've written your headline, you've spent 80 cents of your client's dollar. He estimated that 80 per cent of readers read the headline, but only 20 per cent will go on to read the body copy.

That was back in the 1980s. Forty years on, users are more discerning about headlines than ever. Which means that the difference between a successful headline and a dud can be dramatic.

The headline is yet another place where the two traditions of copywriting – advertising and journalism – converge. Newspapers, of course, have always used headlines to sell copies. As journalism went digital in the early part of the century, news aggregators like Upworthy found they could measure the effectiveness of headlines with unprecedented accuracy. 'When we test headlines,' says Upworthy's founder, Peter Koechley, 'we see 20 per cent difference, 50 per cent difference, 500 per cent difference. A really excellent headline can make something go viral.'

And by 'testing' Koechley means demanding that editors create *at least* 25 headlines for each post and then A/B test the top candidates. That's a habit you could usefully emulate.

What goes for headlines goes for email subject lines as well. Joe Rospars, founder of creative agency Blue State, estimates that the right subject line can easily quintuple engagement – for political campaigns as well as marketing initiatives. 'The key,' he says, 'is to keep finding new ways to engage people with your content by being playful with the creative and ruthless with the testing.' Once again: first-stage thinking (with the creative) and second-stage thinking (with the testing).

To find out more about email subject lines, go to Chapter 14.

In this chapter, we'll look at how to write headlines, and subject lines, that work.

WRITE THE HEADLINE FIRST

Did you write the headline after you wrote the copy? Why not work on the headline first? It might help you discover new angles for your copy – or for other content – or even for a whole new marketing campaign.

Curiosity and the perils of cuteness

Check out the headlines when you open your browser. How do they seduce you?

Curiosity. John Caples would approve.

To remind yourself about curiosity and John Caples, go to Chapter 2.

But curiosity needs to be about something specific. Look at these headlines, gathered more or less at random from an investment news site.

Tomorrow Never Stops Exploring

Tough Just Got Better

Choice is Not an Option, It's a Necessity

Business Can't Wait

Which of these headlines would tempt you to click on its accompanying article?

My guess is: none of them. None of these headlines stimulates curiosity. They give the reader no clue of the content that awaits them.

Why did the copywriters produce those cute headlines? Perhaps someone told them that headlines should be intriguing. But intrigue is not curiosity. Your headline must tell the reader how the copy solves a problem for them. Prioritize clarity over cleverness.

Making a promise

As well as stimulating curiosity, a good headline makes a promise: your reader will be interested in something that's genuinely new to them and genuinely useful. And, obviously, the body copy must fulfil that promise.

If your reader is browsing, answer these questions.

- What are you really selling?
- What's your audience profile?
- What emotional trigger will help them make the buying or conversion decision?
- What's your company and product's story?
- What would your company perceive as the major benefit of anything it sells?
- Is there something unusual about the product, company or manufacturing process?
- What's the call to action?
- What would overcome a perceived objection?

And if your reader is searching – we're talking about content now, rather than copy – answer these questions:

- What is the content's message?
- Who is your target reader?
- What need in the reader is this content addressing?
- What's the story?
- How will your reader benefit from knowing this material?
- What's new here?

- Is there a call to action?
- Why should your reader bother with this information?

To find out more about making promises, go to Chapter 7.

Brainstorming headlines

Whenever you're writing a headline, try to create 10 headlines. Then try to create 25, or even 50. Now, pick three or four. How could you improve them? Can you use fewer words, stronger words, better verbs, more punchy or evocative nouns? Which headline delivers a promise most effectively?

BRAINSTORMING HEADLINES

Do this exercise whenever you need to write a headline or subject line.

Create new headlines beginning with these words. Aim to create *at least* three headlines starting with each word or phrase.

How
How to
Why
Which
Who
Who else
Wanted
This
Because
If
Advice
Introducing
Announcing
Now
At last

Check your headlines against the body copy. Which ones stimulate curiosity and promise what the copy will deliver? How could you test three or four headlines for effectiveness?

The 4U's

I am particularly indebted for this section to my colleague Clare Lynch, who knows a thing or two about writing corporate copy.

The 4U's is a headline-writing technique developed by Michael Masterson. It's often referred to as a writing formula, but it's probably better to think of it as a checklist.

- **Useful:** how does the headline help the reader?
- **Ultra-specific:** how does the headline give details to the reader?
- **Unique:** how does the headline surprise the reader?
- **Urgent:** how does the headline move the reader to act?

Useful

More than anything else, your headline should offer a benefit or promise to solve a problem.

How to be a better dad

A useful headline tells the reader how your product or service can save them money or time; how it will improve their life.

Ultra-specific

Promise information that's specifically useful, or offer a specialized slant that will appeal to the specific reader you're targeting. The headline could promise a story that the body copy will deliver. Accurate and succinct is what we're looking for.

Another way to make your headline ultra-specific is to make it clear who your target reader is. This headline, like the last one, names that reader.

Seven mistakes every new dad makes

Notice, too, how this headline uses a number. Your reader knows exactly how much information they'll get if they read on. We'll see more about numbers in headlines shortly.

By the way, being ultra-specific does *not* necessarily mean specifying a product name. Take a look at these two headlines.

How to use TubeIQ's tag feature

Use this simple trick to get more video views

The first will attract *only* people who have heard of TubeIQ and know what a tag feature is. The second responds to the ultra-specific pain of not getting video views.

Unique

Any headline should offer something useful and ultra-specific. Now we're raising the stakes. Can you offer something that nobody else is offering?

A unique headline is a surprise. It grabs the reader's attention with a shocking fact, unusual statement, special piece of information or distinctive slant.

Now here, you might have to get creative with your choice of words. Remember the clear-and-cool principle. Avoid generalized words like *incredible, amazing, once-in-a-lifetime* and *never-to-be-forgotten*. (Or, indeed, *unique*.) And please – *please!* – avoid all those corporate clichés like *innovative, solution, driving growth* or *delivering success*.

Instead, use words that provoke an emotional response. The trick is to stay ultra-specific. Clare tells me that one of the most successful posts on her blog had this headline.

Ten ways to stop that verbose exec from mangling your copy

Which was quickly followed by this one.

Six more sneaky ways to make them say it your way

What makes those headlines unique? Check out those unusual words: *verbose, mangling* and *sneaky*. They're also useful and specific: they reflect the reader's problem exactly – and promise to solve it.

Urgent

An urgent headline moves the reader to act sooner rather than later. One way to motivate immediate action is to make your offer unignorable. The most obvious way to convey urgency is to include a timeframe or deadline.

Act now.

Limited time offer.

Only ten places left at this price.

Sale ends today.

Prioritizing the 4U's

Very few headlines will be useful, ultra-specific, unique and urgent.

Every headline should be useful. And the more specific your promise, the more attention-grabbing it will be. You might be able to make your offer truly unique or – as we've suggested – you may be able to suggest uniqueness in the way you make your offer. Urgency might be appropriate in certain situations; in others – in technical or academic fields, perhaps – urgency might actually detract from your authority or credibility.

You might also balance or rebalance the 4U's according to the kind of copy you're writing. For blogs and other kinds of content, uniqueness helps to build rapport and grow a following. For authority positioning and B2B content, ultra-specificity establishes credibility and establishes expertise. For headlines and CTAs, urgency makes them more effective.

But whatever you're writing, prioritize usefulness.

USING THE 4U'S

Go back to some of the headlines you created in the last exercise.

Apply one or more of the 4U's and see how the headline changes. Work in this order:

- Useful: how does the headline help the reader?

- Ultra-specific: how does the headline give details to the reader?

- Unique: how does the headline surprise the reader?

- Urgent: how does the headline move the reader to act?

Does a new headline suggest a new piece of copy or content? Note it down; it could be useful.

Using the 4U's in bullet points

What applies to headlines can also apply to bullet points.

Bullet points can look so simple. And that's what can make them so deceptive, and even dangerous. Bullets are easy to read. (That's why you use them, right?) Easy to read means easily read, superficially reviewed and often ignored. Bullets could derail your copy by distracting or diluting your reader's attention.

Writing great bullets is a challenge worth working at. Think of each bullet as a little haiku. A verbal gem. Make each bullet convey as many of the 4U's as possible. And make sure that they work *together* as a list so that the overall effect is coherent.

Which style of headline works best?

Some years ago, tech company Conductor decided to work out which headline styles resonated most with readers. My thanks to them for this useful information.

First, they analysed a sample set of headlines across multiple online publications and social networks and identified five broad categories of headline.

- **Normal** (Ways to Make Drinking Coffee More Delightful)

- **Question** (How Can You Make Drinking Coffee More Delightful?)

- **How to** (How to Make Drinking Coffee More Delightful)

- **Number** (30 Ways to Make Drinking Coffee More Delightful)

- **Reader-Addressing** (What You Need to Make Drinking Coffee More Delightful)

Using actual headlines from multiple content sources including BuzzFeed, HuffPost and Conductor's own blog, the researchers asked respondents to choose the headlines that resonated most with them.

Here's what they found.

Number headlines outperformed all others, at 36 per cent. Reader-addressing headlines came second at 21 per cent, followed by 'How To' headlines at 17 per cent, normal headlines at 15 per cent and question headlines at only 11 per cent.

Next, they tested users' tolerance for superlatives in a headline.

- The 27 Ways to Train a Dog (no superlatives)
- The 27 **Best** Ways to Train a Dog (one superlative)
- The 27 **Best** Ways **Ever** to Train a Dog (two superlatives)
- The 27 **Best** Ways **Ever** to Train a **Perfect** Dog (three superlatives)
- The 27 **Best** and **Smartest** Ways **Ever** to Train a **Perfect** Dog (four superlatives)

Most users (51 per cent) preferred an understated approach: either no superlatives or only one. This result underpins the need for copy that's clear and cool. However, the researchers also found a massive 25 per cent of respondents preferring four superlatives – probably because these users saw the humour in overstating the case. With the right target audience, a jokey over-the-top headline might just capture attention.

Finally, the researchers asked about respondents' capitalization preferences.

- The 5 steps to prepare for the impending zombie apocalypse (sentence case)
- THE 5 STEPS TO PREPARE FOR THE IMPENDING ZOMBIE APOCALYPSE (capitals)
- The 5 Steps to Prepare for the Impending Zombie Apocalypse (title case)
- No preference

The data showed that respondents strongly preferred title case – probably because it remains the most familiar method of capitalizing headlines.

In title case, major words are capitalized and most minor words are lowercase.

- **major words:** nouns, verbs (including linking verbs), adjectives, adverbs, pronouns and all words of four letters or more

- **minor words:** short (three letters or fewer) conjunctions, short preposi-tions and all articles (the, a, an).

Surprisingly, 21 per cent of respondents preferred all-capital headings. If you think you know who makes up that 21 per cent of users, go ahead and yell at them. On the whole, title case is the way to go.

Conductor's survey also underlines the relative ineffectiveness of asking questions – in headlines or in any other prominent parts of your copy.

SUMMARY

A great headline signals your copy's value proposition in language that's familiar to your reader and in a voice that's recognizably your brand voice.

Try writing a headline before you write the copy.

Use headline writing to generate new ideas for copy.

Stimulate curiosity. Avoid cuteness or intrigue. Prioritize clarity over cleverness.

Use a headline to make a promise.

Always brainstorm many more headlines than you will use.

Use the 4U's to develop your headlines:

- Useful: how does the headline help the reader?

- Ultra-specific: how does the headline give details to the reader?

- Unique: how does the headline surprise the reader?

- Urgent: how does the headline move the reader to act?

Prioritize usefulness.

What applies to headlines can also apply to bullet points.

Number headlines can outperform other styles of headline.

Most readers prefer no superlatives or only one. (The clear and cool principle applies here.)

Most readers prefer headlines in title case: major words are capitalized and most minor words are lowercase.

Aristotle and the Three Musketeers

The Ancient Greeks were among the first people in European history to study the arts of persuasion and, crucially, to write about them. Among the most famous was Aristotle, whose treatise *Rhetoric* – probably a set of lecture notes – summarized a three-point strategy for persuasive speaking. That strategy is as relevant to copywriting as it was over 2000 years ago to speaking in the Athenian assembly.

Aristotle suggested that every speech is made up of three elements: the speaker, the audience and the speech itself. It follows that persuasion itself has three components, one based on each element. These three modes of appeal have come to be known as *ethos*, *pathos* and *logos* – in the words of one wit, 'the three musketeers of persuasion'.

- *Pathos* is the appeal to the audience's feelings and imagination.
- *Logos* appeals through the logic of the argument.
- *Ethos* is the mode of appeal based on the authority, credibility, reputation or good name of the speaker.

We can apply these three dimensions of persuasion directly to our own copywriting.

- We create *pathos* by creating a reader persona.
- We develop *logos* by constructing a clear argument or value proposition.
- And we build *ethos* by developing a persuasive brand voice.

I recently saw a great example of the three musketeers in action, on the home page of V&Me, a company that makes and distributes customized baby food.

WHY CHOOSE US?

Cooked today, delivered today

We cook local and seasonal produce from scratch and deliver fresh to your door. The fresher the food, the more nutrition it keeps. That means more tantalizing flavours for your baby to enjoy.

Developed by children's dieticians

'What should I make today?' Don't worry about it. Our baby health experts decide every meal according to evidence-based research to help your baby grow up smarter and stronger.

Happy mummy, full wee tummy

Don't slave away in the kitchen when you could be having a much-needed nap. We serve 54 delicious dishes every season. Your baby will be licking the plate. You'll be skipping the prep and clean-up!

Each paragraph fits one of Aristotle's three modes of appeal: *logos*; *ethos*; *pathos*. Can you tell which is which? (Hint: how does the copy order them?)

PART THREE

Shaping the copy

Copywriters often use structural frameworks or formulas. But a good copywriter never deploys a formula blindly; they adjust and adapt it as the need arises. Very often, the content will suggest its own structure.

So, which structure to choose? As you might guess, it comes back to that distinction between browsing and searching we explored in Chapter 2. A browsing reader needs to be led from where they are to where we want them to be; a searching reader needs to see the information they're looking for at once and then navigate it easily. Journeys and pyramids form the basis of the structures we look at in this section.

- In **Chapter 7**, we look at structures for browsing: how to shape your copy to capture your reader's attention and guide them towards taking action.
- In **Chapter 8**, we investigate narrative structures. Why are we so drawn to stories? How can you construct stories that will hold your reader's attention from start to finish? And does narrative have any other uses beyond storytelling?
- In **Chapter 9**, we explore structures that will work for a reader who's searching for useful information. Use these structures whenever you're creating content to raise your reader's awareness, direct their thinking, instruct them or argue a case.

These structures aren't mutually exclusive. A single piece of content might use two or more structures. Think of these different structures as tools in your copywriting toolkit and try them out in different situations.

7

Structures for browsing

A browsing reader scans and skims you need to capture their attention and then take them where you want them to go. That destination is likely to be a call to action: buying something, signing up or subscribing, donating, completing a task – or simply clicking through to another web page.

The structures in this chapter all take your reader on that journey. Use them for social media, short-form ads, newsletters, emails and contributions to chat rooms or forums. But they can also help you structure longer-form content, especially scripts for videos or podcasts. And whenever you need to hook your reader – at the start of an article or blog post – these structures will be useful.

Arouse and fulfil

In 1998, a marine biologist and filmmaker called Randy Olson was making a video called *Talking Science: The elusive art of the science talk*. Olson wanted to improve the way scientists communicated their ideas, especially to non-scientists.

At one point, he interviewed Tom Hollihan, Professor of Communication at the USC Annenberg School for Communication and Journalism. Hollihan talked about how to hold an audience's attention. 'Some of the most effective theories about communication,' he said, 'talk about the arousal and fulfilment of your audience's desires. You want to pique their interest and then you want to satisfy that interest. If you don't arouse them, they never get engaged, they never connect, they never listen; if you don't fulfil them, they walk away saying, "That wasn't a very satisfying talk."'

What applies to talks or presentations applies also to copy. Too much copy fails because it doesn't arouse and fulfil. Some copy arouses without fulfilling, like a bad movie: all arousal, teasing, flashy effects, explosions – and no substantial payoff. And we're left feeling cheated, let down, disappointed. Some copy ignores the arousal and cuts straight to the fulfilment. Think of much technical copy, specialist copy, bureaucratic copy or scientific copy: bombarding the reader with facts and details, details and facts. No arousal of expectations. No acknowledgement of a need or desire in the reader. And we're left feeling confused, bored, insulted or hostile.

Arouse and fulfil. The two must go together.

How to attract attention

We attract attention by making a gesture. A gesture is a single, isolated, unusual or surprising movement. We notice gestures because they stand out from their background. They might be physical: a sudden, unexpected movement, like pointing. They might be visual, like a flashing light or a sudden cut in a film. And they might be vocal, like suddenly shouting or breaking into song.

We can also gesture using words. We might suddenly use an unusual word. We might utter a proverb. ('Ah well, you know… hope springs eternal in the human breast…') Advertising slogans are prime examples of verbal gestures.

> Don't leave home without it.

> I'm lovin' it.

> Every little helps.

Many animals gesture to each other, physically and vocally – usually to threaten or to attract each other. But humans are the only animals that gesture to each other *about something else*. It's called declarative gesturing: 'Look at this,' the gesture says. 'This is interesting!'

It's exactly this kind of gesture – declarative gesturing, using words – that we're interested in.

CREATE A SLOGAN

A slogan encompasses a brand's value proposition in a single, unforgettable phrase. Creating a slogan is an art in itself.

Have a go. Pick a brand that you know well. It could be your own brand, it could be a brand that you use regularly. Create three possible slogans for that brand.

1 Identify the customer persona for this brand. If you've already created a customer persona from the exercises in Chapter 3, use that – and maybe adjust your brand to one that fits that persona.

2 Identify the value proposition of the brand for that persona.

3 Write down some sentences expressing that value proposition.

4 Think about the emotion you want to evoke in your reader.

5 Simplify and condense each sentence. Try to create a slogan using no more than about six words. Use rhyme, alliteration, contrast or wordplay. Imagine creating a proverb...

Which slogan seems to work best? Can you say why?

If you're writing any copy longer than a slogan, begin by making a verbal gesture. Here are three possible gestures.

- Ask a question.
- State a problem.
- Make a promise.

(There's at least one other kind of gesture that you could use. And it might just be the most powerful of all. But we'll come to that later in this chapter.)

How to fulfil your reader's expectation

Having aroused their curiosity, you must now set about fulfilling their expectation.

- Ask a question – and answer it.
- State a problem – and solve it.
- Make a promise – and keep it.

Arouse one expectation at a time. and then fulfil it. Don't set up multiple expectations.

And there's the structure we're looking for. It has a beginning and an ending. It begins with arousal; it ends with fulfilment.

Arouse, withhold, fulfil

You've aroused your reader's interest and created an expectation. Suppose, now, that you *withheld* the fulfilment of that expectation. What would be the effect?

We love having an expectation aroused and then having its fulfilment withheld. In a crime story, we love not knowing who the killer is; in a love story, we love wondering whether they'll finally get together or not. That frustration of our expectation is what keeps us reading or watching.

We're talking about suspense.

By withholding fulfilment, you create suspense, which intensifies the arousal – especially the emotional arousal. Which, in turn, will make the fulfilment all the more – well, fulfilling.

Arouse; withhold; fulfil. Let's apply this three-part structure in some typical marketing situations.

Problem, agitate, solution

How do you withhold solving a problem? By making the problem more emotionally intense.

PAS stands for:

- **Problem**
- **Agitate**
- **Solution**

First, **identify a problem**: one that the reader will immediately recognize and identify with.

Now **agitate the problem**. Paint a picture of how that problem feels. Make the reader *experience* the problem. Don't be afraid to show the problem in its worst light. But remember to be clear and cool: don't let your copy become too overtly emotional. Describe the problem in specific, concrete terms so that the *reader* feels the emotion: frustration, fear, irritation…

And finally, **solve the problem**. Your product or service will remove the suspense. Present your solution as the best one available. You're creating a value proposition. On a social media channel, the solution will often be a link to a web page or another piece of content.

To find out more about value propositions, go to Chapter 4.

Here are two examples of PAS at work.

[*Problem*]
   Peter Drucker once wrote, 'If you can't measure it, you can't improve it.'
   According to a recent survey by Hubspan, 61 per cent of marketers rate generating traffic as their most significant challenge. When the C-suite aren't seeing the leads they expect, they start to question the value of your work – and your position in the organization.

[*Agitate*]
   That's when data becomes crucial.
   Without data, you'll have no idea what effect your SEO strategies are having on your marketing performance. But with access to clear, intelligible data, you can justify your marketing budget to the most sceptical of executives.

[*Solution*]
   We've produced a user's guide to Google Analytics, the most robust free analytics tool available. It will help turn you into an SEO pro in just a few days.
   Click here to receive your free copy.

[*Problem*]
A cake is a great way to bring the whole family or office together. But what about people with major food allergies? They can so easily be left out of the fun.

[*Agitate*]
Sure, you could find an alternative for them. But who's ever happy with that? And what if you forget? Worse still, what if a loved one or colleague accidentally ingested an allergen? Even momentary contact can be extremely harmful – or deadly.

[*Solution*]

Help is at hand. Spare yourself the stress and worry by purchasing one of our yummy, allergen-free cakes. Each of our regular cakes comes in an allergen-free version, making it safe for all while retaining the same handmade, delicious flavour.

Which means that everyone can help themselves – and enjoy the fun together.

WRITING PAS COPY

Go back to your reader persona and identify three problems that they face.

Find a solution for each problem. Let your imagination run free: the solutions don't have to be related to your own work as a copywriter.

Write three pieces of PAS copy marketing each solution.

Check your copy's voice. Is it:

- sure and steady?
- clear and cool?
- smart and specific?

AIDA and AIDCA

In 1915, Business Books of Whitefriars House, Tallis Street, London EC4 published the *Encyclopedia of Advertising and Selling*. At one point, the anonymous author presented what has become a classic structure in direct marketing. Here, in its own words, is how the encyclopedia laid out this structure. Notice the words I've put in bold.

1 The opening, which wins the reader's **attention** and prompts them to go further into the letter.

2 Description and explanation that gains **interest** by picturing the position in their mind.

3 Argument or proof, which creates **desire** for the article you have to sell by showing its value and advantages.

4 Persuasion, which draws the reader to your way of thinking by showing the adaptation of the article to his needs and his need of it now.

5 Inducement, which gives him a particular or extra reason for buying.

6 The climax, which makes it easy for the reader to order and prompts him to **act** at once.

Thus was born AIDA, perhaps the most famous copywriting structure of them all.

(Culture-vulture moment: to avoid embarrassment, know that this acronym is pronounced 'eye-ee-dah'. The reference is to an opera by that great Italian composer Giuseppi Verdi. Don't be caught out by talking about 'ay-dah'.)

As time went on, AIDA acquired a fifth letter: 'C', standing for 'Commitment' or 'Conviction'. Step 5 in the encyclopedia's explanation – the step about inducement – provides the conviction that will help the reader commit to the final action.

AIDCA stretches the 'arouse, withhold, fulfil' structure. 'Attention' and 'Interest' arouse an expectation; 'Desire' and 'Conviction' withhold fulfilment, intensifying emotional arousal in the reader – making the final 'Action' step all the more compelling.

ATTENTION

The most obvious tool for capturing attention is a headline – in an email, the subject line. Rouse curiosity. Make a promise. Use the 4U's.

To find out more about headlines and the 4U's, go to Chapter 6.

You can also hook your reader's attention in the opening lines of the body copy. A good way to do that, of course, is to focus on a problem.

INTEREST

Generate interest by guiding the reader from the problem to the solution. Focus on *one* problem. Agitate it. And then guide your reader to the solution. Focus on the benefits of the solution – what's in it for the reader – rather than enumerating all the features of the product or service.

> *To find out more about benefits, go to Chapter 3 and Chapter 4.*

DESIRE

Now stimulate your reader's senses and imagination. Paint a picture of the solution making a difference in their life. Don't overdo the adjectives: use them to describe, not to emphasize. (Avoid, for instance, *incredible*, *fantastic* and *amazing*.)

> *To find out more about adjectives, go to Chapter 5.*

CONVICTION

Will your reader believe you? Use evidence: testimonials, statistics from authoritative sources, information that lends credibility to your offer. Is the benefit worth the cost? You could also offer evidence that your solution has minimal costs.

ACTION

Make the action as simple as possible. A single click would be ideal.

For decades, AIDCA has ruled as the go-to structure for all advertising copy. You might not use every step in every ad or direct-marketing email. And you might even decide to disrupt the sequence. But AIDCA provides a useful template. If in doubt, use it. It will serve you well.

MAPPING AIDCA

Fast Track offers a fitness regime based on a technology called EMS. Here's how the company introduces the technology on its website. I've altered the wording very slightly.

Map the AIDCA structure onto this copy. When you've finished, check out our solution at the end of this chapter.

> EMS is quite simply the Fast Track to fitness. Just one twenty-minute session a week at Fast Track could help you achieve exceptional results in muscle strengthening, body toning and all-round fitness. EMS is also extremely effective at helping overcome back pain and knee injuries, as well as being an excellent training method for asthmatics and emphysema sufferers.

EMS (or Electro Muscle Stimulation) is medically approved and has been used in training by Olympic athletes since the 1970s. The technology is German and there are over 2000 specialist EMS studios across Europe. But although EMS is now used by sports stars such as Usain Bolt and Rafa Nadal, it has been little known in the UK.

Until now.

So, whether you are an elite athlete, an 80-year-old looking to stay in shape, or wanting to overcome an injury, EMS at Fast Track can change your life. Book a free trial today at either of Fast Track's venues, or let us come to you.

The power of the promise

Why would your reader buy anything from you? Because of what you provide? No. They will buy from you because of what you promise. (This section is indebted to Andy Maslen, with thanks.)

I'm not talking about this kind of promise.

I promise to send the bird food you ordered.

I'm talking about a promise that looks something like this.

I promise you that within minutes of filling your feeder with our bird seed, you'll have birds flocking into your garden.

A promise goes beyond the product's benefit and fulfils an emotional need. A car might have satnav fitted as standard: that's a feature. As a result, you'll find your way to any destination efficiently: that's the benefit. But what does the reader *really* want from pre-installed satnav? Why would they pay the premium for that feature? What's the deeply buried emotional lever that we could throw here? What are we promising?

You'll never be lost again.

They'll process the benefit rationally. They'll process the promise emotionally.

How to make a promise

In short-form copy, the best way to make a promise is usually as an order. And make it specific.

Earn a year's salary in a week.

Get a good night's sleep without using drugs.

Never lose data again.

By promising in this way, you're doing two things. First, you're immediately engaging an emotional expectation: in these three cases, greed, anxiety and insecurity. Second, the fact that the promise is incomplete means that you trigger curiosity. The reader now needs to know the crucial thing: 'How do I do this?' Which prompts you to find the material you need for the rest of your copy.

MAKING A PROMISE

Pick a product or service that you're writing copy for. Identify the benefit for your customer.

Now take one step beyond the benefit and find the emotional promise. Phrase it as a command – or maybe a prediction: *after buying this product, you'll...* Or: *after buying this product, you'll never ... again.*

Imagine your reader asking 'How?'

Now write 100 words answering that question. Let the material go where it wants to go. Or return to AIDCA if it helps. Remember to close with a clear call to action.

When promises don't come true

Now, I can already hear you saying, 'This is all very well, but what if...?' Yes. Indeed. What if the promise fails to materialize? What then?

Things do go wrong. Some customers, in some situations, will simply shrug and put it down to experience – or admit that they got it wrong. But you should write something that acknowledges the possibility of failure. In fact, your reader will probably find your promise more than a little suspicious if you *don't* make that acknowledgement.

The money-back guarantee is probably your first option. Phrase it positively. So, not like this.

> If you're not completely satisfied, just contact us for a full refund.

But like this.

> I think you'll be delighted when you see how our widget makes your life easier. But if at any time and for any reason you decide that you're not completely satisfied, please contact us and we'll happily offer you a complete refund.

You could also try something a little more subtle.

> Will our widget change your life overnight? Maybe not. But if it hasn't made cleaning your home more enjoyable and less stressful, let us know. We'll happily offer you a complete refund.

What's the secret?

Earlier in this chapter, I promised you another verbal gesture that you could use to arouse your reader's curiosity. And I told you that it might be the most powerful of all.

You can probably guess what it is.

'I'm going to tell you a secret. But you mustn't tell anyone.'

A secret pushes two emotional buttons. First: if something seems to be hard to get, we feel a need to get it. And secrets, by definition, are not widely available. Which makes them highly desirable. And second: knowing a secret makes us part of an in-crowd. Knowing a secret gives us social power. Who doesn't want to feel more powerful?

Secrets – and the promises of secrets – have an astonishing power to attract attention and arouse emotional expectations. So, how can you use them in your copy?

Try headlines that begin in these ways.

The secret [X] that [professional group] don't want you to know about.

The secret ingredient that makes [X] so effective.

Three [X] secrets that they don't teach you at [Y].

Top [customer or business category] all love this [X]. But they'll never tell you why.

Revealed, the [X] that was known only to the Romans.

REVEALING A SECRET

Pick a product or service you're writing copy for. Identify a secret that you could use to promote the product or service.

Write a headline and 50 words of copy exploiting that secret to promote the product or service.

You can use a secret to create brand loyalty. You might even be able to encourage satisfied customers to become influencers and advocates for your brand by allowing them to share a secret with their friends.

MAPPING AIDCA: SOLUTION

Here's how the Fast Track copy breaks down, using the AIDCA structure.

[Attention] EMS is quite simply the Fast Track to fitness. **[Interest]** Just one twenty-minute session a week at Fast Track could help you achieve exceptional results in muscle strengthening, body toning and all-round fitness. **[Desire]** EMS is also extremely effective at helping overcome back pain and knee injuries, as well as being an excellent training method for asthmatics and emphysema sufferers.

[Commitment] EMS (or Electro Muscle Stimulation) is medically approved and has been used in training by Olympic athletes since the 1970s. The technology is German and there are over 2000 specialist EMS studios across Europe. But although EMS is now used by sports stars such as Usain Bolt and Rafa Nadal, it has been little known in the UK.

Until now.

[Action] So, whether you are an elite athlete, an 80-year-old looking to stay in shape, or wanting to overcome an injury, EMS at Fast Track can change your life. Book a free trial today at either of Fast Track's venues, or let us come to you.

SUMMARY

Browsing readers must be captured and taken on a journey.

The basic principle is: 'Arouse and fulfil.'

We attract attention by making a gesture. We can also gesture using words. In marketing, slogans and taglines are such gestures.

You can gesture in three ways:

- Ask a question.
- State a problem.
- Make a promise.

To fulfil the arousal created by the gesture:

- Ask a question – and answer it.
- State a problem – and solve it.
- Make a promise – and keep it.

Arouse one expectation at a time. And then fulfil it. Don't set up multiple expectations.

We can develop this structure into 'Arouse; withhold; fulfil'.

PAS stands for:

- Problem
- Agitate
- Solution

We can develop it further into AIDA and AIDCA:

- Attention
- Interest
- Desire
- Conviction or Commitment
- Actlon

Make your promises specific. It should fulfil an emotional need as well as a functional need.

You may need to acknowledge that promises can fail. The money-back guarantee is probably your first option.

You can also use secrets to hook a browsing reader. You can use a secret to create brand loyalty or to encourage customers to become brand advocates.

8

Storytelling and the uses of narrative

Marketers have fallen in love with storytelling. 'Marketing is no longer about the stuff that you make,' says permission marketer Seth Godin, 'but about the stories you tell.' And the stats seem to prove him right. According to Sprout Social, 84 per cent of consumers say that they buy from brands they feel an emotional connection to – and stories, it seems, provide just such a connection.

But how do stories create that connection?

The aura of authenticity

Here's one answer, offered by a content marketing consultancy's website, picked more or less at random.

'Storytelling isn't just about pushing a product or service,' says Lauren Basiura of Marketing Insider Group. 'It's about crafting an aura around your brand that grabs your customers, stirs up their feelings, and gets them to take action.'

Ah. So that's it. Stories create an *aura*. Interesting word. It was used by Walter Benjamin, a major cultural critic of the early 20th century. In an essay called 'The Work of Art in the Age of Mechanical Reproduction', Benjamin explained that an original, authentic work of art has an aura that's lost when it's reproduced. The Mona Lisa, for example – the real, the authentic Mona Lisa – has an aura that a poster of the Mona Lisa completely lacks.

So maybe stories carry an aura because they make a brand or a product seem more authentic. How might they do that?

- **First, stories create a sense of identification.** Our brain seems to respond to a story about an event in roughly the same way it does when we experience the event directly. If you tell me about your frustration at missing a train, for instance, I'll feel something of that same frustration. I identify with your feelings.

- **Second, stories seem to act on our senses and even our muscles.** We all know, for instance, that hearing a description of a tasty meal will make us salivate. The words *she smiled and kicked the ball into the long grass* will stimulate the part of the brain that controls your facial muscles and your leg movements. You might even twitch your leg or smile slightly when you hear or read those words.

- **Stories activate hormones.** If we're watching a tense thriller in which the hero is battling a deadly enemy, the suspense raises our levels of cortisol and adrenaline, heightening our attention. (That word again!) When our hero finally wins out against the odds, serotonin is released, which makes us feel happy. And the satisfying conclusion of a story can give us a dopamine rush, which rewards us with a feeling of pleasure – and, crucially, the desire to *repeat* the experience. (Which is probably why children love to hear the same story over and over again.)

Who wouldn't want to exploit all those effects to market a product?

How stories work

My guess is that you've already told several stories today. Maybe it was about what happened on the way to work; or about a friend; or about a problem that you encountered at home the night before. You probably found the story so easy to tell that you hardly thought about *how* you told it.

Three key features of a story

What do all good stories have in common?

First, a story has characters. They'll often be people. But a character doesn't have to be human. It could be the deer that ran out in front of our car last night; or the computer that crashed just when we were rushing to complete a crucial email; or the sponge in the oven that failed to rise.

Second, the characters are always doing something. A story is always about things happening. The storyteller chooses which actions or events to highlight and presents them in a particular order. That sequence is critical to the story's success: if we disrupt that sequence – if we narrate the actions in the wrong order – our audience might, literally, lose the plot.

Most stories revolve around two key actions.

- The first action is usually called *the inciting incident*. It sets the story in motion. A person accosts us in the street and asks a question. We decide to go to a wedding. We hear water dripping onto the ceiling above our bed.

- The second key event is a *crisis*. The person in the street suddenly makes a grab for our bag. The bride at the wedding turns out to be our ex-partner. The ceiling collapses onto the bed. That crisis is the climax of the story.

Third, stories generate meaning. In every case, the crisis triggers a question in our audience. The question is likely to be, 'So what happened?' or 'So what did you do?'

The answer to that question resolves the crisis. We crave certainty or closure. Once a story has hooked us, we desperately need to know how it ends.

The end of the story usually points to a lesson or a moral. Whenever you tell me a story, you're not just telling me what happened, you're telling me what that event means to you. And you're inviting me to share that meaning.

The people we tell stories to, in fact, *expect* us to share that meaning. I vividly remember telling my young daughter stories, only for her to ask, more or less politely, 'Your point being?'

I think that this 'so what' element is fundamental to the deep magic of storytelling. That lesson or moral helps to make life less uncertain, more predictable.

WHAT DOES A STORY MEAN?

Think of a story that you know really well. It might be the story of Cinderella, or the latest episode of a soap opera.

Tell the story in your own words. Now ask yourself: what is this story about? What does it mean? What is the moral of the story?

To make the exercise even more interesting, share a story with a friend. Ask them to tell the same story in their own words. Then ask them what they think the story means.

It's highly unlikely that both of you will come up with the same answer. Why should the same story mean such different things to different people?

What does this exercise suggest about the way you use stories in your copy at work?

Marketing copy, too, seeks to make life less uncertain for its reader. 'Should I buy this product?' 'Should I trust this person with my money?' A story can help your reader navigate that uncertainty. By showing how a character solves a problem, for example, the story creates a safe space in which the reader can imagine how *they* might solve it.

The narrative arc

We all know that stories have three parts: a beginning, a middle and an end. In the nineteenth century, a German novelist and literary critic called Gustav Freytag added two elements to that three-part structure. Freytag's terms – 'rising action' and 'falling action' – have led to this structure being called a narrative arc.

- **Exposition.** This initial material establishes the theme of the story, its setting and the major characters.
- **Rising action.** Tension increases because of a conflict or a developing sense of uncertainty. The rising action usually begins with an inciting incident.
- **Crisis.** This is the moment of greatest tension or uncertainty. The conflict comes to a head or the protagonist must make a decisive choice.
- **Falling action.** The falling action is triggered by the protagonist's action at the crisis point. Tension is released.
- **Resolution.** Everyone lives happily ever after. Or not. The resolution supplies and underlies the story's moral or meaning.

Finding a plot

The narrative arc shows you how to lay out a series of events. The events you choose determine the story's plot.

Alfred Hitchcock once famously described plot as 'life with the boring bits taken out'. So, how do you distinguish the interesting bits from the boring bits?

Here's the plot of Charles Dickens' famous tale, *A Christmas Carol*, set out in the framework of the narrative arc.

- **Exposition.** Ebenezer Scrooge is a miserly merchant and money lender in Victorian England. He cruelly dismisses poor men seeking money for food and turns down an invitation to have dinner with his nephew.

- **Rising action.** In the inciting incident, Scrooge is visited by the ghost of Jacob Marley, his late business partner, who warns him he'll be visited by three spirits. The Ghost of Christmas Past takes Scrooge back to his unhappy childhood and shows him how his fiancée, Belle, ended their relationship because he was too obsessed with money. The Ghost of Christmas Present then shows him his employee Bob Cratchit's bleak Christmas dinner. Scrooge learns that Cratchit's son, Tiny Tim, is gravely ill; if the family's circumstances don't change, Tiny Tim is likely to die.

- **Climax.** The Ghost of Christmas Yet to Come shows Scrooge a future where he, Scrooge, dies and nobody mourns his loss. Scrooge breaks down and promises to become a better person if he is offered the chance to go back to the present.

- **Falling action.** Scrooge wakes up on Christmas morning a changed man. To make amends for his previous cruelty, he donates money to charity, provides Christmas dinner for the Cratchit family and raises Bob's salary.

- **Resolution.** Scrooge vows to embody the spirit of Christmas spirit in all he does. Tiny Tim does not die and Scrooge vows to become a second father to him.

Cause and effect – the key to a good plot

Whenever you tell a story, the events *must* all be causally linked.

Cause-and-effect thinking is one of the basic ways in which we understand how the world works. We drop a glass on the floor and it smashes. We throw a switch and the light comes on. We take a pill and the headache disappears. In each case, we don't need to understand the technicalities; simple cause-and-effect thinking explains what happens.

SPQR: the bare bones of the plot

Here's a structure that will give you the bare bones of a plot. You can remember these four terms because their initial letters spell SPQR: the motto of the Roman Empire.

SITUATION
Once upon a time…

The Situation sets out an initial state of affairs. We meet the key characters and the setting or context in which the story will play out. The Situation might include the physical location – where the story takes place – and other elements, such as when the story happened, the kind of business or organization involved, and so on.

The trick in writing a good Situation is to make it immediately recognizable to the reader. Don't start your story somewhere the reader will find unfamiliar. Sales presentations, for example, that begin with *What We Do* risk alienating the audience immediately.

PROBLEM

Within the Situation, a Problem arises. The Problem complicates the Situation in some way. Perhaps something has gone wrong or a threat has suddenly appeared. Maybe improvements are necessary.

If you possibly can, make your Problem an event: something should happen that disturbs the equilibrium of the Situation.

The Problem must create suspense. You need to set up a sense of rising tension that leads to a...

QUESTION

In narrative terms, the Question stands for the crisis. How will the Problem be solved?

RESPONSE

The Response answers the Question and solves the Problem. We might also call it the Resolution: it resolves the Problem and brings the story to a satisfying close. The Response also provides the all-important 'so what?' element that gives the story its meaning.

The 'so what' should relate directly to your value proposition. If the story demonstrates that proposition, then the story's worth telling.

How to use SPQR

One of the most common ways to use SPQR is to tell your company's backstory. Here's a brilliant example, written by Christopher Dobbing, which sits on the home page of the company he founded, the Cambridge Mask Company.

I founded Cambridge Mask Co after moving to Beijing. I saw a lot of young kids get sick from air pollution. They were growing up thinking the air should be coloured in grey in pictures and coughing all day was normal. No one, especially not children, should have to sacrifice their health just by breathing. I developed a family-friendly science-led mask that can help protect children and adults from air pollution. I believe everyone should be able to get out and enjoy life without having to worry about what they breathe or the way they look. Today we have helped over 1 million people in over 100 countries get the mask they need to help them stay safe from pathogens, urban air pollution, wildfire smoke, traffic fumes or whatever might be damaging their health.

MAPPING SPQR ONTO A STORY

Map Situation, Problem, Question and Response onto Christopher Dobbings' founding story.

Where is the 'So what?' element in this story? My solution is at the end of this chapter.

SPQR is also a great structure for introducing proposals and business cases.

Our business is rapidly expanding. Our current premises are too small and are not ideally located. We need to find both an assembly site and distribution hub. In this report, we recommend relocating both facilities to Freeborough.

Use it, also, for the introduction of a formal report or thought leadership piece.

Farmers in marginal economies use traditional systems to feed livestock. However, changes in agricultural systems and environmental degradation have made fodder both increasingly scarce and less nutritious. How, then, can we help these traditional farmers to improve their feeding systems? In this report, we suggest five strategies.

Notice how, in these examples, the Question tends to disappear: it's implied and the reader can infer the Question from the way the Problem is stated.

Bring on the characters

Stories, as we've seen, need characters. Characters focus that all-important sense of identification.

Finding the hero

The most important character, of course, is the hero. Otherwise known as the protagonist, the hero must meet a challenge or solve a problem. We always want the hero to succeed, but success can come at a cost: they may need to grow or learn.

If you're using a story to dramatize a value proposition, you'll need to choose your hero with care. You'll want your reader to identify with them.

So, who could your hero be? The most obvious answer is: you. Or your company. And that might work. What matters is not who you are, but what you've done. The founding story of Cambridge Mask Company is a good example.

Unfortunately, many companies don't tell an interesting story. They simply describe themselves as a hero.

> We are the acknowledged experts in our field because we have been working in this industry for over 25 years. Our people are trained to a high level of competence and every one of them is a certified professional. Our products are rigorously tested, which means that we can guarantee you, our valued customer, the very highest quality. And our customer service is second to none. Click here to see all the awards we've won. And then give us a call.

No challenges overcome. No conflict. No suspense. Whoever wrote this has forgotten that the story's most important task is helping the customer solve their problem.

Rather than yourself or your company, how about making the hero of your story a product?

The Austin Mini had been launched in 1959 with a campaign highlighting its practicality. When it was relaunched in 2001, BMW wanted to promote the Mini as a premium car for motorists who wanted to downsize without losing status. The problem was liberating the car from its past image.

The solution was to make the car itself the hero of the campaign.

Andy Brittain, working for ad agency WCRS, wrote a 15-second advertisement in which the Mini saves the world: the ultimate heroic task. Brittain's script – all 37 words of it – follows the narrative arc to the letter. The tagline – *It's a Mini adventure* – ties the story directly into the value proposition of the brand: the Mini will give you a sense of adventure, whatever your budget and wherever your drive.

Here's the complete script.

> Annoyingly, Martians appear, all over planet Earth.
>
> Nothing can stand in their way.
>
> Or could it?
>
> Acting as bait, new Mini leads Martian into trap.
>
> Invasion cancelled.
>
> Mini saves the world.
>
> The End.
>
> It's a Mini adventure.

So, you could make the product or service the hero of your story. But there's a third possibility. The hero could be your reader. It's the ultimate in identifying with the hero.

If your reader or customer becomes the hero, you – or your brand – become the mentor: the wise guide. Think Obi-Wan Kenobi or Gandalf. Or Wonder Woman. Or Mary Poppins. Your task is to instil confidence and provide the magical gifts that will help the hero fulfil their destiny – or at least, solve their problem.

Also starring…

Beyond the hero and the wise guide, stories will often include other characters. Villains create problems or cause pain to other characters. In a marketing context, villains might be household germs, or unscrupulous salespeople, or irritating family relations. Victims suffer the consequences of the villain's action and need to be rescued by the hero. A typical victim might be someone the customer needs to help: their children, a neighbour, a much-loved pet.

A victim might even be an object: a car in need of repair, a moss-infested lawn, a business losing its way.

SPOT THE CHARACTERS

Spend an hour watching adverts on television. Spot as many of the following characters as you can:

Hero

Victim

Villain

Mentor

Remember that characters need not be human.

You can play this exercise in two ways. You could look out for particular characters and note them down. Alternatively, you could note a character in an ad and assign a role to them. The househusband who discovers a product that cleans the kitchen floor faster? The dentist who advises us to use a particular toothpaste?

Writing a case study

We write case studies precisely to give a brand or a company the aura of authenticity. The case study tells the story of a challenge faced by a customer or company and how you or your brand helped to overcome it. Your reader will see that people like them have benefited from it. You can even quote your customer or business partner. Along with this powerful sense of identification, the case study gives you lots of opportunities to write sensory-rich, muscle-twitching, hormone-inducing copy.

Researching the case study

The hero of the case study is usually a customer. What is their problem? How will they have succeeded at the end of the story? Choose a customer who's genuinely solved a problem with you rather than simply used your product. (One of the side benefits of a case study: you can use it to market your customer as well as your own company.)

Next, work out how you'll tell the story. It doesn't have to be a printed one-pager. The material can be repurposed for different channels: social media, video, podcasts, infographics…

Work with your hero to create the story. Your customer must, of course, approve of the project. You might need to sell the idea to them: how the case study could benefit them.

You might even need to draw up a plan or a release form, explaining why you're creating the case study and what it will contain, as well as what you might expect from the customer.

Gather all the material you need. Ask the right questions and get detailed answers, with lots of real-life experience included. 'What was the problem? How did it affect you? What did you try before contacting us? How did we work together? How did you feel about our contribution? What's the "so what?" factor? How are you going to live happily ever after?'

Structuring the case study

A case study can build on the SPQR sequence we've already looked at. Develop that sequence into seven steps, highlighting the role of the mentor – you! These steps are based on the work of Donald Miller, in his book *Building a StoryBrand*.

1 Introduce the hero.

2 Identify the problem or challenge they must face.

3 Enter the mentor.

4 The mentor offers a plan.

5 The mentor tells the hero what to do.

6 The problem is solved.

7 Failure is averted.

Introduce the hero. What did your customer want? Identify their goal, their aspiration, their dream.

Identify the problem or challenge they must face. What prevented them from achieving their goal? Remember that the challenge – like the Problem in the SPQR sequence – will be more compelling if it's an event. It should also have had an emotional effect on the customer.

Enter the mentor. Here's where you come into the story.

Your customer wanted to do something, but something was stopping them. Or so they thought. Luckily for them, *you* were there. And you had exactly what they needed: your product or service. But you had to help the hero decide to use that product or service. To be an effective mentor, you had to demonstrate both empathy and authority. By your actions in the story, you showed that you understood their situation and their problem and that you knew, without a shadow of a doubt, how to help them.

The mentor offers a plan. In this step, the wise guide tells the hero exactly how to meet the challenge and achieve their goal. The plan must be simple: as simple as 1-2-3. Even if it took 50 or more steps to solve the problem, your plan in the story must be rigorously simple.

The mentor tells the hero what to do. And offers the magical gift that will make it happen: the product itself.

The problem is solved. What did success look like for your customer or reader? Paint a vivid picture so that your reader can see, hear and feel what success looked like. Include sensory information and as much physical action as you can. Focus on the final, overwhelming benefit of doing what you suggested.

And failure is averted. Success is not a single event. In the fairy tale, the hero and heroine didn't just slay the dragon once; they lived happily ever after. The success that ends this case study must be permanent and long-lasting.

And, But, Therefore: Linking narrative to argument

Randy Olson – whom we met in the previous chapter, discussing arousal and fulfilment – offers a powerful structure that links narrative to argument. He calls it *And, But, Therefore* (ABT).

We can map that sequence onto the SPQR structure we've explored in this chapter.

AND: THE SITUATION
Write two sentences that establish the Situation. String together the setup with *and*.

BUT: PROBLEM/CRISIS
Introduce the element that creates tension within the Situation. Rack up the tension to create a crisis or internal contradiction.

THEREFORE: RESOLUTION

Therefore is both a term of logic and what Olson calls a 'time word'. It links a reason to a conclusion in an argument, just as *because* links the conclusion to a reason, in the opposite direction. But it also lays out the argument as a kind of narrative. The argument thus takes on the quality of a story.

> *To remind yourself about how arguments work, go to Chapter 4.*

ABT is especially useful if you're writing technical copy or communicating specialist material to non-specialists. Here's an example of ABT used in copy to explain how vaccines work.

> The immune system has cells that fight infection.
>
> [*AND*]
>
> After they've fought off disease, some cells hang around as memory cells, ready to fight another day – ready for when the body is attacked again.
>
> [*BUT*]
>
> Cell memory doesn't last forever. Especially against microbes that don't occur naturally where we live.
>
> [*THEREFORE*]
>
> We use vaccines and other techniques to trigger this memory function and keep our immune systems strong.

And here's an example from an advocacy leaflet.

> In our society, we have a serious obesity problem.
>
> *AND*
>
> Currently, we tackle the problem with government campaigns based on individual behaviour: eat well, exercise, lose weight.
>
> *BUT*
>
> These programmes are failing. The incidence of obesity continues to rise because we're failing to address the social causes of the problem.
>
> *THEREFORE*
>
> We need to address the social and economic factors that contribute to obesity.

The ABT framework is also great for creating elevator pitches, social media posts and other kinds of short-form copy. Here's an example: a mocked-up post for LinkedIn for a journalist turned consultant.

In a world where interruption marketing is failing, I help businesses tell their story in a way that grabs attention, generates interest and builds credibility.

How do I do that? Here's my backstory.

I'm a writer by trade. I've become known, over the years, as a specialist in project management and systems development.

And much of my writing tackles complicated technical subjects so that non-technical managers can understand them more easily.

But recently I've discovered that the techniques I use all the time – vivid description, lucid explanation and compelling storytelling – can also help corporations that want to grow sales, attract talent and secure funding.

That's why, in 2023, I launched Fircomm Communications Ltd, a consultancy specializing in strategic storytelling. I've found that my clients can use the skills I offer in a wide range of formats and channels. All of them help to grow their business and their bottom line.

SOLUTION: MAPPING SPQR ONTO A STORY

Here's how SPQR fits Christopher Dobbings' founding story.

[Situation] I founded Cambridge Mask Co after moving to Beijing. **[Problem]** I saw a lot of young kids get sick from air pollution. They were growing up thinking the air should be coloured in grey in pictures and coughing all day was normal. **[Question – implied]** No one, especially not children, should have to sacrifice their health just by breathing. **[Response]** I developed a family-friendly science-led mask that can help protect children and adults from air pollution. **['So what?']** I believe everyone should be able to get out and enjoy life, without having to worry about what they breathe or the way they look. Today we have helped over 1 million people in over 100 countries get the mask they need to help them stay safe from pathogens, urban air pollution, wildfire smoke, traffic fumes or whatever might be damaging their health.

SUMMARY

Stories can give brands an aura of authenticity by:

- creating a sense of identification with the characters in the story
- stimulating our senses and muscles
- elevating levels of some hormones

A good story has three key features.

- It has characters.
- The characters are always doing something.
- The story generates meaning through a moral or conclusion.

These elements combine into a narrative arc, made up of exposition, rising action (including an inciting action), crisis, falling action and resolution.

The events in the story constitute its plot. The events in the plot must be related through a process of cause and effect.

SPQR offers a clear, concise model of a narrative:

- Situation
- Problem
- Question
- Response

Use SPQR to tell a company's backstory or to create a case study.

The characters in a story include a hero. The hero could be your company; it could be a product; it could be the reader or customer.

Other characters include villains, victims and wise guides. These characters need not be human.

Case studies can give a brand the aura of authenticity. The hero of the case study is usually a customer. Your brand or organization can act as a wise guide.

Structure the case study in seven steps.

1 Introduce the hero.
2 Identify the problem or challenge they must face.
3 Enter the mentor.
4 The mentor offers a plan.

5 The mentor tells the hero what to do.

6 The problem is solved.

7 Failure is averted.

Use *And, But, Therefore* to give an argument a narrative structure.

9

Building pyramids: Structures for searching

In this chapter, we'll think about a reader who's not browsing but searching. Maybe they've found your website by using a search engine. Perhaps you've hooked them with attention-grabbing copy on the cover of a brochure; they've now opened the brochure to learn more about what you're offering. Perhaps they've been guided through a newsletter to a piece of in-depth content: a blog post or white paper, an advertorial or an ebook.

A reader who's searching already knows what they're looking for. Your copy needs to deliver the information they're seeking as quickly and efficiently as possible, and maintain their interest, as they read, by keeping that information relevant and useful.

Make your point, then support it

Your reader will usually assume that ideas presented in a sequence must fit together somehow. If you say in advance *how* they fit together – by offering reader a summarizing idea before going into detail – your reader will more easily make sense of the other ideas. If you *don't* offer an initial summarizing idea, your reader will automatically try to group together all the ideas for themselves.

In other words, make your point, then support it.

This is the controlling principle of the new structure we're exploring in this chapter. It's the structure not of a journey but of a pyramid.

Question: what's at the top of a pyramid? Answer: a point. The point you want to make. (Apologies for the pun.) Having made your point, you can then support and expand upon it. You're writing a paragraph. A well-constructed paragraph makes its point and then supports it, surely and steadily.

That's the theory. Let's see how it works in practice.

What's the big idea?

A paragraph is a group of sentences related to one idea. Everything in the paragraph should support that single idea. If you feel that you need to keep to the point, then you're looking for a paragraph's governing idea.

To find that big idea, you need to do two things.

1 First, find your topic.

2 Then, convert that topic into a topic sentence.

Finding your topic

To find the topic of a paragraph, ask two questions.

- 'What is the paragraph about?' That is the paragraph's subject.
- 'How do I want to write about the subject?' That is the paragraph's topic.

Your topic gives you your point of view on the subject. The word 'topic' comes from the Greek word *topos*, meaning 'place' or 'location'. To generate a range of topics at speed, start with the Six Ws: *why, what, who, when, where, how*. (Call *how* an honorary W.)

Suppose you're promoting a new brand of washing-up liquid. The product is your subject. Potential topics for this subject include the following.

Why our new product is better than any other washing-up liquid

Why we decided to create it

Who developed it

Who already likes it

What makes it different

What ingredients it includes – and which ones make the critical difference

When we realized that we needed to create it

Where it can be used

How to use it most effectively

Each one of those topics could generate a paragraph. Indeed, each one could generate a whole range of copy, from ads to packaging, from social media posts to blog posts. In fact, a single topic might help you generate a whole marketing strategy.

Another way to generate a topic is to check out what your customers are thinking or saying about your products. Sites like answerthepublic.com display phrases and questions that people are keying into search engines, relating to your products, services or keywords. Every phrase and question could generate a new topic.

FINDING YOUR TOPIC

Try generating some topics for yourself. It's a great exercise in creative thinking.

First, identify your subject. What are you going to write about? One of your products? A new service? The sector you work in?

Now use the Six Ws to generate a range of potential topics about that subject. Let your thinking range far and wide. Don't censor any ideas. Create as long a list of topics as you can.

Look at each topic idea and ask how you might be able to use it. Keep this list of topics to hand. You're going to use it in the next exercise.

Writing a topic sentence: the top-down approach

You now need to convert the paragraph's topic into an idea. To do that, you need to write a sentence. It's called, unsurprisingly, a *topic sentence*.

To create a topic sentence, convert your topic into a question and then answer it. Let's go back to that washing-up liquid example. Here are the first three topics in the list, converted into questions, with potential topic sentences as answers.

Topic: *Why our new product is better than any other washing-up liquid*

→ 'What makes this new product better than any other?'

→ Topic sentence: Our new product is more environmentally friendly than any other washing-up liquid.

Topic: *Why we decided to create it*

→ 'Why did you decide to create this new product?'

→ Topic sentence: We decided to create this product because we could see how existing detergents were causing serious environmental damage.

Topic: *Who developed it*

→ 'Who developed this product?'

→ Topic sentence: This new product was developed by our in-house research team, working in collaboration with scientists from two universities.

FINDING A TOPIC SENTENCE

Take one of the topics you discovered in the previous exercise. Convert it into a question and then answer the question to create a topic sentence.

Make sure that your topic sentence makes only one point. It should be 'short and striking': use as few words as possible to make your point.

Save that sentence. You'll use it in the next exercise.

The best place to put the topic sentence is at the start of the paragraph. It will then prime the reader for what they're about to read in the paragraph.

Make your point, then support it.

Writing a topic sentence: the bottom-up approach

So far, we've created topic sentences top-down. We started with a subject, sharpened our focus to create a topic and then wrote a sentence that expressed that topic clearly.

subject → topic → topic sentence

But we often discover topic sentences using a different, bottom-up approach. And you might find this approach easier, more natural, or more creative. We often write in order to work out what we think. Creative writing gurus sometimes call this a 'process-oriented' approach to writing – Julia Cameron's Morning Pages is a good example.

To find out more about Morning Pages, go to Chapter 1.

We can create paragraphs this way and to do so we need to add an extra step to the process. That step comes at the *end* of the process. You've written and written and discovered – hopefully – what it is you want to say. What conclusion have you come to? Being a conclusion, it's probably at the end of your piece of writing. If you can express that conclusion in a single, striking sentence – well, *that's* your topic sentence.

Move your conclusion sentence to the beginning. Then reconstruct the paragraph to support it. You may need to do two things as you rebuild your paragraph.

1 You may need to reorder the sentences.

2 You may need to remove sentences that don't directly support the topic sentence; perhaps they will form part of another paragraph, before or after this one.

By editing the paragraph in this way, you're making it more coherent.

INSTANT PARAGRAPHING

Set yourself a time limit for this exercise.

Pick something technical in your work or your organization's work: something specialized that you would need to explain to a friend in ordinary conversation. Write down the name of the thing you're going to write about.

Now: give yourself 60 seconds to write down an explanation of what that thing is. Write whatever comes into your head, just as you might speak this explanation to your friend. Don't think too hard, just write. After 60 seconds, stop – even if you haven't finished.

Now pause.

Step away from the copy you're written. (If you've typed it on the computer, make sure you save it before stepping away.) After a couple of minutes, come back to the copy and look for a sentence that *summarizes* everything you've written.

That single summarizing sentence might be there, somewhere, in the copy you've written. It might be at the beginning. It might be the very last sentence you wrote. It might be buried somewhere in the middle. It might not be there at all, in which case, write it down as a separate sentence.

That's your topic sentence.

Now, if the topic sentence is not already at the beginning, place it at the start of your copy. All the other sentences in your paragraph should expand on, support or develop that topic sentence.

Edit the paragraph in whatever way you think might make it easier to understand. Keep the paragraph. You can review it later.

Organizing the sentences in a paragraph

In a coherent paragraph, all the ideas fit together to support the topic sentence. And they should be arranged so that they make sense in order.

Using old-to-new sequencing

If your reader reads something familiar at the start of a sentence, they'll find new information easier to process and recall. Old-to-new sequencing exploits that idea.

- Begin a sentence with old information: information that the reader already knows, either because they've just read it – in a preceding sentence or paragraph – or because it's the kind of information that they're likely to know anyway.
- Find the new information that you want to offer the reader. Put it at the very end of the sentence.
- Now write the words that link the old information to the new information.

The new information at the end of your sentence then provides the 'old information' for the *next* sentence. And so on.

Here's an example, adapted from one provided by the Harris School of Public Policy at the University of Chicago. Imagine that this is copy from an editorial in a newspaper. Notice that the paragraph begins with a concise topic sentence. (Old information is <u>underlined</u>; new information is in **bold**.)

<u>The forthcoming election</u> will be dominated by a complex **debate about taxes**. <u>This debate</u> provides an opportunity for the country to take **a new direction in tax policy**. <u>We can move away</u> from the flawed trickle-down policies of the past decade and towards **a more progressive and fair policy**. <u>This new policy</u> should include **three key measures**: letting regressive and repressive tax laws expire on schedule; reducing the huge and unpopular tax cuts offered to international companies and their shareholders; and lowering the threshold for the highest rates of domestic income tax. <u>The income generated by these three measures</u> can fund **urgently needed social programmes**, including child tax benefit and investment in healthcare.

Using schemas

Schemas are the mental patterns we use to help us prepare for what's coming and so to make sense of what we're reading. Put simply, schemas link different words together into clusters of meaning. The word *restaurant*, for instance, is part of a schema that includes words like *food*, *menu*, *waiter* – and *bill*. Schemas link words into networks of meaning.

Here's an example.

> Our new mentoring programme will help small businesses unlock their potential. SMEs need not only expert advice but a process for putting new ideas into action. Our in-house experts are trained to deliver exactly the step-by-step advice that will help small businesses to grow sustainably.

Where are the schemas here?

- The word *mentoring* sets up a schema to do with helping and supporting people.
- The phrase *small businesses* sets up the schema locating the context for mentoring.
- The word *programme* provides the schema of a planned sequence of activities.

The words *unlock their potential* provide a schema of achieving a goal or objective. By placing that set of words at the end of the topic sentence, we prime the reader to give that particular schema a certain emphasis. (We'll look at emphasis in more detail in a moment.)

Having identified these various schemas, we can choose words and phrases that align with them.

- *SMEs* echoes *small businesses* – which is repeated at the end of the paragraph.
- The phrase *step-by-step* aligns with programme.
- The words *grow sustainably* echo *potential* in the schema of achieving a goal or objective.
- And of course, *experts* and *advice* continue the governing schema of *mentoring*.

Using schemas is a great way to help you vary your word use without confusing your reader. Copywriters often worry about repeating the same words too often; schemas help you find different words within the same network of meaning.

Keeping the paragraph in proportion

Your paragraph should say as much as you need to say to support your topic sentence – and no more.

Deciding whether your paragraph says enough – or not enough, or too much – is sometimes tricky. Think about it from your reader's point of view. Once they've finished the paragraph, they should feel that they don't need to know any more – or, at least, that they're ready to move on to the next paragraph.

Include everything you need to include

First, make sure that nothing essential is missing. Can you reduce the elements in the paragraph without sacrificing something essential?

Look also at the expectations you set up in your topic sentence. Take a look at this one.

> We're currently running four campaigns in Europe.

Now, if the paragraph refers to only three campaigns, something's clearly lacking. (Of course, if you mention *five* campaigns, then you'll need to adjust your topic sentence.)

Manage detail

What about detail? How much is too much?

Think about the number of sentences in the paragraph. Three is a good working minimum; seven might be a reasonable maximum. The more detailed ideas will probably appear later in the paragraph. As a result, you might find that sentence length increases gently as the paragraph proceeds. The topic sentence might well be the shortest sentence in the paragraph. Experiment with alternating longer sentences with shorter ones. Think about why the sentences are ordered as they are. Could you change the order?

To find out more about sentence length, go to Chapter 10.

There are no rules here. I'm describing design principles for paragraphs. See what works.

The one-sentence paragraph

Paragraphs constructed in the way we've explored are more formal than the linear structures we looked at in the last chapter. They're less 'spoken' and more 'written'. If your paragraphs are all of a similar length – or if the sentences within a paragraph are all of a similar length – your reader might start to feel a bit sleepy. A one-sentence paragraph can change the pace and jolt them awake.

> For many in-house copywriters, writing technical copy can be a chore. It's detailed work, requiring hours of research. And it requires both expertise and experience, someone who can combine specialist know-how with the communication skills of a good writer.
>
> That's where I can help.

Where to use paragraphs

Paragraphs will appear in any kind of more formal content. Use paragraphs within brochures or below the fold on websites. Use them in central parts of emails, beyond the first-line hook. And, as we'll see later, paragraphs are essential components of blog posts, articles and newsletters. Your reader's attention is constantly on the move. You must capture your reader's attention so that you can get your message across. If you do that, they might read on. Paragraphs help you to do both.

To find out more about writing blog posts and articles, go to Chapter 17.

Working on paragraphs can also help you develop your brand voice. A well-constructed paragraph develops its ideas surely and steadily. It feels clear and coolly assured. And it should make your reader feel smarter for having read it.

RINGING THE CHANGES

Here's an exercise to develop your structural versatility.

Pick a product, component or service that you know a lot about. Something complicated or technical, which you might need to explain to a non-specialist reader. First, build a pyramid-shaped paragraph, as follows:

1 Explain what the service is or does, in one simple sentence. That's your topic sentence.

2 Now write two or three more sentences explaining what it is or how it works, in more detail.

3 Check your paragraph for coherence and emphasis.

Second, write a piece of copy marketing or promoting this service or feature to a customer. Use PAS or AIDCA. Or any other linear structure that works for you. Finally, try writing a mini-narrative telling the story of how someone used this service or feature successfully.

Compare the three pieces of copy. How do they differ in terms of energy and tone? How do the words differ in each piece of copy? And the sentences? Are you able to find a brand voice that works for all three? In all three cases, the voice should be:

• sure and steady

• clear and cool and

• smart and specific

SUMMARY

The best way to structure material for a reader who is searching is to make your point and then support it. The image to have in mind is a pyramid. We use the pyramid principle to create paragraphs.

A paragraph is a group of sentences related to one idea. To find that idea:

• find a topic and

• create a topic sentence

You can also find topic sentences by using a bottom-up approach: write a paragraph freeform, then extract or add a topic sentence and restructure the paragraph. Organize the sentences in the paragraph using old-to-new sequencing.

- Begin a sentence with old information.
- Put new information at the end of the sentence.
- Recast the sentence so that it moves as easily as possible from old information to new information.

Bind together the words in your paragraph using schemas: clusters of meaning linking different words. Include everything you need to support your topic sentence – and no more.

Most paragraphs should include at least three sentences. Most need no more than six or seven.

One-sentence paragraphs can be dramatically effective.

Use paragraphs in longer-form content, but also in emails and shorter copy where necessary.

Working on paragraphs can also help you develop your brand voice.

Six patterns of influence

American psychologist Robert Cialdini suggests that, in an age of information overload, we need signals to help us decide whether to do something. These signals focus our attention on what's new, different and potentially useful. Cialdini identified six such signals; we could call them patterns of influence.

- Reciprocity
- Authority
- Scarcity
- Consistency
- Alignment
- Liking

You can remember these six patterns using the word RASCAL. You can use all six to generate new ideas for copy.

RECIPROCITY: THE OLD GIVE AND TAKE (AND TAKE)

We feel a strong urge to repay a favour. Do something for your reader and they may do something for you. But you should give generously. Create useful content, for example, and give it away for free. (Or at least, some of it.)

Decide what you can give away. If you've been producing content for some time, you should know what content resonates most strongly with your readers. Use that content to guide your free gifts.

Repurpose. Once you've selected (or created) the content to offer to your visitors, find ways to convert it into a format that will look good: a brochure or an ebook, a simple PDF.

Decide how you want the reader to reciprocate. Do you want their email address? Do you want them to opt in to something? Your free content should be valuable enough to your reader to persuade them to return the favour.

Promote the gift. Use all the usual channels: social, home page, email newsletters.

Concessions count as favours. Discounts, free gifts, after-sales service... Promote these and your reader may feel obliged to repay the favour.

Authority: directed deference

We are extraordinarily compliant to the requests of people we see as authority figures. How can you increase your authority with your reader?

Authority in the mind of the reader can translate into making a purchase. (Or making a donation, if you're a charity.)

Be transparent. Don't just give your reader the facts, tell them how you assembled the facts. Take the reader behind the scenes. Introduce team members and let them speak to your reader.

Use content that reinforces your authority. Offer technical information from impressive sources, your experience as a provider, your position in the rankings, customer testimonials (see *Alignment* below). **Don't blag; be specific.**

Make yourself available. Signal prominently how people can contact you and ask for help.

Publish content consistently. Create an editorial calendar and stick to your schedule. Consistency confers authority. (See *Consistency*, below.)

Scarcity: offer ends Monday

Scarcity triggers the fear of missing out. (Copywriters often talk about FOMO.) The more scarce a resource, the more value we attach to it. Intriguingly, we're more motivated by the prospect of losing something than by the hope of gaining something. Part of this pattern is emphasizing the dangers of not doing something.

Invite only: limit the people you make your content available to. You could try this with interactive content, for example quizzes, calculators, online tools.

On demand: Ask the reader to request the resource so that they can download it. This works well for content like white papers, thought leadership pieces or videos.

If you're going to use offers to trigger the fear of missing out, you've got four main options.

Limited time offer: the offer runs until a specific date.

Limited units offer: Limit the number of rooms/spaces/places/items available.

One time offer: clarify that this offer will never appear again.

Charter offer: typically offered when a product launches: a pre-launch discount or an exclusive opportunity.

Consistency: I am what i say

We hate to be seen to be inconsistent in our behaviour. Parents learn this from bitter experience. ('But you *promised* we would go to Disneyland!') If you know that your reader has already acted in the past in a way that's consistent with buying (or donating), remind them.

You kindly subscribed last year.

You have already bought three of our products. We thought you'd like to know about this new addition to our range.

As a long-term customer, you've already proved that you Alignment: social proof

We're strongly influenced to feel and do what we see others feeling and doing. Social proof is evident in lots of marketing content. Testimonials are an obvious example. Here are a few other ways that you can integrate alignment or social proof into your content strategy.

Add social sharing options. Most social sharing tools offer the option to display the share count. The share count is a great indicator to the visitor of the quality of your content.

Get influencers to share your content. Encourage influencers in your field to share your content.

Display social followings: The strength of your social following also acts as social proof.

Use badges and drop names. If your content is the most read content in your field, or if it's been featured in leading publications, promote that fact loud and clear.

Liking: I like you, you're like me

'If I'm like you, you'll like me.' We'd all prefer to say 'yes' to someone we know and like. Make your content more likeable and show how you are like your reader. Here are some tips to get you going.

Talk to one reader. Create a reader persona (Chapter 3 of this book!) and produce content for that reader.

Display shared values. For instance: *Like you, we believe that travelling abroad should not cost the earth.* Or: *We set up this company because we wanted our own children to live healthier lives.*

Write a compelling title. In other words, write your headlines as personal remarks to your persona. Address specific concerns. Avoid generalizations.

Talk directly to your reader. Every time your reader reads 'you', they feel a little more that you know them – and understand them.

Speak in the first person. The more personal your content sounds, the more your reader will identify with you.

Be positive. Prefer to say what something *is* rather than what it *isn't*. Don't say *inexpensive;* your reader will subconsciously focus on *expensive*.

In 2016, Cialdini proposed a seventh pattern of influence. He called it the unity principle. Unity is about identification: it can come from being part of a family or a close-knit team, but also can be based on race, ethnicity, nationality, religion, political affiliation and other factors. The more we identify ourselves with others, the more we're influenced by them. Reminding someone of a shared identity makes you more persuasive. The unity principle lies behind the developing idea of brand communities.

To find out more about brand communities, go to Chapter 12.

PART FOUR

Bringing your copy to life

Your words will come to life only when your reader reads them. Your task is to make the copy as easy to read as possible.

Some copy never comes alive. It doesn't talk to the reader. Instead, it mutters to itself. Copywriters call it zombie copy.

> We have a reputation for delivering excellent higher education facilities, as well as facilitating the growth of the science and technology sector in the region...

> Leveraging world-class infrastructure capabilities, mature quality control processes and industry benchmarked people management practices...

> As a premium provider, we partner frontrunners in our sector who aim to optimize their efficiency and are constantly looking for better and more sustainable ways to operate.

That's not the kind of copy you want to write.

In Part 4, you'll discover how to give your copy the spark of life. We'll look at two skills: how to choose the right words and how to put them in order.

- **Chapter 10** is all about writing powerful sentences and how to connect them.
- In **Chapter 11**, we explore the subtle relationship between verbs and nouns. How do they work together? When does the relationship go sour? How can we keep it sweet?

10

Sentences: Putting your words in order

The easier the sentence is to read, the more life it will have. Sentences that are hard to read will lose life; they will start to zombify.

Sentences put words in order. The technical name for word order is **syntax**. The rules governing word order are the rules of **grammar**. But grammar isn't really a set of rules; it's actually a set of conventions describing how we usually put words together. Copywriters often break those conventions. That's why you need to understand them: if you flout a grammatical convention, you should look as if you know what you're doing and not just making a mistake.

The techniques in this chapter aren't rules either. Think of them as practical suggestions to help you write sentences that live. If a technique works for you, great. If not, try another one.

How does it sound?

To know whether a sentence has life, read it aloud. If it sounds good, leave it alone. Only if it *doesn't* sound good do you need to work on it. Better still, ask a colleague or friend to read it aloud. You're trying to hear the sentence as if you haven't written it. Where does your reader stumble when they read the sentence? That might give you a clue about how to improve it.

Your sentences should speak – but remember that they won't be heard. Your copy should retain the easiness of speech – its beats and pauses – but fitted into the tighter structures of writing. There's a sweet spot somewhere between the ease of speech and the discipline of writing. That's the spot you're aiming for.

To find out more about voice, go to Chapter 5.

Vary your sentence length

When sentences vary in length, reading becomes easier. In his book *100 Ways to Improve Your Writing*, Gary Provost brilliantly demonstrates the power of varying your sentence length.

> This sentence has five words. Here are five more words. Five-word sentences are fine. But several together become monotonous. Listen to what is happening. The writing is getting boring. The sound of it drones. It's like a stuck record. The ear demands some variety. Now listen. I vary the sentence length and I create music. Music. The writing sings. It has a pleasant rhythm, a lilt, a harmony. I use short sentences. And I use sentences of medium length. And sometimes, when I am certain the reader is rested, I will engage him with a sentence of considerable length, a sentence that burns with energy and builds with all the impetus of a crescendo, the roll of the drums, the crash of the cymbals – sounds that say, listen to this, it is important.

Provost focuses on the music of sentences. We talk about 'content' – as if a sentence is merely a container for something else. We should also think about the form of a sentence: its pattern of stresses, its rhythm, the play of vowel and consonant sounds. Form *is* content. And vice versa.

You don't need any technical knowledge to vary sentence length. You just need to be able to count.

VARYING SENTENCE LENGTH

Write a piece of copy: a paragraph of about five or six sentences. Save that first version. Make a copy. Then edit the copy in the following way.

1 Start with a sentence of no more than 15 words. That sentence should state the paragraph's main point.

2 Now create a second sentence that is *either* shorter than the first sentence – by at least five words – or longer than the first sentence, by at least five words.

3 Now alternate short and long sentences until the paragraph is complete. Each sentence must be at least five words shorter or longer than the sentence before it.

Compare the original and the copy. What has improved? What has not improved? Can you improve the copy still further? If so, try to maintain the technique of alternating short and long sentences.

How sentences work

Nobody can agree on what a sentence is. Some say that a sentence starts with a capital letter and ends with a full stop. That's not a bad definition – except that not all sentences begin with a capital letter and not all end with a full stop. Some sentences begin with a quotation mark; some sentences end with a question mark or an exclamation mark.

To find out more about full stops and other ways of ending a sentence, go to Interlude 4.

Some say that a sentence expresses a complete thought. That, too, is not a bad definition – except that it doesn't include a sentence like *Fish and chips* as an answer to the question *What did you have for dinner last night?*; or *The more, the merrier* as a comment on the statement *Julia's parents have suddenly told us they're coming to dinner*. Answers like this are sometimes called **minor sentences**. They make sense only in relation to a preceding sentence.

Copy often uses minor sentences, or single-word sentences, for effect. (I use a lot of minor sentences in this book.)

A **major sentence** must have a **subject**. The subject is the thing or person that the sentence is about and it will always be a **noun** – or a **noun phrase**, which is simply a group of words doing the job of a noun. *Fish and chips* is just such a noun phrase.

A major sentence says something about that subject. What it says is called the **predicate**. The predicate is everything in the sentence that isn't the subject. And – just one more technical point at this stage – the predicate must (usually) contain a **main verb**.

Most major sentences have subjects and predicates. Some don't. Here, for instance, is a major sentence where the subject is invisible.

Claim your free gift now!

In this sentence, the subject – *you* – is implied. The reader supplies the subject: *they* are the subject.

How we read a sentence

Whenever your reader reads a sentence, they want to know two things.

- What is this sentence about?
- What does the sentence say about it?

In other words, your reader will always look for the subject and predicate. If the reader can't find the sentence's subject, they'll spend time and energy looking for it. So, to make reading easier, place the sentence's subject at the start of the sentence.

THINKING ABOUT SUBJECTS

The sentence's subject will not always be at the very start of the sentence.

Look at a sentence you've written and ask yourself: What is this sentence about? Underline the word or phrase that you think is the subject of the sentence. Is that word or phrase at the start of the sentence? If not, why not? (There may be a good reason why not.)

Try putting the subject at the very start of the sentence and rewrite the sentence as necessary. Has the sense of the sentence changed? Is the sentence easier to understand? If not, why not?

Once the reader has understood what the sentence is about, they'll want to know what the sentence says about it. To do that, they'll have to read the predicate. The shorter and simpler the predicate, the easier the sentence will be to read.

Some predicates contain nothing but the main verb:

Linda [subject] was reading [main verb].

To find out more about verbs, go to Chapter 11.

Most predicates add extra information to the verb.

Linda was reading a book.

Linda was reading a book that Ben gave her.

Linda was reading a book that Ben gave her as a present.

Linda was reading a book that Ben gave her as a present for her birthday.

In each of these sentences, the subject – Linda – sits at the very start. However long the sentence becomes, we're never in any doubt what – or who – this sentence is about.

Notice also that the main verb of this sentence – *was reading* – comes immediately after the subject. Why? Because your reader knows – if only intuitively – that the sentence must contain a verb. If they can't find it quickly, they'll spend more energy searching for it than in reading all the other words in the sentence. And because that energy isn't being used to read the sentence as a whole, the sentence will start to lose its life. It will start to zombify.

PLACING THE SUBJECT AND MAIN VERB

Here's the first principle of good sentence writing:

- Put the subject of the sentence at the very beginning – or as near the beginning as you can.

The second principle follows hard on from the first:

- Place the main verb of the sentence as close to the subject as you can.

Once your reader has identified the subject and main verb of the sentence, they'll start to *predict* how the sentence will continue. They'll also predict that, once the sentence has made its point, it will stop. So, they'll look for the end of the sentence. In fact, the point of maximum attention in any sentence for your reader will always be the end – not the beginning.

In each of those sentences about Linda, for example, the point of the sentence is embodied in the final word. In the first sentence, the point is that Linda was *reading* – rather than singing, swimming or eating an apple. In the second, she was reading *a book* – rather than a comic, a technical report or the back of the cereal packet. In the third, the book was *a gift*. And so on.

PLACING NEW INFORMATION

The third principle of good sentence writing is:

Put the most important new information at the end of the sentence.

Characters in a story

Your reader will understand a sentence more easily if its subject acts like a character in a story. That character might be a person; it might be an organization, an animal, a product, or even an idea. The subject should *act* like a character in a story: the main verb should tell us what the character is doing.

I call this technique 'characters in a story'.

Sentences can zombify because the characters disappear. Take a look at this sentence.

An annual reduction of 50 per cent in the introduction of new products by the agrochemical industry is estimated in the event that new legislation is introduced.

Where are the characters here? The agrochemical industry is a character. Presumably the government is another; after all, someone must be introducing new legislation. And someone must be estimating a 50 per cent reduction.

Suppose we put those three characters into the sentence.

We estimate that **the agrochemical industry** will introduce 50 per cent fewer new products each year in the event that **the government** introduces new legislation.

The sentence has – almost magically – come alive. We could take the story-telling one stage further and place the actions in a narrative order. (I've also quietly reduced *in the event that* to the simple word *if*.)

> If the government introduces new legislation, we estimate that the agrochemical industry will introduce 50 per cent fewer new products per year.

Of course, we could rewrite this sentence in a number of other ways.

> The agrochemical industry is likely to introduce 50 per cent fewer new products per year if the government introduces new legislation, according to our estimates.

> According to our estimates, the agrochemical industry will probably introduce 50 per cent fewer new products per year if the government introduces new legislation.

You could find yet more ways to rewrite this sentence. All of these options become available once you liberate the characters in the sentence and say what they're doing.

HOW TO USE 'CHARACTERS IN A STORY'

1   Make the *subject* of your sentence name the main character.

2   Make the *main verb* express what the character is doing in the sentence.

3   Reveal any other characters in the sentence as necessary.

What's really wrong with long sentences

Copywriters love short sentences. Look at this bit of copy by Ed McCabe.

> My chickens eat better than you do. They eat what I give them. And I only give them the best.

Three sharp jabs: left, right, left. But then, McCabe adds a longer sentence.

> My chickens eat better than you do. They eat what I give them. And I only give them the best. Their diet consists mainly of pure yellow corn, soybean meal, marigold petals – you'd call it health food.

That's one way to lengthen a sentence: write a list. But beware: lists are major zombiefiers. The moment your reader comes to a list, they assume that the real point of the sentence has passed. They're likely to skim over the list in pursuit of the next interesting point. David Abbott once said, 'If you believe that facts persuade (as I do), you'd better learn how to write a list so that it doesn't read like a list.' Ed McCabe does precisely that. He limits the list to three items, places the item with the most syllables last (*marigold petals*) and sums up the list with a little nod to the reader.

We can lengthen sentences in other ways. For example, we can add descriptive detail with adjectives.

> The **incessant** ticking and chiming of a **hundred** clocks echoed off the **weathered** walls of the **old** shop in a **lonely** part of the city.

Or we can imitate the energy we're trying to describe.

> The eye-popping, limb-contorting swirl of magic and colour that is the tribal dance of the Nomads of the Niger has reached its mesmeric climax. (*Tim Mellors*)

Long sentences can also stretch out an idea and allow the reader to ponder it at greater, well, length.

> If you are under 40, with no history of breast cancer, your doctor is the best person to talk to about breast health and a detection regime most appropriate for you. (*John Bevins*)

So, how long is long? Is there a maximum length we should aim for? Most authorities will answer that question by talking about word count. The consensus seems to be that 25 words is a reasonable maximum.

Don't be fooled.

Sentences are not too long because they contain too many words. Sentences become too long when they contain too many *bits of information*. Your reader has to understand each new bit of information *and* assemble those bits mentally into one idea. If they can do all that, they'll understand the sentence. But if they can't, then they won't.

REMEMBERING A SENTENCE

Read a sentence, then immediately try to repeat it from memory – without deliberately memorizing it. Try a few different sentences. Are some sentences easier to remember than others? Why?

You *can* write long sentences, if you write them in such a way that the reader can find their way through them. It's to do with the number of *sections* you put into a sentence and how those sections fit together. We're talking about chunking.

The power of chunking

When we speak, we divide our sentences into little chunks of sound, about two seconds long. These chunks are sometimes called **intonation units**. They help us focus on one element at a time and they help our listener do the same thing.

We can also chunk our written sentences. Each chunk – each group of words sitting naturally together – has a smooth, natural syntax. It creates a bundle of meaning and *sounds* like a bundle when we speak it. A simple sentence might be a single chunk. That last sentence is probably made up of two chunks.

A simple sentence // might be a single chunk.

Or possibly three, depending on how we read it.

A simple sentence // might be // a single chunk.

Intonation is something we hear. That's why it helps to read your copy aloud: you'll hear the intonation units more clearly. We can indicate the chunks using commas, semi-colons, colons or dashes. Take a look at this sentence. Better still, read it aloud.

> The technology renders ultra-realistic 3D images of our watches for customers to explore every dimension in their own way and see intricate characteristics of the designs with a level of detail that static images and even video can't provide.

Use punctuation to chunk the sentence and – with a little subtle rewording – we can save it.

> The technology creates ultra-realistic 3D images. Customers can now explore a watch in every dimension; they can examine intricate design characteristics with a level of detail that static images – and even video – can't provide.

A sentence sculpted into chunks will combine sound and sense. Copy that's chunked sounds more spoken and more alive.

B2B CLIENTS ARE HUMAN, TOO

If you're writing B2B copy, get to know the way your business client chunks their sentences. Not in their copy but in the way they speak. Try to replicate that chunking in your copy.

Branching right and left

Sentences become longer by branching outwards from the subject. And they can branch in two directions. Here's some well-chunked copy by John Stingley.

> The new Porsche 968. It is the latest vision to come down from Porsche's legendary development centre, perched high on a hill overlooking the ancient village of Weissach. And, like each and every Porsche which has rolled down the hill before it, it is a dichotomy.

The first sentence fragment introduces the product. The second, major sentence branches right from its subject and main verb. (The double slashes mark the intonation units.)

> It [subject] is [main verb] the latest vision // to come down // from Porsche's legendary development centre, // perched high on a hill // overlooking the ancient village // of Weissach.

The next sentence branches left from the subject and main verb.

> And, // like each and every Porsche // which has rolled down the hill before it, // it [subject] is [main verb] a dichotomy.

A right-branching sentence is usually easier to understand than a left-branching one. Most spoken sentences branch to the right. A left-branching sentence demands more of its listener or reader. They have to hold everything to the left of the sentence's subject in their short-term memory while they wait for the main idea to arrive.

John Stingley's left-branching sentence works well. He carefully places it *after* a right-branching one and uses elements from the previous sentence (rolling down the hill; Porsche's celebrated brand name) to help the reader through the left-leaning branch. The reward is a little frisson of suspense (where is this sentence heading?) before we land on that unexpected and intriguing final word, *dichotomy*.

Cumulative sentences

To create a right-branching sentence, put the subject and main verb first, then attach intonation units in a loose, colourful sequence. The result is a **cumulative sentence**. It's a bit like a tracking shot in a movie. Cumulative sentences are great for descriptive copy.

> This hotel mixes the beauty of the past with the comfort of the present, tucked down a quiet, cobbled street in the historic heart of this tranquil Cretan coastal town, where modern design rubs shoulders with Ottoman relics and Venetian stonework. You'll have glorious views from first light as you breakfast on the hotel's sun-soaked roof terrace, overlooking terracotta roofs and the minarets of mosques towards the ancient port...

Subordinate clauses and complex sentences

Left-branching sentences tend to be more formal, and less spontaneous, than right-branching ones. They're less 'spoken' and more 'written'.

> In the three weeks since he sacked his long-serving defence minister, the president has pursued a series of high-level corruption cases against members of his own cabinet.

That left branch contains a subject, 'he', and a verb: 'sacked'. That makes it a **clause**. A phrase becomes a clause when it acquires a subject and a main verb. A simple sentence is also a clause. But *this* left-branching clause about the defence minister can't sit alone as a sentence. It depends for its existence on the main clause, the part of the sentence following the comma. (For the record, the subject of the main clause is *the president* and the main verb is *has pursued*.) That makes the left-branching clause a **subordinate clause** – and subordinate clauses are often responsible for left-branching sentences.

Sentences with subordinate clauses are classed as **complex sentences**. They appear frequently in technical copy, op-ed pieces, advertorials and thought leadership papers.

(In each of these examples below, the subordinate clause comes before the comma. I've marked the subjects and main verbs in every clause. Where a subject is a lengthy noun phrase, I've underlined it.)

> While a number of measures recently introduced by the FCA [subject] will take effect [verb] in the course of 2024, the FCA's focus [subject] has turned [main verb] from rule-making to supervision and enforcement of existing requirements.

> If the UK [subject] adopts [verb] a digital and data-centric approach for the design and delivery of its new energy infrastructure, the country [subject] has [main verb] a chance to become a leader in the green energy transition.

> While <u>initiatives developed in one context</u> [subject] cannot usually be
> transposed [verb] completely unchanged to a new location, we [subject] see
> [main verb] real potential for adoption and adaptation of these approaches
> in new places.

A subordinate clause is usually introduced by a **subordinating conjunction**.
Here are the most common:

after	so long as
although	though
as	unless
because	until
before	when
even though	whenever
if	whereas
once	wherever
since	while

A complex sentence can branch left or right:

> Because our satnav updates every few seconds, you'll never be lost again.
> →
> You'll never be lost again because our satnav updates every few seconds.

Which of those two would you choose? Left-branching, or right-branching?

You could invoke the earlier principle of putting the most important new
idea at the end of the sentence. Which is the most important idea here? I
would probably choose the benefit over the feature – *you'll never be lost
again* – but your decision will also be influenced by the context of the sentence.

Compound sentences

Instead of using a subordinating conjunction, we could join clauses together
by using a **coordinating conjunction**. The most common are *and* and *but*.
Five others make up the mnemonic FANBOYS:

for

and

nor

but

or

yet

so

We could rewrite the sentence we've just looked at like this:

> Our satnav updates every few seconds so you'll never be lost again.

That sentence is looser, less logically rigorous, more conversational. Technically, it's a **compound sentence**: a pair of simple sentences bolted together with a coordinating conjunction.

We could even dispense with the conjunction altogether and write two short sentences.

> Our satnav updates every few seconds. You'll never be lost again.

Now the reader makes the connection. By doing a bit more work, maybe the reader adds just a little more life to the copy.

Complex sentences tend to appear in longer content. Perhaps we see them as more sophisticated, more mature, than sentences bolted together with *ands* and *buts*. Maybe we think complex sentences give our content a bit of intellectual heft.

> As industry practice has begun to shift from document sharing to data sharing, the role of established technology providers may also need to change.

> After extensive consultation with impacted teams, it has been agreed that the primary zone for both teams will be on the fourth floor of the Praxis building.

In contrast, while a number of measures recently introduced by the FCA will take effect in the course of 2024, the FCA's focus has turned from rule-making to supervision and enforcement of existing requirements.

But complex sentences can make reading harder. If you create too many, your reader might get lost. And if you create a chain of complex sentences, your copy will risk terminal zombiedom.

USING THE THREE TYPES OF SENTENCE

Mix and match these three types of sentence in your copy:

- **Complex sentences** slow your reader down and make them think more precisely. Use them for complex explanations and arguments, but don't overuse them: what they offer in precision they lose in energy.

- **Compound sentences** link ideas easily and casually. They feel closer to scurrying rhythms of speech than complex sentences.

- **Simple sentences** can package well-digested insights with pithy directness. When you want a slogan, a simple sentence will do the job for you.

Knitting sentences together

We've seen that we can join sentences together by using old-to-new sequencing.

To find out more about old-to-new sequencing, go to Chapter 9.

Add energy to this sequencing technique by using full stops, repetition, substitution and transitions.

Using full stops

Full stops give your sentences life. The longer a sentence goes on without a full stop, the more life will drain from it. And full stops don't just end sentences, they also announce the arrival of the next sentence.

Repetition

Don't be afraid to repeat words across sentence breaks. Repeating reinforces the importance of the repeated word and helps your reader remember it. It also helps them predict what comes next in the new sentence.

You can repeat words exactly.

> You want a pen that's beautifully engineered. As beautifully engineered as a sports car or an ocean-going yacht.

And you can use a variant of the same word.

> Take a moment to compare these two products. The comparison should tell you all you need to know to decide which is best for you.

Substitution

Substitution uses one word or phrase in place of another. For example, you can use a **pronoun** in place of a noun. (Pronouns are words like *I, you, he, she, it, they, we, them, which* or *that*.)

> These new biodegradable **gloves** will help a business to become more environmentally friendly. **They're** an essential buy if you care about the environment.

Take particular care with **relative pronouns** (*this, these, those…*). They're called 'relative' because they relate to a noun you've already used. If the reader can't work out what noun they relate to, they may get confused. For example:

> It was hard to decide whether to offer our clients a free gift or a full refund. **This** complicated the customer service plan.

What does *this* refer to? What, precisely, caused the complication? Better, in a situation like this, to add the relevant noun.

It was hard to decide whether to offer our clients a free gift or a full refund. **This confusion** complicated the customer service plan.

Transition

Transitional devices signal to your reader how one sentence relates to the next. They also help you to vary the rhythm of your copy. Some transitional devices point up a comparison: *on the other hand, however, conversely.* Some contribute to an argument: *because, for the same reason, indeed.* Some highlight summaries or conclusions: *in brief, therefore, thus.* And transitions can show time, sequence or introduce examples. Google the phrase *transitional devices* and you'll soon find exhaustive lists of them.

Avoid transitions like *in addition, additionally, also* or *moreover.* They're variants on *and here's another thing.* You don't need them.

But the most problematic transitional device of them all is *as such.* It means 'in the exact meaning of the word' or 'in itself'. The phrase must relate back to a noun: a thing or person. If you find yourself writing it, ask simply, 'As what?' For instance:

Fido was leader of the pack. As such, he commanded obedience from the other dogs. (As what? As the leader of the pack. No problem.)

As such often pops up in copy when the writer wants to say *as a result, consequently* or *therefore*:

We wanted to understand how well geriatric patients could make decisions. As such, we designed a cross-sectional study of nursing home residents.

Bad news. Rewrite.

We wanted to understand the decision-making capability of geriatric patients. We therefore designed a cross-sectional study of nursing home residents.

SUMMARY

Sentences put words in order. The technical name for word order is syntax. The rules governing word order are grammar.

Read your sentences aloud. Or ask a friend to read them aloud. Aim to retain the easiness of speech, fitted into the tighter structures of writing.

Vary your sentence length. Experiment with alternating longer and shorter sentences.

A major sentence must have a subject and a predicate. The predicate must always include a finite verb. The best place for the sentence's subject is (usually) at the very beginning. The best place for the main verb is (usually) directly after the subject.

Put old information at the start of the sentence and new information at the end.

Where possible, make your subject act like a character in a story.

You can make sentences longer by:

- creating lists (but you should be able to write a list so that it doesn't sound like a list)
- adding descriptive detail
- imitating the energy you're describing
- stretching an idea so that the reader ponders it more fully

Sentences become too long when they contain too many bits of information. Break your sentences into chunks or intonation units. Copy that's chunked sounds more spoken and more alive. Don't put too many chunks into one sentence.

Right-branching sentences are usually easier to understand than left-branching sentences. Right-branching sentences often join clauses with coordinating conjunctions to create compound sentences. Cumulative right-branching sentences are great for copy that describes, evokes or stimulates the senses.

Left-branching sentences tend to be more formal, and less spontaneous, than right-branching ones. They're less 'spoken' and more 'written'. They often include subordinate clauses to create complex sentences. Content probably uses more complex sentences than copy. Don't use too many.

Mix and match these three types of sentence in your copy:

- simple
- compound
- complex

Knit sentences together using full stops, repetition, substitution or transition.

11

Doing and being: How verbs and nouns live together

Learning to speak as babies, we name things. *Mama, dada, doggie, juice.* The first words we speak tend to be nouns. We soon realize that these nouns often *do* things and, even more excitingly, that we can *make* things happen. And so we start to speak verbs. *Mama eat cake. Dada fall over. Doggie chase stick. Drink juice.*

A noun and a verb: that's all a sentence needs. Everything else is extra.

Verb-spotting for beginners

Verbs bring your copy most vividly to life. But verbs can be tricky to spot: they continually change their shape, depending on the role they play in the sentence. Many of those shapes are unpredictable. Verbs help to save your copy from zombiedom, but they can be volatile and hard to control.

As we explore verbs, don't worry too much about the technical details. Develop your skill in *spotting* verbs.

VERB-SPOTTING

Identify the verbs in this passage. Handy hint: no verb appears more than once. The answer is at the end of this chapter.

Comic book superheroes have a number of traits in common. They often display extraordinary powers. These powers vary greatly, but among the most prevalent are superhuman strength, the ability to fly and the capacity to project energy. Batman and Green Hornet possess no superpowers but they practise martial arts. Most superheroes risk their own safety in the service of good. Many refuse to kill an opponent, even though that opponent threatens the safety of others or presents a menace to society at large. Many superheroes use a descriptive or symbolic code name. The cast of characters in a comic book usually includes the hero's friends and family. Superheroes often work from a secret headquarters or base.

(Adapted from a page on the website of De Anza College, California)

Action verbs

Most of us remember verbs as 'doing words'. And many verbs are just that: we call them **action verbs**. Action verbs describe something we do, physically or mentally. They create movement in your reader's mind, stimulating their senses and imagination.

Finding the best action verbs

The best action verbs are specific, vivid and evocative.

FOCUS ON VALUE

Find the verb that persuades your reader to do more than read on. You're trying to evoke the *experience* that your value proposition will create for them.

Hire one of our consultants today.

→

Rebuild your business model. **Hire** one of our consultants.

MAKE IT PHYSICAL

Your reader will find an action verb easier to process if it suggests physical action – either real or metaphorical.

Maximize your core competencies.

→

Grow your skill set.

EVOKE EMOTION

The trick is to find the action that generates the emotion rather than focusing on the feeling itself. Let the reader supply the emotion.

Dabble

Delve

Dig up

Dip into

Dive

Extract

Plunge

Probe

Turn up

Uncover

Unearth

If you're focusing on solving a customer's problem, look for verbs that give problem solving a physical dimension.

Deflate

Demolish

Ditch

Expand

Fire up

Ignite

Jumpstart

Lift

Make strides

Pick up

Polish

Shape up

Sharpen

Spark

Step up

Take off

USING ACTION VERBS

Take one of the lists we've just looked at and create single sentences using each of the words in the list. Some sentences can relate directly to your current work. Feel free to write some sentences that relate to completely different sectors.

Active and passive – and something in between

An **active verb** expresses what its subject does.

> Deborah **wrote** the report.

A **passive verb** expresses what its subject has done to it.

> The report **was written** by Deborah.

That passive verb is made up of a part of the verb *to be* – in this case, *was* – and a **past participle** (*written*). We'll have more to say about participles shortly.

Most style guides tell us to prefer active verbs. And for good reason: a passive verb disrupts the reader's flow of thought by turning actions back to front. Its two-part construction also tends to add to your word count. And a passive verb can allow us to sidestep responsibility for an action.

> An error has been made.

But passive verbs have their uses. They allow us to talk truthfully about an event when we don't *know* who was responsible.

> The files **were stolen** from our Bradford office.

A passive verb can also allow us to put an important new idea at the end of a sentence.

> This new product **was developed** by our research team in Munich.

Here, the passive verb allows us to emphasize the team and its location rather than the product (which we've probably already mentioned in a previous sentence).

Active verbs will add life to your copy; passive verbs will drain energy from it. Passive verbs will make your copy more formal and less personal; more written, less conversational. Used too often, passive verbs will zombify your copy.

DEALING WITH PASSIVE VERBS

Get into the habit of spotting passive verbs. Whenever you find one, check to see whether the sentence would work better with an active verb. Aim to use more active verbs than passive ones.

There is a middle way between active and passive. It's called the **mediopassive**. A mediopassive looks like an active verb but its subject is really the object of the verb. Take a look at this sentence.

This copy **reads** well.

The copy is not actively reading but is being passively read. But the verb *looks* active. Used like this, the mediopassive can bring inert objects to life.

Our tip-and-turn window **opens** easily.

Our top-of-the-range mobility scooter **handles** like a sports car.

These cakes **sell** well, especially in Chicago.

The wine **drinks** beautifully and smoothly.

This shirt **washes** easily.

You'll also find the mediopassive turning up in reviews and testimonials.

Unfortunately, the game at times **plays** a bit like multiplayer solitaire.

The mediopassive is a neat solution to the active–passive conundrum.

Non-action verbs

Verbs don't always express action. A verb can also express a state of being, a sense or a feeling, or a desire. The verb *to have* expresses possession; the verb *to think* helps us express an opinion.

These **non-action verbs** are less energetic than action verbs. Here are the most common.

appear	like
believe	look *
consider *	love *
feel *	matter

own	sound *
possess	taste *
prefer	think *
seem	want
smell *	

Asterisks indicate verbs that can also be used as action verbs.

> I **feel** happy. (non-action)
>
> The customer **was feeling** the material. (action)
>
> This coffee **smells** good. (non-action)
>
> The dog **smelled** every lamppost in the street. (action)

To be: the most invisible verb

To be is the ultimate non-action verb. It says nothing about what its subject does, it merely asserts that the subject is the same thing as something else (*I* **am** *a copywriter*) or that it's something else (*poverty* **is** *a scourge on society*) or that it has some quality (*our deodorant* **is** *fully organic*).

To be cools your copy down. Sometimes, that's useful.

> It's winter. Time to plan this year's holiday.

But if you use it too much, your copy will lose energy – bringing zombiedom a step closer.

To be can be hard to spot. We sometimes use it to create a kind of verbal scaffolding.

> It **is** important to note that…
>
> It **is** evident that…
>
> It**'s** unclear whether…
>
> There **are** a number of ways in which…
>
> There **is** no doubt that…

In these sentences, *to be* drags in an **empty subject**. The words *it* and *there* are placeholders, fulfilling the role of a subject in the sentence without actually referring to anything.

Why do we start sentences like this? I think that, sometimes, we feel uncertain about what we're saying: that, under scrutiny, the sentence might collapse like a house of cards. And so we protect it with scaffolding. Remove the scaffolding and see whether the sentence remains standing. If it falls down, maybe you should replace it.

To be works best when it tells us that something is something *else*: something we might not have expected it to be.

A beach holiday is an opportunity to be crushingly bored for a whole fortnight.

ELIMINATING *TO BE*

Take a piece of your copy and see how many instances of *to be* you can eliminate. Not sure whether you can spot *to be*? Use the Find function on your computer to look for these eight words:

am

are

be

been

being

is

was

were

The finer points of verbing

To understand more about how verbs work, we must delve deeper into the murky waters of grammar.

Finite verbs

A major sentence needs at least one **finite verb**. A finite verb is limited by its subject and by time. We normally say that a finite verb agrees with its subject.

Our client **pays** us once a month.

Our clients **pay** us once a month.

To show when an action was, is or will be occurring, the finite verb must have **tense**. The simple present and simple past use just one word.

> We **build** a new housing estate every six months.

> We **built** the housing estate in 1995.

Other tenses need an **auxiliary verb** to create them.

> We **have built** a new housing estate on the edge of town.

> We **are building** a new housing estate.

> We **shall build** the housing estate next year.

Some of these tenses use **participles**. The **present participle** always ends -*ing*. The **past participle** often ends -*ed*, -*en*, -*n* or -*t*. Some past participles have irregular endings.

Infinitive verbs and lonely participles

An **infinitive verb**, unlike a finite verb, is not limited by subject or time. Infinitives come in two forms: the basic form, using the word *to*, and participles operating on their own, without an accompanying verb. Here are two famous instances of the basic infinitive.

> **To be** or not **to be**: that is the question.

> ... **to boldly go** where no one has gone before!

(That second example is probably the most notorious example of a **split infinitive**: an infinitive split in two by a word or phrase. Some say that split infinitives are wrong. I'm not one of them. If Captain Picard can split an infinitive, so can you.)

Participles on their own operate as either adjectives or nouns. A past participle, for example, can act as an adjective.

> Stella's new dress designs are beautifully **embroidered**.

> We can repair any **broken** vase, if we have every part.

> We need to create a sustainable **built** environment.

A present participle can also act as an adjective.

> It's a **growing** market.

> This new movie is extremely **annoying**.

> **Flying** over two thousand miles a day, our executive jets are much in demand.

And present participles can sometimes operate as nouns.

Walking is the gentlest and most enjoyable form of exercise I know.

Brushing your teeth twice a day will help maintain healthy teeth and gums.

It's not the **winning** that matters.

Present participles used as nouns are called **gerunds.** (Now you know.)

As well as using participles alone, we can create **participial phrases**: groups of words that include a participle. The participle in these phrases injects some verbal energy into the copy, even though it's not actually a verb.

> Queen olives, bursting with a luscious fruitiness, are the largest olives grown in Spain.

> You want a car waiting for you at the airport, not sitting outside an office three miles away.

> When you build a castle for a king who's renowned for chopping people's heads off, you build a really nice castle.

Participles, then, can inoculate your copy against zombiedom.

Moods

As well as having tenses and aspects, verbs come in different **moods.** A mood tells your reader whether something is a fact or an opinion; whether it's definite or only possible.

English has three primary moods: indicative, imperative and subjunctive. The **indicative mood** states, asks or denies a fact. Most of the verbs in your copy will be indicative.

Newspapers **have become** now a secondary communication medium.

Are newspapers now a secondary communication medium?

Newspapers **are not** at all a secondary communication medium.

The **imperative mood** gives orders, instructions or advice. Marketing copy often uses the imperative.

> **Be** the best.
>
> **Make** this the best holiday ever.
>
> Just **do** it.

Most calls to action use the imperative.

> **Do not walk** on the grass.
>
> **Click** here for more information.
>
> **Call** us now if you need further help.

Imperatives are also helpful when you're writing instructions. Your reader won't thank you for wrapping up instructions in complicated language – especially if that language includes passive verbs. They *will* welcome being told, simply, what to do.

> Every section of this form **must be completed** before submission.
>
> →
>
> **Complete** every section of this form before you submit it.

The **subjunctive mood** suggests, recommends or wishes.

> I suggest that you **be** there on time.
>
> We recommend that you **not drink** more than two units of alcohol a day.
>
> I suggest that you **consult** a physiotherapist.
>
> I wish I **had** a more interesting job.

In English, the subjunctive is fading away. It survives in some set phrases: *as it were; if I **were** you; **be** that as it may; **bless** my soul; heaven **forbid**; far **be** it from me to…*

Modals

Modal verbs alter the emphasis of a sentence. They can show possibility.

> It **might** rain today.

They can show ability.

> I **can** work on Friday.

And they can suggest or advise.

You **should** always wear protective gear.

These are the main modal verbs:

can

could

dare

may

might

must

should

will

would

We often use modals to blur the sharp edges of our copy with politeness.

Please could you return the form by next Thursday.

But that use of a modal can become irritating. Often, the word 'please' will do the job just as well.

Please return the form by next Thursday.

VERBS: TOP TIPS

Build your skill in spotting verbs.

Prefer action verbs to non-action verbs.

Prefer active verbs to passive verbs.

Look for instances of *to be* in your sentences. Replace as many as you can with more interesting action verbs.

Use mediopassive verbs to give a little more life to inanimate objects.

Check your tenses.

Don't be afraid to use imperative verbs to give clear instructions or calls to action.

Use participles as adjectives and nouns to give a sense of action.

Use participial phrases to add colour and energy to your sentences.

Cut down on the modals – especially *could, should* and *would*.

Nouns: concrete and abstract

Verbs bring your copy to life; nouns pin it down. Nouns name the things and people doing the actions – or, if the verb is passive, having the actions done to them. But nouns can do more. By naming something, we can literally bring it into existence. We all use nouns in this magical way: in ceremonies (*I name this ship Triumphant*); in curses (*You idiot!*); and in oaths (*I now declare you husband and wife*). And, as we'll see, this word magic extends into other areas – not always for the better.

We can divide nouns into two categories. **Concrete nouns** name things that exist physically. These nouns include living things (*man, frog, oak, virus*), places (*park, city, mountain*) or material objects (*table, car, pen*). Concrete nouns can also refer to anything else that we can sense with our five senses (*noise, picture, smell*). **Abstract nouns** name things that don't exist physically or that we can't experience with any of our five senses. They include emotions or feelings (*anger, happiness, bliss*), states of being (*chaos, comfort, luxury*), units of time (*second, minute, hour, day*) or concepts (*management, bravery, value*).

Abstract nouns are problematic. On the one hand, they tend to zombify because, unlike concrete nouns, they evoke no physical sensations. On the other hand, abstract nouns often name the things that are most important to us: our thoughts, feelings and vague hunches; our ambitions and dreams.

We need to use abstract nouns. How can we bring them to life?

The Ladder of Abstraction

In the late 1930s, an American linguist called Sam Hayakawa invented a tool to answer that question. Imagine, said Hayakawa, that all the nouns in the world sit on a ladder. Nouns on the bottom rung are unambiguously concrete: *dog, chair, paper*. As we climb each rung of the ladder, we climb through various categories or classes of word: *pets, furniture, stationery*. At the top of the ladder sit the most general concepts: *life, relaxation, expression*.

Here's the point: we communicate most effectively when we keep moving up and down the ladder. Your reader needs both concrete details and abstract concepts to make sense of things. Concrete details bring abstract ideas to life; concepts tell us what the concrete details mean in the broader scheme of things.

Copy that gets stuck on one rung engages in 'dead level abstraction'. At the bottom of the ladder, a project manager might cite vast amounts of data with exquisite precision but fail to explain what the data mean. At the top of the ladder, a CEO might invoke a string of corporate values – *respect, integrity, excellence* – without giving concrete examples. Copy that's stuck on one of the middle rungs is worst of all. On these rungs sit categories which give the illusion of concreteness: words like *values, stakeholders, goals*.

This single sentence slips elegantly down the ladder.

Usain Bolt has achieved greatness through dedication, discipline and perseverance on the running track.

We could also walk up the ladder.

On the running track, Usain Bolt applied perseverance, discipline and dedication to achieve lasting greatness.

In marketing copy, products and services typically sit on a middle rung as a category: *kettle, policy, computer*. The product's features are lower down: *switch, no-claims bonus, hard drive*. The benefits to the customer will sit towards the top of the ladder: *efficiency, peace of mind, power*.

Use the Ladder of Abstraction to bind all three elements together.

USING THE LADDER OF ABSTRACTION

Use this exercise to help you plan a new piece of copy.

List the topics you plan to talk about on different rungs of the ladder and think about how to connect them together.

- If you want to move down the ladder, ask questions like, 'How will this happen? What's an example of this idea in practice? What will this mean to a real customer or employee?' Use vivid descriptions to show your reader what the idea looks and sounds like. Give examples, data or statistics. Tell stories.

- If you want to climb the ladder, ask questions like, 'So what? What does this mean? What categories am I talking about? Why?' Show patterns or trends. Paint the bigger picture. Summarize.

Nominalization

One kind of abstract noun is especially dangerous. **Nominalization** is a form of zombification in which verbs (or adjectives) mutate into nouns. Nominalization turns *act* into *action, measure* into *measurement* and *maintain* into *maintenance*. In fact, *nominalization* is itself a nominalization.

We usually nominalize by adding a suffix to a verb. The most common suffixes *are -ion, -ment and -ence* or *-ance*. (Some nominalizations are short words with no added suffix: *use, cost, thought*.) Here are just a few.

achievement	consideration
agreement	implementation
appearance	payment
application	performance
approval	reduction
transition	replacement
commitment	solution
communication	

Nominalizations flourish particularly strongly in the upper reaches of management, in academia, in government and in the not-for-profit sector.

SPOTTING NOMINALIZATIONS

Where do you see the most nominalizations in your work?

   Do you see them in the briefs that your clients give you?

   Do some clients use them more frequently than others?

   Do you see more nominalizations in some sectors than others?

   Do some parts of a client organization use nominalizations more than other parts?

   Where do nominalizations breed most successfully?

   Why?

How nominalization arose

According to the linguist Michael Halliday, nominalization emerged in the seventeenth century. It allowed scientists – they were called 'natural philosophers' back then – to objectify the phenomena they were trying to understand and to pin them down as objects of thinking. Processes and qualities could be named as things, which made them easier to explain and think about.

Starting in the hard sciences – physics, chemistry, astronomy – nominalization slowly spread to biology during the eighteenth century and by the twentieth century to the new social sciences, whence it migrated into government, politics and business.

And then it took off. Increasingly, adjectives were nominalized along with verbs and a new suffix appeared: *-ity*. *Available* became *availability*; *suitable* became *suitability*; *profit* became *profitability*. Then other endings – *-ism*, *-ology* and *-ization* – generated new nominalizations: *social* begat *socialism*; *method* spawned *methodology*.

Some existing nominalizations mutated into meta-nominalizations: *transport* became *transportation*; *function* became *functionality*. Nouns began to pair with cloudy categories, on the middle rung of Hayakawa's Ladder of Abstraction: *weather conditions*; *an ongoing conflict situation*; *a content delivery mechanism*. Worst of all, nominalizations began to coalesce into deadly strings: *hybrid resource structures*, *risk mitigation instruments*, *sector systems analysis*.

This is word magic gone wild. By endlessly chanting these abstract nouns back and forth, writers create echo chambers in which we convince ourselves that we all know what we're talking about – and, because they hint at verbs, that these abstract concepts actually *live*.

> These interdisciplinary initiatives are key vehicles for the co-design and co-delivery of innovation, capacity development and policy change, matching capabilities to regional demand.

> Our organization's success is dependent on our employees' competence, engagement and ability to execute customer assignments with great integrity, excellence and empathy.

Nominalization allows us to say something without fully explaining it. It allows us to hide our personalities behind systemic processes: *modernization initiatives were implemented throughout the organization*. At its worst, nominalization can make the insane sound reasonable and provide a cover for atrocities: *collateral damage*, *intensive interrogation*, *ethnic cleansing*.

When abstract nouns take over your sentences, they squeeze the life out of them. All the imaginative energy and potential of your ideas has been reduced to a tasteless mush, offering neither sustenance nor delight. It's the ultimate in zombie copy: neither living nor entirely moribund. It can even be toxic.

How to denominalize

Simple. Use verbs. Or adjectives.

With many abstract nouns, you can root out the buried verb and reinstate it.

We reached an agreement last Friday on **the implementation** of the systems improvement plan.

→

We agreed last Friday **to implement** the plan to improve our systems.

Abstract nouns ending in *-ity* can sometimes be transformed into adjectives.

There was a lack of **availability** in the schedule.

→

There were no dates **available** in the schedule.

Untie the strings of abstract nouns by linking them to verbs, prepositions and adjectives.

We undertook underground mine worker safety protection procedures development.

→

We developed procedures to protect the safety of mine workers underground.

→

We developed procedures to make working underground safer for miners.

Transform phrases using a noun and a weak verb into a single, stronger verb.

Gives consideration to

→

Considers

You can also slip sideways a little from verbs to adverbs: replace adjective+noun combinations with single adverbs.

In an efficient manner → Efficiently

On a daily basis → Daily

NOUNS: TOP TIPS

Prefer concrete nouns to abstract ones.

Use the Ladder of Abstraction to link concrete nouns to abstract concepts.

Use categories to link concrete examples to abstract ideas.

Seek out nominalizations and convert as many as possible to verbs or adjectives.

VERB-SPOTTING: ANSWERS

This passage contains both finite verbs and infinitives. Finite verbs are underlined; infinitives are in **bold**. The passage includes no verb forms using participles and no floating participles acting as either adjectives or nouns.

Comic book superheroes have a number of traits in common. They often display extraordinary powers. These powers vary greatly, but among the most prevalent are superhuman strength, the ability **to fly** and the capacity **to project** energy. Batman and Green Hornet possess no superpowers but they practise martial arts. Most superheroes risk their own safety in the service of good. Many refuse **to kill** an opponent, even though that opponent threatens the safety of others or presents a menace to society at large. Many superheroes use a descriptive or symbolic code name. The cast of characters in a comic book usually includes the hero's friends and family. Superheroes often work from a secret headquarters or base.

SUMMARY

Verbs bring your copy most vividly to life.

Develop your skill in being able to spot verbs.

Action verbs describe something we do, physically or mentally. The best action verbs are specific, vivid and evocative.

Focus on value.

Make it physical.

Evoke emotion.

An **active verb** expresses what its subject does. A **passive verb** expresses what its subject has done to it.

Most style guides tell us to prefer active verbs. But passive verbs can allow us to talk truthfully about an event when we don't know who was responsible, or to put an important idea at the end of a sentence.

Active verbs will add life to your copy; passive verbs will drain energy from it.

A mediopassive looks like an active verb but its subject is really the object of the verb. The mediopassive can bring inert objects to life.

Verbs don't always express action. A verb can also express a state of being, a sense or a feeling or a desire. These **non-action verbs** are less energetic than action verbs.

To be is the ultimate non-action verb. But if you use it too much, your copy will lose energy – bringing zombiedom a step closer. *To be* works best when it tells us that something is something *else*: something we might not have expected it to be.

A major sentence needs at least one **finite verb**. A finite verb is limited by its subject and by time.

An **infinitive verb**, unlike a finite verb, is not limited by subject or time. Infinitives come in two forms: the basic form, using the word *to*, and participles operating on their own, without an accompanying verb.

Participles on their own act as either adjectives or nouns.

As well as using participles alone, we can create **participial phrases**: groups of words that include a participle. The participle in these phrases injects some verbal energy into the copy, even though it's not actually a verb.

English verbs have three primary moods: indicative, imperative and subjunctive.

Modal verbs alter the emphasis of a sentence. They can show possibility, ability or advice.

Verbs bring your copy to life; nouns pin it down.

Nouns name the things and people doing the actions – or, if the verb is passive, having the actions done to them.

We can divide nouns into two categories:

- Concrete nouns name things that exist physically.

- Abstract nouns name things that don't exist physically or that we can't experience with any of our five senses.

To manage abstract nouns, move up and down the Ladder of Abstraction.

Nominalization is a form of zombification in which verbs (or adjectives) mutate into abstract nouns.

When abstract nouns take over your sentences, they squeeze the life out of them.

To denominalize, transform abstract nouns into verbs or adjectives.

A pocket guide to punctuation

Good copy relies on good punctuation. But 'good' can mean different things.

Punctuation helps your copy 'sound' good: suggesting the rhythm and beat of your phrasing, the pauses and breaths that help it speak.

Punctuation can also make your meaning clearer. The commas in Lynne Truss's famous *Eats, Shoots, and Leaves* tell us what the clause means, as well as – subtly – how to speak it.

Sound and sense: when you use punctuation, think about both.

This interlude looks at punctuation from these two points of view. As you read each example, think about how the punctuation makes the example sound, as well as how it helps you understand what the example means.

This interlude is not intended to be a full explanation of how every punctuation mark operates; for that, I suggest you consult some of the resources I've listed at the end of this book – and, in particular, David Crystal's excellent (and highly entertaining) *Making a Point*.

Full stop

Full stops give your copy energy. They stop sentences collapsing under their own weight or dribbling away into oblivion.

Generally, full stops mark the end of full sentences. But not always. Copy often includes minor sentences or sentence fragments for dramatic effect; the full stops create a powerful kick that drives the copy along.

> What a week. Three rail crashes, two murders and an outbreak of foot and mouth disease at an urban farm. Ken was under pressure, no question.

> Don't worry about what your friends think. Just. Say. No.

Sentences don't always end in full stops. We can use question marks (?) or exclamation marks (!). We can use repeated question marks or exclamation marks to convey excitability. (I don't recommend it!!! What do you think you're doing???) We can use an ellipsis (...) to indicate an unfinished sentence; we can use a dash (–) – to indicate an interrupted sentence. We can use an interrobang (‽) to suggest something like *You cannot be serious.* Sometimes – on a poster, for instance – we might even write a sentence with no full stop at all.

Comma

Commas mark tiny micro-pauses. But they also change the meaning of sentences – sometimes dramatically.

Use commas to separate lists of adjectives.

She was a strong-willed, principled, radical entrepreneur.

Omit commas in lists of adjectives where the last adjective is more closely related to the noun than the others, or where the adjectives can be read as a single unit of meaning.

He was a good little boy.

We have nothing but praise for the response of London's emergency, transport, health, and police services.

Omit the comma where *and, or* or *but* join adjectives.

This is a limited and temporary measure.

We met several competent but unadventurous marketing managers.

This may prove to be a protracted or extensive campaign.

In a list, a comma can precede *and*. This is the Oxford comma, which in the United States is called a Harvard comma.

> We examined areas of natural beauty, architectural monuments, and sites of special scientific interest.

> Stores were opened in the area by Marks and Spencer, Jaeger, and Dixons.

Some writers regard the Oxford comma as essential; others see it as optional. Personally, I sit somewhere between these two camps.

> We ate bread, scones and cake.

But on occasions it's very useful.

> We had tea, bread and butter, and cake.

Use a comma between main clauses joined by a conjunction, to separate subordinate clauses, or to mark out separate intonation units.

> Prices are low, and customers are flocking to this holiday destination.

> Some towns have many allotments available, but others have ten-year waiting lists.

> Parliament has not been dissolved, only suspended.

> Because it is one of the most densely populated countries in Europe, the Netherlands continues to reclaim land from the sea.

The comma between coordinating conjunctions – *and*, *but*, *yet* and so on – is controversial, and not always necessary. Think about how you want the sentence to *sound*.

Words or phrases in parentheses will be surrounded by commas.

> There is a chance that, despite the media coverage, the event will be a failure.

> The atmosphere, even in the most dangerous areas, was calm and orderly.

Use commas for non-defining clauses, and not for defining clauses.

> The car, which was in the garage awaiting repair, continued to leak petrol. (non-defining clause)

> The car that is in the garage is older than the car on the driveway. (defining clause)

Non-defining clauses nearly always start with *which*; defining clauses nearly always start with *that*.

Use commas for adverbs when used alone as the first word in a sentence. (And, sometimes, when used in the middle of a sentence).

Already, sales are rocketing.

However, some parks remain centres of crime and anti-social behaviour.

Some products, however, contain non-organic ingredients.

Moreover, the CEO was slow to respond to media criticism.

The CEO, moreover, has overseen a 57 per cent leap in annual profits.

Use a comma to avoid ambiguity.

Mr Smith said that he had shot, himself, in the past.

Use commas for appositives.

The capital of France, Paris, is a popular tourist destination.

Jane Austen is best known for her second novel, *Pride and Prejudice*.

An appositive is a noun or noun phrase following another noun phrase and providing additional information about it.

Avoid separating sentences with commas.

We had a holiday in Florence, it was wonderful, the food was delicious.

We encountered countless acts of individual bravery, many of them remain to this day unreported.

This is the most common 'comma crime'. These commas are called 'comma splices'. Avoid them.

Do not place a comma between the subject of a sentence and the verb it governs.

The reason that utilities are expanding their unregulated activities, is the potential for higher returns.

The key to an effective marketing campaign in an international context, is communication.

Apostrophe

Apostrophes can indicate missing letters. Using an apostrophe in this way is called contraction.

It's a beautiful day.

I can't do it.

They're the best shoes on the market.

Contractions strongly indicate an informal style. As a copywriter, you should always be considering whether to use them or not. You don't need to be consistent (*you do not need to be consistent...*), even within one piece of copy. You can use contractions sparingly, regularly, habitually, or not at all. Using contractions as a general feature of your voice allows you to make a point of *not* using one.

> You're able to use the red button in an emergency. You must not use it in any other circumstances.

Apostrophes also indicate possession. The basic principle is: *place the apostrophe after the agent of possession.*

The manager's office (= belonging to one manager)

The managers' office (= belonging to more than one manager)

Possessives based on plural nouns can cause difficulties. Note these examples.

in a week's time

three months' notice

a children's hospital

men's boots

women's shoes

Use -*s* for all possessives of first names and surnames wherever possible:

Jones's

Burns's

Cousins's

Dickens's

James's (though the football ground in Newcastle is St James' Park)

Thomas's (although the London hospital calls itself St Thomas' Hospital)

Note that the rule changes if the name ends in a sounded /-is/.

Bridges'

Moses'

Most classical names will create possessives similarly.

Mars'

Venus'

Herodotus'

Thucydides'

Note also this major confusion.

It's = It is or It has.

It's a glorious day.

It's been a difficult year.

The word *its* is a possessive adjective, like *his* or *her*.

I ate my dinner. My wife ate her dinner. The dog ate its dinner.

Colons and semi-colons

A colon introduces something. It can introduce a list (including a bullet list).

Everything was ready: the house was clean, the table was set and the porch light was on.

It can introduce an explanation.

I heard a loud thump: the cat had upset the goldfish bowl.

Semi-colons have two main uses.

Use a semi-colon to separate items in a list. Use semi-colons especially when the items themselves are clauses or include commas, or when the list is organized vertically with bullets.

The committee included Dr Smith, Professor of Multitasking at Glasgow University; Dr Stepan Buchesky, Dean of Peckham Cathedral; and Professor Serge Speakalot, of the University of the Third Sphere.

Use a semi-colon to separate two main clauses in one sentence. Use one especially when the balance is between contrasted or qualifying clauses.

I prefer to paint in oils; I've never liked watercolour.

London has many open spaces; New York, in contrast, has relatively few.

Hyphens

The hyphen can be used in many different ways. Try to use it consistently.

Use a hyphen to join two or more words to form a single expression.

The meeting descended into a violent free-for-all.

Hyphenate some adjectival phrases and noun phrases used adjectivally.

It was a kids-free festival. (Note the difference between this and a kids' free festival.)

The strategy was discussed with community-based organizations.

Progress will depend on a number of executive-level decisions.

Use hyphens to join prefixes to words.

She met her ex-husband.

I never claimed to be anti-vegetarian.

Hyphens are sometimes used to join a prefix ending in a vowel to a word beginning with a vowel: *co-ordinate, pre-empt, anti-industrial.*

Use hyphens for e-words – except where a word has become so common that the hyphen has disappeared, like *email.*

Use a hyphen to prevent misunderstanding.

There were thirty-odd people at the meeting.

The conference met to discuss extra-territorial rights.

I was unable to re-cover the book.

If you send me the contract, I shall re-sign.

Dashes

The dash is longer than a hyphen and is normally surrounded by spaces.

Use a pair of dashes to indicate a part of a sentence that could be removed, leaving the outer part complete.

> Our latest model – available in cheery crimson or sultry purple – can be yours for just £68.

Dashes are also used to show a span, a period of time, or between linked names:

volumes 23–40

the 1939–1945 war

the London–Manchester line

Pairs of dashes work very like brackets but are more 'open'; they don't suggest an aside in quite the same way.

Copy often uses a single dash. It can indicate an interruption, a shift in tone or a sudden gear-change in the energy of a sentence. Use one at the end of a sentence to segue into a related idea, as if you're so excited you can't wait for a new sentence.

> Schedule a consultation today – slots are filling fast, so don't miss out.

These single dashes, like contractions, indicate a more informal voice. I use quite a few in this book – check them out and ask whether they work for you. I suggest that you use them sparingly.

Brackets

Round brackets generally enclose explanations and asides. Use them both within sentences and to surround sentences.

> Investment bankers (who organize large, complex financial transactions) have to have their fingers on the pulse of the current investment climate.

We've all been there. You sit down to write a blog post and the next thing you know, it's lunchtime and your screen is still blank. (Yeah, it happens to us, too.)

Quotation marks

Quotation marks show that the words you're using aren't yours. Use them when you're directly quoting someone, quoting a definition, or referring to a word or phrase your audience may not be familiar with.

'Where's the showroom?' he asked.

He asked, 'Where's the showroom?'

Stephen Hawking warned that the Higgs boson could potentially lead to 'catastrophic vacuum decay' in the universe, caused by 'a bubble of the true vacuum expanding at the speed of light'.

A playing field is defined as 'the whole of a site which encompasses at least one playing pitch'.

The simultaneous occurrence of multiple crises is sometimes called a 'polycrisis'.

A lengthy quotation might be indented rather than using quotation marks.

You might place titles of short-form works in quotation marks: poems, short stories and songs, for instance. Long-form works like books, films and stage plays would probably use italics.

Quotations within quotations generally alternate single and double quotation marks. You're not likely to be doing much of that as a copywriter; if in doubt, find an authoritative guide.

Bullet points

Bullet points are not punctuation; they are graphic devices to help the reader recognize a list of items more easily.

Do not use bullet points except when you want to present a list. Each item in the list should be written in the same way.

You can punctuate bullet points in two ways.

Introducing a list with an unfinished sentence

The first way is to introduce the list with an unfinished sentence.

The applications are likely to be for:

- large-scale development;
- major infrastructure or
- redevelopment of existing sites.

Note the use of the colon, the semi-colons and the full stop to punctuate the list.

In this format, the 'platform' or introductory text determines the structure of the items in the list. Each item should be written so that it could fit onto the end of the platform.

Introducing a list with a complete sentence

In the second format, the platform text introducing the list is a complete sentence.

The report raises a number of issues.

- The number of people living in our cities is rising.
- Older people are more likely to be poor.
- Inner-city areas generally have a higher proportion of people living in poverty than the outer suburbs.

As a general rule, have no more than two bullet point lists on any one page or screen and no more than five or six items in any one list.

Bullet points become less useful when the items in the list use more words. They may not work well to mark sub-paragraphs, for example. Try to avoid using bullet points if the text of any one item exceeds two lines in length.

Content planning

In Part Five, we apply all the skills we've developed to different types of copy and content.

We begin by investigating how to manage that range of content. You might be responsible for your brand's content strategy; you might simply contribute to it. Either way, you'll need to understand the broader canvas into which your copy fits.

- **Chapter 12** is all about creating and running a content strategy. At the heart of your strategy, almost certainly, will sit your website. It's where your brand makes itself known to the world.

- **Chapter 13** looks at how websites work and how to make the content on yours maximally effective.

Email is a sophisticated and multi-functional channel for holding conversations with your customers, but capturing your reader's attention on this most transient of media is challenging.

- **Chapter 14** explores the benefits and pitfalls of email and how to use it to generate ongoing customer conversations.

Most brands and organizations create email newsletters. If used well, they are powerful marketing tools, but they demand regular hard work and adequate resources.

- In **Chapter 15**, we look at how to make email newsletters more effective.

With press releases, marketing shades into journalism and public relations. Press releases demand very specific skills.

- **Chapter 16** covers the skills of writing great press releases – and how you can repurpose them within your content strategy.

Most longer-form content appears as articles, advertorials, white papers, blog posts and thought leadership pieces. They stretch your skills to the limit: every structural and stylistic technique is available to you to deliver content that educates and entertains.

- **Chapter 17** pulls together all the skills required to produce long-form content.

12

Creating a content strategy

Content strategy is the discipline of planning, creating, publishing and managing content. To create a content strategy, you'll need to do everything we've covered so far in this book: understand your reader, develop powerful value propositions and speak in a clear, consistent voice. But you must then organize and structure content for different channels. And you'll need to work out *why* you're producing content and *what* you want that content to achieve.

As a copywriter, you might have one of three possible relationships to content strategy.

- You might be responsible for the strategy in your company or organization.
- You might be writing copy to align with the strategy created by a colleague in the marketing department.
- You might be a freelancer aligning with your client's content strategy.

Of course, there's a fourth possibility. You might – for whatever reason – not have a content strategy at all. In which case, keep reading.

You can take two approaches to content strategy.

- The first approach focuses on the architecture of your content: how it all fits together.
- The second approach looks at how your user navigates your content.

These approaches complement each other. Whichever approach you adopt, focus on two things: your business goals and the needs of your reader.

In this chapter, we look at:

- the role played by content pillars and key messages and how to create them;
- the Hero, Hub and Hygiene model and how to apply it to your content;
- how to plan content for all stages in the customer journey and
- the ultimate goal of content strategy – which is to create a brand community.

Content pillars: grounding your content strategy

Content pillars provide the foundations of the architectural approach to strategy. They're called 'content pillars' because they support the overall mission of your brand. Content pillars are broad themes. Look for three or four of them. They help you align your copy and content more consistently with your content and brand strategy.

REVIEWING YOUR BRAND STRATEGY

Answer these questions to focus on your brand's overall strategy. If you find yourself reaching for your company's brand guidelines, review what you read there, critically. Can you improve your current guidelines?

Why does your brand exist?

[Vision, long-term aspirations]

What's your brand's mission?

[Based on: the products or services you provide; your customers; your unique proposition; the benefits your brand promises]

What values does your brand embody?

[Focus on no more than six]

How would satisfied customers describe you?

[single adjectives, no more than six]

With your brand strategy clear in your mind, look for the three or four content pillars that can support it.

Finding key themes

Content pillars should cover themes that respond to your customers' needs. You're looking for:

- topics and trends that your customer base is passionate about;
- ways for your company to outshine your competitors and
- which types of marketing messages really resonate.

Combine this research with some social listening. You might use specialized tools to listen socially; you might just hang out for a few hours in your industry's social communities.

Find the keywords, key phrases and questions people are asking about the themes that are emerging. Tools such as AnswerThePublic are invaluable. Gather these elements into clusters that suggest potential themes for content pillars.

Unless you're breaking new ground, you'll have company. Look for gaps and seize opportunities to outshine them. What themes are they missing? How can you address those issues more effectively?

Audit your content to see how you could repurpose it. Think about how different topics can be treated in different kinds of content.

By now, a small number of themes for your content pillars should be emerging. Review them. A successful content pillar is:

- **informative**: providing in-depth insights into how your brand pursues its mission;
- **up to date:** remaining relevant as the world changes; and
- **user-friendly:** immediately understandable to your customers or users, wherever they encounter it.

Content pillars can be product-based: *how we produce our products*; *the research behind our products*; *how our customers use our products*. Or they might reflect the way users interact with the brand: educational tips; case studies and testimonials; product information; company updates.

A company that provides AI to improve performance at call centres might create content pillars like this.

- Our products
- The sectors where we work
- Success stories
- Our story

FamilyWorld, a (fictional) global chain of resorts, might have content pillars like these.

- FamilyWorld resorts around the globe
- Key attractions at FamilyWorld
- Planning your trip to FamilyWorld on a budget
- FamilyWorld packages this year

Think MECE

Your content themes should be mutually exclusive and collectively exhaustive. (Think MECE – which I always pronounce 'mee-see'.)

Mutually exclusive

Each content pillar should embody a theme that's distinctly different from the other content pillars.

Collectively exhaustive

Between them, the content pillars should support your brand mission completely and provide locations for all the content you want to create. MECE gives you a tough but useful tool for auditing your content pillars.

To find out more about pillar pages, see Chapter 13.

Topic clusters

Develop topic clusters relating to the theme of each content pillar. Use keyword search tools; 'People also ask' and 'related searches' sections can be helpful here. Study the articles and other content that rank highly. Jot down ideas for structures, formats and channels.

A topic has a tighter focus than a pillar theme. Good topics often start with the words *How* or *Why*. Or you could use one of the other honorary Ws: *who, when, where* or *what*.

To find out more about topics, go to Chapter 9.

For example, if you've created a content pillar such as *What is bankruptcy?*, the topic cluster around it might include these topics.

- What happens if I file for bankruptcy?
- How does bankruptcy work in this country?
- What are the benefits of declaring bankruptcy?
- What assets can I keep if I go bankrupt?

Each piece of content needs both to focus on one topic in detail and point back towards the content pillar's broader theme. Maintaining that balance will be a constant discipline.

Mix it up. Include a range of content types: case studies, how-to guides, advertorials, videos… You'll always be able to treat a topic in more than one way.

Finding your key messages

Key messages form the next supporting layer of your content. They're derived from topics and are expressed as sentences. You can build key messages into your copy to reinforce topics and echo the themes of your content pillars. Indeed, writing a collection of key messages can help you distil your brand values, company vision and mission statement.

Creating key messages

Imagine your reader – a typical reader persona – asking you these questions.

What does your company do?

What's unique about the way you do it?

What do you stand for?

What do you want to be known for?

How do your products or services make a difference – in a different way – to me?

How do you aim to make the world a better place?

What's your role in your industry?

How do your products or services contribute to wider trends in your industry, your market or society as a whole?

Try to create simple, one-sentence answers to these questions. Speak your answers aloud.

- Do they sound straightforward, using 'real-world' language rather than in-house jargon?
- Are they the kind of sentence you might speak in an informal conversation?
- Can you imagine your reader asking further questions as a result of hearing your answers?

If the answer to all three of these questions is 'yes', your answers are good candidates for key message sentences.

Involving colleagues in the search for key messages

As you work on key messages, include key stakeholders. Different people will have different ideas about how to answer your reader's questions. Gather ideas in meetings – on site or online – or create a shared document and invite contributions. If you include your colleagues' input, they'll be much more likely to use these messages themselves: in client presentations and meetings, as call centre scripts or responding to customer queries.

Use key messages to help you develop content ideas. Collate messages into a hierarchy: a master message, and primary and secondary messages grouped by customer segment.

INVESTIGATING CONTENT PILLARS AND KEY MESSAGES

Look at a competitor's website. From their home page, try to identify the content pillars that support their overall brand proposition. Now review a blog post produced by a competitor in your sector.

- What content pillar do you think this blog post is supporting?
- What key message or messages for the company do you think the blog post is supporting or conveying?
- How effectively is the blog post supporting those content pillars or key messages?
- How do you think your organization might communicate those content pillars or key messages more effectively?

The Hero, Hub and Hygiene model

The Hero, Hub and Hygiene model helps you prioritize the projects in your content strategy. The model is widely credited to Google: the company developed it to help YouTube creators plan their content schedules.

Think of this model as a pyramid.

- At the bottom is **hygiene content**, which people regularly search for.
- On the level above, **hub content** is regularly produced to improve awareness, engagement and user experience.
- And at the summit, **hero content** is the 'Go Big' campaigns, delivering authority and credibility.

HERO, HUB AND HYGIENE EXPLAINED

Hero content

- It's a big-ticket, big-budget, big-resource, high-production, campaign-style piece.
- It aligns with your key messages and content pillars.
- It can also introduce new people to the brand.
- It might be a video or event: high profile and thematic, less product- and sales-driven.
- Components can form part of a wider campaign.
- You might produce only a small number of pieces of hero content each year.

Hub content

- This is thought leadership or topical content.
- It targets prospects to learn more about your brand.
- It links topics more closely to your brand.
- It is regularly scheduled on social media or newsletters.
- You might produce this content quarterly or monthly, budget and team resources permitting.

Hygiene content

- This is practical content such as tips and how-to guides.
- Your reader might be searching directly for hygiene content; SEO is really important.
- You might produce this content weekly or daily, budget and team resources permitting.

The customer journey

So much for the architectural approach to content strategy. Now for a more dynamic approach. We can develop a content strategy around a customer journey. That journey models the path that someone takes from the moment they realize they have a problem to the moment they purchase something that helps them solve the problem – and beyond.

Received wisdom has it that the idea of a customer journey was first formulated in the mid-1980s by Chip Bell and Ron Zemke. It's often connected with a much older idea: the sales funnel. The funnel works on the assumption that if you capture enough prospects at the top, they will be filtered down until some of them buy. (You'll still hear marketers talking about 'TOFU', 'MOFU' and 'BOFU': the top, middle and bottom of the funnel.)

The customer journey typically has five stages. You, the copywriter, are intervening in that journey.

Awareness

Most prospective customers start at the awareness stage. They have a problem and they're searching for a solution.

Some prospects might be browsing. They may not have defined the problem clearly. For example, they may not yet be considering buying a car, but they're aware of the difficulties of using public transport or travelling with a family. They might ask: 'What are the pros and cons of public transport?' or 'How cost-effective is car ownership?' A reader might not know about your charity that distributes books to remote villages, but they might be asking, 'What are the literacy rates in these countries?'

- What are the reader's challenges and goals?
- How do they prioritize their goals?
- How do they like to consume information?
- How urgent is the problem?
- What would be the result of doing nothing?

Think of yourself as a consultant. Your copy can help a prospect define their problem more clearly. Respond to problems that are topical or urgent. Don't ignore existing users and customers – they might alert you to new issues or problems that can generate new customer journeys.

COPY FOR THE AWARENESS STAGE

White papers

Thought leadership articles

Books

Ebooks

Detailed guides

Checklists

Blog posts

Press releases

Articles in relevant ezines, websites or magazines

Email

Social media posts

Issue-based campaigns

You have a wide range of channels to choose from. Blog posts can unpack and develop ideas. Ebooks can do the same but require more effort and time to produce. Videos can offer practical advice or discuss a topic in more depth. Keep videos short and tightly focused, with high production values. Webinars, in which specialists discuss a specific topic, present an opportunity to build authority and credibility. Podcasts are increasingly popular: unlike other formats, a podcast doesn't require full user concentration and can be consumed while working, driving or exercising. Align your podcast topics with blog posts: there's no shame in repurposing material you've worked hard to research.

Other potential visual content at this stage includes slideshows or slide decks, infographics and interactive infographics. These can be especially helpful in B2B marketing.

Consideration

At the consideration stage, the reader has defined the problem and is now searching for different ways to solve it. They've also realized that solving the problem requires some level of investment. They need to choose.

- What types of solution is the reader searching for?
- How do they inform themselves about these solutions?
- How do they judge between alternatives?
- How do they decide on the best option?

Product-focused information is the most valuable content at this stage. The reader is hungry for knowledge and might be 75 per cent of the way to deciding on a purchase. Make information detailed and specific. Focus on your offer's specific benefits. Show the range of possibilities your brand offers: different models, detailed specs. Offers of trials, free tools and demo versions will go down well. Point the way *beyond* the sale and paint a picture of how life will look once the purchase has been made.

Create social proof: case studies, product reviews, endorsements and testimonials. Use FAQs, live chat and customer reviews.

Three warnings at this stage. Don't oversell; don't offer content that's irrelevant to the reader's interests; and never hide the price.

COPY FOR THE CONSIDERATION STAGE

Ebooks

Comparison tools

Blog guides

Case studies

Newsletters

Live chat

Decision

Otherwise known as 'conversion'. The prospect is on the verge of making a purchase. All they need is a nudge.

- What do prospects appreciate most about your offer?
- What scares them off?
- How many people are involved in the purchasing process?
- What influences the decision?
- Do prospects expect a trial before making the final decision?
- Do prospects have to make any preparations before making a purchase?

Focus on the purchasing *process*. Keep it reassuringly simple: as few clicks as possible. Ask only for info that's critical to the transaction. Use incentives to purchase: discounts, promotions, free gifts or access. And assure the prospect that the purchase will be confirmed in an email.

COPY FOR THE DECISION STAGE

Catalogues

Product landing pages

Product profiles

Spec sheets

FAQ pages

Retention

The customer journey isn't over. Retaining customers is much more cost-effective than finding new ones. And we generate that loyalty by offering help.

- What generates loyalty in your customer?
- What does loyalty look like – for you and for your customer?
- What would destroy loyalty?
- How important for your customer is loyalty to your brand?
- How can you generate more loyalty?

Some retention techniques are obvious. A simple email can demonstrate that you value the customer's decision to choose your brand and that you're still ready to help them. You might also set up regular newsletters, establish regular training sessions or offer new promotions.

But the best way to generate brand loyalty is to help your reader solve problems for themselves. Your customer will feel happier if you make them feel smarter. Guide them towards content that helps them make the most of their purchase: information about associated products or activities, how-to content that develops their skills or interests.

Gather this content into a well-organized knowledge base or help centre. You can include articles, your blog, instructional copy and the all-important FAQs. The centre should be easy to navigate and optimized for mobile.

COPY FOR THE RETENTION STAGE

Special offers

Instructional videos

Specialized support

How-to docs

Educational content:

Explanations, narratives, opinion pieces

Articles to expand interest

After-sales info and service

Advanced tutorials about your product or service

Thought leadership

White papers [offered exclusively]

Advocacy

Loyalty becomes advocacy when your customers start to promote your brand themselves.

Brands have always benefited from customers selling to each other. Word-of-mouth advocacy has been around for hundreds of years and various brands have exploited it by creating schemes in which customers sell to their friends. Now, word-of-mouth advocacy is replicated online, with a burgeoning sub-culture of influencing, celebrity endorsements and online reviews. Nine out of ten consumers apparently consult reviews before buying. But we tend not to trust them as much as face-to-face advocacy from real friends. Advocacy marketing works best when your advocates have real relationships to potential customers.

- How can your customers act as advocates for your brand?
- How can you build partnerships with your customers?
- How can your customers create more customers?

Find your brand's closest friends. Look for the most engaged, satisfied and influential customers – especially the ones who communicate brilliantly. These people can write reviews, join conversations or refer new customers to your brand. 'The strongest consumer endorsement is one that is unprompted, positive and, ideally, done on a public platform,' says Jamie Michaels, digital marketing executive. 'When brands engage and acknowledge this support, that's where the magic happens.'

Advocates can even create content for you. User-generated content can carry great credibility. But you may feel that you're losing control of the content. After all, when user-produced content becomes criticism, brand advocacy can become brand assassination.

The trick is to do what you want your customers to do: *engage*. Become part of the conversation. When advocates start creating content, you can extend its reach. Share it; repurpose it.

One way to encourage advocacy is to set up a referral programme. Provide customers with a safe, easy way to refer you to others; offer simple rewards or incentives for each new customer referred.

You could even develop a full-scale loyalty programme. Make a splash with a big launch. Add incentives to join. Don't be afraid to offer members the opportunity to promote themselves: it's one of the most powerful incentives. But be careful to avoid clashes of interest or the potential for direct competition.

CREATING A LOYALTY PROGRAMME

- Use all your owned channels that are appropriate: the company blog, Facebook, X, Instagram, Pinterest, etc.

- Email news about the programme with links to more information.

- Use website content, featured prominently.

- Use direct mail.

- Have business cards.

- Make use of brochures.

- Fold it into traditional media (direct mail, business cards, brochures).

Lastly, take the time to acknowledge and recognize your advocates. A simple thank-you tweet or Facebook update could be effective. But you could go further: offer your advocates exclusive access to content; invite them to join exclusive initiatives. The more creative you are with your recognition programme, the more it will generate word-of-mouth marketing itself.

COPY FOR THE ADVOCACY STAGE

Surveys

Reviews

Ratings

Testimonials

Social media posts

Emails

Best practice guidelines

Links to information resources

Transforming employees into brand advocates

If you're working in internal comms, think of your organization's staff as potential advocates. Pick your brand ambassadors with care: not every colleague will want to become a brand advocate. And prepare them well. Simple likes and comments are great, but make sure your advocates understand the business's goals and strategy, so that their advocacy aligns with them. Publicize their involvement through the company newsletter and intranet.

Inbound marketing: from customer journeys to flywheels

In recent decades, the last two stages of the customer journey – retention and advocacy – have come to dominate conversations in marketing. In the new marketplace, advocacy feeds back into awareness and the linear customer journey has become a cycle.

Co-founder and CEO of HubSpot, Brian Halligan, has developed the idea of inbound marketing. It grows your brand, says Halligan, 'by building meaningful, lasting relationships with consumers, prospects, and customers'. HubSpot now models its three-part inbound marketing methodology as a 'flywheel', in which delighted customers attract new ones. Inbound marketing creates a virtuous circle, in which *logos*, *ethos* and *pathos* reinforce each other.

1 **Attract**: engaging the customer you want with valuable content and conversations that establish you as credible and trustworthy. (This is *ethos* at work.)

2 **Engage**: presenting insights and solutions that align with your customer's pain points and goals. (Think of this as *logos*.)

3 **Delight**: appealing to your customer's feelings and imagination; offering help and support so that the customer lives comfortably with your product or service. (This is *pathos*.)

Welcome to the brand community

The ultimate incarnation of this increasingly complex set of customer relationships is a brand community. It can offer people a place to make an emotional connection with your brand – and with each other.

In an influential 2009 article in *Harvard Business Review*, Susan Fournier and Lara Lee showed how a brand facing extinction – in this case, Harley-Davidson – can be resurrected by creating 'a group of ardent consumers organized around the lifestyle, activities, and ethos of the brand'. Management at Harley-Davidson realized that the community had itself reinvented the brand and they sought to maximize on that customer-driven innovation.

Community-building is not just a marketing strategy. A community exists to serve the people in it and to meet their needs. The brand should contribute to that ambition.

BUILDING A BRAND COMMUNITY

What kind of brand community could you help build for your company or organization?

Strategy consultancy Jump Associates has identified three basic forms of community affiliation. Effective brand community strategies combine all three in a mutually reinforcing system.

- **Pools.** In a pool, people have strong associations with a shared activity or goal, or shared values, and loose associations. Members of pools are united by shared goals or values (think Republicans, Democrats or Apple devotees).

- **Webs.** Web affiliations are based on strong one-to-one connections (think social networking sites or the Cancer Survivors Network).

- **Hubs.** Members of hubs are united by their admiration of an individual (think Deepak Chopra or Madonna).

Brand communities cannot exist solely online. Social networks online can be powerful and useful, but they have limitations. The anonymity of web encounters often encourages antisocial behaviour; shallow, transient online interactions, which create only weak social bonds – or even destroy them. Think about how you can strengthen your brand community by holding events where people can actually meet each other.

Managing a brand community is a form of stewardship. It's not a corporate asset and you can't completely control it. But loosening control does not mean abdicating responsibility. 'Companies build effective communities through a design philosophy that replaces control with a balance of structure and flexibility,' say Fournier and Lee.

As a copywriter, you can be at the heart of that work, nurturing and facilitating the community. You can do that by creating three types of content (thanks to Dusty DiMercurio of Autodesk for these ideas):

- **Content that builds affinity**: for personifying the brand and the vision of the company. This content helps the community understand your brand's personality, aesthetic and values. This content doesn't try to sell anything. It succeeds when it gets attention and exerts gentle influence.

- **Content that drives demand**: for attracting and converting. This content helps to move people through the traditional customer journey. It succeeds when it creates new customers.

- **Content that supports success**: for helping customers realize the value of your services. The content benefits customers and helps them be successful. This can be onboarding content, which teaches customers about your services or products so they can make use of them for maximum benefit. It can include education, training and tutorials. It succeeds when it helps people contribute to the community.

SUMMARY

Content strategy is the discipline of planning, creating, publishing and managing content. You can take two approaches to content strategy:

- The first approach focuses on the architecture of your content: how it all fits together.
- The second approach looks at how your user navigates your content.

Content pillars provide the foundations of the architectural approach to strategy. Content pillars are broad themes. Content pillars should respond to your customers' needs.

- Perform keyword research.
- Check out your competitors.
- Review existing content.
- Identify content pillar themes.
- Map the pillar content.

Key messages form the next supporting layer of your content. They're derived from topics and are expressed as sentences.

As you work on key messages, include key stakeholders.

Use key messages to help you develop content ideas.

The Hero, Hub and Hygiene model helps you prioritize the projects in your content strategy.

We can develop a content strategy around a customer journey. The customer journey typically has five stages:

- Awareness
- Consideration
- Decision
- Retention
- Advocacy

HubSpot now models its three-part inbound marketing methodology as a 'flywheel', in which delighted customers attract new ones. Copy can attract, engage and delight as part of this iterative process.

A brand community can offer people a place to make an emotional connection with your brand – and with each other.

Community-building is not just a marketing strategy. A community exists to serve the people in it and to meet their needs. The brand should contribute to that ambition. Create:

- content that builds affinity
- content that drives demand
- content that supports success

13

Writing website copy

Much of your copy will be digital. For most businesses, thinking digital means, first and foremost, creating an effective website.

Your role in website development

You could be involved in website development in two ways.

- If the site is brand new, you might be brought in during the initial stages, designing the structure of the site and the content of sections and individual pages.
- If a website is being redeveloped, you might be helping the business reposition itself, restructure the site and update the copy.

In either case, you'll need to work on your relationship with the website designer. You both need the same vision of what you're creating. Some website designers insist on having the copy to work with before they begin designing; others may have begun to design the site by the time you meet them. 'Design' means more than formatting and visuals; both of you need to understand and agree the site's structure.

I believe that leading with the copy brings three key advantages.

- **A site is only as good as the ideas it communicates.** And those ideas can be articulated only by good copy. Without clear messaging, users – and search engines – will remain confused and frustrated.
- **Well-written copy will suggest the nature of the design.** The alternative would be clever, beautiful visuals that do nothing to express the brand's mission, values and activities.

- **Leading with the copy makes for a more efficient project.** Once you have the content in place, even in first-draft form, you reduce the number of iterations the project will go through.

Why have a website?

Seems a ludicrous question. Most marketers would regard a website as a fundamental resource. Heck, if you don't have a website, you ain't got a business. Right?

Here's the bottom line – well, *three* bottom lines.

- A website should generate sales (directly or otherwise).
- It should also present a brand to the world.
- And it should reinforce, link to and complement all the other communication channels you're using.

Of course, a website can do much more.

WHAT ARE YOU USING YOUR WEBSITE FOR?

Here's a list of ideas by Andy Maslen in his *Copywriting Sourcebook.*

- Promote your business
- Sell your products and services
- Get people to apply for a job with you
- Make investors want to buy your shares
- Push your political views
- Attack 'unfair' regulation in your industry
- Sign up new clients
- Get people to register to join your service
- Find out more about your customers
- Get people to sell their stuff through your site
- Gain new subscribers to your service
- Deliver your service itself
- Show how your products work

- Give examples of successful projects you've undertaken
- Act as a forum for users to exchange information
- Build a network of like-minded professionals
- Create a marketplace
- Get journalists to write positive stories about you
- Create a community of people with similar hobbies, interests or ideas

Now, make your own list. Think about your company's website and list all the things it *could* do. Choose some activities from Andy's list, if you wish; add your own.

Use the four rules of brainstorming here.

1   Look for *more* ideas. Aim for quantity, not quality.

2   Don't censor, reject or filter out any ideas.

3   Freewheel. Look for wild ideas and then try to make them wilder.

4   Combine and improve. Put two ideas together and see what new idea emerges.

That's the first-stage thinking done. The ideas you've just generated are a resource you can draw on as you start to design the website.

Websites have five main strengths.

- **Websites are familiar.** Most of us use websites as a first port of call when we look for information about companies, brands, products and services. We also expect websites to work in more or less the same way: home page, sections, links within and out of the site; different kinds of page; familiar navigation aids…

- **Websites are flexible.** If you can dream it up, someone can probably build it. If the business grows or changes, the website can change with it.

- **Websites are efficient.** Gone are the days of printing massive catalogues, user guides, instruction booklets, brochures and flyers… well, almost gone. Compared with the cost of paper, ink and postage, it's relatively cheap to build a site, launch it and maintain it.

- **A good website carries authority.** The stunning imagery that fills your screen when you hit the home page – and, of course, the cool copy that accompanies it – can make a powerful impression in a microsecond.

- **A good website creates rapport with your reader.** It's a chance for you to start a conversation.

We're so familiar with websites that we can forget their weaknesses. And there are a few.

- **Websites aren't easy to find.** A brochure or a flyer landing on someone's doormat will, at the very least, be seen. Your website is forever hiding in cyberspace until someone searches it out.

- **Promoting your website might be costly.** You might have to spend money on Google Ads campaigns or social media hustling; you might have to build a whole strategy involving networking sites, blogs, public relations and articles in magazines or ezines. And you may need to invest heavily in efforts to optimize your SEO rankings.

- **Navigating a website can be tricky.** All those directional cues might interfere with our experience of all the gorgeous copy you've spent so much time writing.

- **And websites are easy – very, very easy – to leave.** According to Nielsen Norman, most people spend no longer than 20 seconds on a website; many leave after 10 seconds. We simply don't feel as connected to images on a screen as we do to a piece of paper or object in our hand. Fewer senses are involved.

If we're creating a website, we need to reinforce the strengths and mitigate the weaknesses. Here's how.

Designing the website

You should be involved as early as possible in the process of designing the site. A typical project team will include the client, the web designer and the copywriter. You may be both the client and the copywriter. In any case, the important thing is to decide from the outset on a few key points.

What are you trying to achieve?

You're spending money on this. How do you want the website to generate a return on your investment?

What ideas and information do you want to include?

Think about your brand's mission, the content pillars that will support that mission, the topic clusters that will surround the content pillars and the key messages that you want to promote. Think, also, about your users. What will they *want* to find on your website? How will they want that information to be structured? The answers to these questions will help you create your site map.

To find out more about constructing a content strategy, go to Chapter 12.

A site map is the website's plan. Creating a clear site map helps you to avoid duplicating pages or making incoherent connections. It helps the designer create a visually coherent design. And it helps users find their way around. You might find yourself morphing into an information design consultant. Different media can demonstrate or illustrate your key messages.

Site sections: start here

If you're creating a site from scratch and structuring the whole thing, the specific pages you include will depend on your content strategy. Sites of different kinds will tend to have different sections.

E-COMMERCE

- Product pages
- Checkout and payment pages
- Discussion boards
- Corporate background
- Terms and conditions
- Privacy policy

CORPORATE SITE

- Home
- About us
- Our services/products
- Our team

- Client area
- For investors
- Testimonials/case studies
- Press
- Careers
- Corporate social responsibility
- Privacy policy
- Contact us
- Sitemap

These are the generic sections that the average reader will expect to see. Deviate too far from them and you risk causing confusion. Adhere too rigidly to them and you risk being boring.

Visitors to the site may not be landing on the home page. Neither are they likely to proceed in an orderly manner through the structure you have so carefully designed. If they're coming via a search engine, who knows which page they'll land on? Don't assume prior knowledge. You don't have to repeat your entire company profile on every page; you *do* have to give users the means to find their way around, wherever they happen to be.

Finding your voice

Obviously, your website needs to speak with the brand voice that you've nurtured so carefully. The reader needs to hear that voice at once. It should sound in the headlines, in the sub-headings, in the micro-copy accompanying images – everywhere the visitor looks.

To find out more about brand voice, go to Chapter 5.

A website is not a document. Most visitors don't want to read, they want to move on. *Talk* to the reader: imagine speaking to one person. Use short sentences and short, simple words – everyday language that your visitor can hear themselves using. Use 'you' and 'your' more than 'I' or 'we'. Prefer active verbs over passive ones. Whatever voice you choose, it needs to be:

- sure and steady;

- clear and cool;

- inspiringly smart.

Avoid anything that puts a barrier between you and the reader. Avoid phrases like *Welcome to our website*, for instance, or *as a valued client*, or *whether you're [doing x] or [doing y]*. This lazy copy simply draws attention to itself rather than directing your reader's attention to the idea you want them to understand. Don't try to sound impressive. But avoid, also, the temptation to sound trendy or slangy. Your copy is likely to go out of date almost before the website is launched.

Perhaps the most irritating sin in writing web copy is pasting in copy from an offline source. At least, it's a sin when the original offline copy is overwritten, corporate or academic in tone. And that offline copy is, by definition, older than the website into which it's being shoehorned; it won't fit with the surrounding copy. Rewrite it.

What about SEO?

How long have we got? SEO is all about matching terms. You're trying to write copy that matches your reader's language when they're searching for something. These days, search engines are primed to look for key phrases as well as keywords: for example, *best smartphones*, *digital marketing advice* or *how to make a lemon meringue pie*. So, you first have to identify the keywords and phrases that people are typing into their search engine. Then, you need to weave those search terms – skilfully – into your copy so that your keyword density (the ratio of keywords to all the words you've written) is high enough to register with the search engine.

The keyword here, of course, is: *skilfully*. I still regularly come across copy like this.

> Our boutique hotel in London's Marylebone is one of the finest boutique hotels in the Marylebone district of London. If you're looking for a boutique hotel in London's Marylebone, then our boutique hotel in Marylebone is the boutique hotel in London's Marylebone you're looking for.

Guess which words the copywriter identified as keywords. Now, your reader might indeed have used those words, but the search engines are now much,

much smarter than they used to be. They can identify this practice of cramming keywords into copy and penalize it. What's more, they measure not just the frequency of keywords or phrases but also how long people stay on a webpage and whether they click on links. If you want to improve your SEO rankings, you need to keep readers engaged and offer them valuable content – especially by linking it between pages.

EEAT and what it means

To improve its search results, Google contracts 16,000 Search Quality Raters around the world. These are real people. In Google's own words: 'Quality Raters are highly trained using our extensive guidelines.' (You can find these guidelines online.) 'Their feedback helps us understand which changes make Search more useful,' continues Google, before adding – rather coyly – 'we use responses from Raters to evaluate changes, but they don't directly impact how our search results are ranked.'

Here are four key factors that Search Quality Raters are asked to consider when looking at webpages.

- **Experience:** How much first-hand life experience do you have of the topic you're writing about? If you can demonstrate that experience, your content will be rated highly.
- **Expertise:** Can you demonstrate the knowledge and skill necessary to advise on a topic? Different topics require different levels and types of expertise to be trustworthy. How can you demonstrate your expertise?
- **Authoritativeness:** Are you the go-to authority on the topic? Most topics do not have one official website or content creator, but when they do, that website or content creator is often among the most reliable and trustworthy sources.
- **Trust:** Can your reader trust your content to be accurate, honest, safe and reliable?

The type and amount of trust required depends on the content itself. Online stores need secure online payment systems and reliable customer service. Product reviews should be honest and written to help others make informed purchasing decisions (rather than solely to sell the product). Social media posts may not need a high level of trust, as long as the content doesn't risk causing harm.

My advice?

- Create content that your readers will find valuable.
- Do whatever you can to hold readers on pages for longer.
- Use your readers' language – or language that they will easily understand *and read.*

The search engines will do the rest.

Creating homepages

The homepage is your website's front door. Most of your website traffic will enter here. People will probably also visit your homepage to find contact details. So, it needs to welcome everyone. And it has to work fast. When a user visits your site, they decide whether to stay in milliseconds.

Create a compelling headline

You need to tell your reader what you're offering at once. Avoid headlines about *What We Do*. Focus on *Why You Should Stay*. Keep it clear and simple. Be clever and stylish, by all means – but don't get overcomplicated.

> Everything you need for work, all in one place.
>
> (Dropbox)

> Music for everyone.
>
> (Spotify)

Avoid generalizations. The visitor should know, within those first few fractions of a second, what your brand does for them – specifically.

Write a clear sub-heading

The sub-heading on a home page supports the headline by explaining briefly what you offer. 'Briefly' here means in two or three sentences, together containing not more than 50 or 60 words.

Being that brief, and that clear, isn't easy. Focus, as ever, on benefits: not so much on the detail of what you do as the difference it makes to your visitor.

- Be specific. Make your copy cool and clear – not vague and overheated.
- Concentrate on value. Explain how you help people: the specific problems you solve, how – precisely – you make life better for your customers.
- Use conversational language. Avoid in-house jargon and 'talking up' the brand. Keep the copy light and easy to read. Use your customer's language.

Include primary calls-to-action

You want visitors to enter the site. Your calls to action (CTAs), then, should be visual invitations to move on through the homepage. They should be visually striking: choose a colour that stands out from the design of the homepage – while fitting in with the overall design concept, of course. The CTA should tell the visitor *exactly* where they can go. You might want the user to do something specific; if so, state that action simply and specifically.

Sign up.

Make an appointment.

Book a free demo.

You could create secondary calls to action for visitors who want to know more before buying. For example, if you have a range of products or styles, you could have two CTAs.

Start shopping.

Browse our range.

A third option: you might create a set of information sections based on your content pillars. Create pillar blocks beneath your sub-heading and encourage the visitor to click on them. As the visitor's cursor moves into the pillar block, you could reveal another piece of mini-copy summarizing what the visitor will find when they enter that part of the site.

You could also make a content offer as a CTA: a download of an ebook, a guide or an infographic, maybe in exchange for an email address. With this gift, your visitor might be more willing to stay on the site and even consider buying. Content of this kind also helps you establish your authority as a thought leader in your sector.

Stay above the fold

This is a design matter, but as the copywriter you should keep an eye on it. Headline, sub-heading and primary CTAs should be 'above the fold': the visitor shouldn't need to scroll down to see any of them. If they like what they see, they'll either continue scrolling or they'll take the action you ask them to. But if they can't *see* these elements at once, they may not scroll at all.

If your page is simple, keeping these elements above the fold is relatively easy.

> Learn a language for free. Forever.
>
> [Get started.]
>
> (Duolingo)

If your offering is more complicated, you may find the task more of a challenge.

Suppose you're a web agency offering consultancy, brand development, web design, content strategy and training. That would be a lot to explain in the limited space above the fold. Instead, use all three elements.

> Let's make your web experience brilliant. Together.
>
> We are a full-service web agency that helps you help your clients discover, create and share knowledge through your website.

[*Pillar boxes: <consultancy> <site design> <training>*]
[*CTA:*]Get in touch

Include testimonials if you've got room

Social proof is a powerful persuader. Include a few of your best testimonials on the homepage. You could create a horizontal scroll, so that testimonials swim into view as the reader sits on the page.

Awards and success statistics can also act as testimonials. Are you critically acclaimed? Have you won trophies? Let your visitor know.

1 Make the navigation clear.

2 You'll probably have a banner menu across the top of your homepage. Give each element a simple label: *About us, Tools and services, Knowhow, Downloads, Contact us*. Each heading will probably generate a sub-menu: as you develop the hierarchy of content, keep everything rigorously simple so that navigation is intuitive.

3 Use striking imagery.

You'll need an image that underlines your brand offer, drives action and carries emotional charge. A stunning full-width image can work wonders. But the copy in front of it must be just as striking.

Simplicity is all. Whatever the visuals do, the design of the homepage should accentuate the key features that deliver your ideas and encourage your visitor to go further: the headline, sub-heading, CTA and any other elements for which you've written copy.

Creating pillar pages

A pillar page offers an overview of one broad theme. It should cover the major points and questions related to that theme. You're demonstrating that you know what you're talking about and that the detailed information in smaller pages – all of which are linked hierarchically to the pillar page – is valuable. Pillar pages are typically aimed at readers at the awareness and consideration stages of the customer journey.

Identify the topics that support that broad theme. Use the pillar page to present that topic cluster and help the user navigate it; back-link from topic pages to the pillar page.

To find out more about content pillars and topic clusters, go to Chapter 12.

This clustering strategy will improve your SEO rankings. By linking all the content to the pillar page, you funnel all your visitors to that pillar page. Rather than having 30 people visiting one page and 40 visiting another, you have 70 people visiting the cluster. That raises the ranking of the pillar page in the search engines and moves you nicely up the search rankings.

Clustering will also encourage visitors to stay on your site for longer. When people see how the information they've searched for relates to other, closely related information, they'll go to those other pages – rather than away from the site.

Pillar pages are usually a few thousand words long. Starting with your head term (give that an H1 heading), define the main theme and then lay out the next layer of sub-topics. Move through headings – H2, H3 if necessary – and outline a head term for each topic. You're building a pyramid: one pillar theme, a small number of H2 sub-topics and under each of those, if necessary, another small number of H3 minor topics. ('Small' means 'about three or four'. This isn't a rule, it's a guideline.)

To find out more about constructing pyramids, go to Chapter 9.

Here's a very simple example. If you provide digital marketing solutions, your H1 pillar pages might look like this.

- Website design
- Content marketing
- Link building
- SEO

You might open the 'website design' page with a statement of broad principles and then introduce these H2 sub-topics.

- Web design tools
- Functional components of a website

- Website layouts
- Visual elements of web design

All of this material gives you ample opportunities to generate other kinds of content: blog posts, videos, infographics, and so on – all of which you can link back to these pillar pages. Prioritize the links *upward* to the main pillar page. You can also include links from each page to other pages on the site – including landing pages.

Creating landing pages

Where a pillar page gives your user information, a landing page seeks to sell them something. Most often, landing pages have visual elements and a natural flow to a CTA, which is the purchase.

Landing pages can work at any stage of the customer journey. They're probably most powerful at the decision stage, when the prospect is on the verge of buying. But they can also help at the awareness or consideration stages. They could offer informational or educational content, perhaps in return for an email address. And later in the journey, you could create a landing page that links to product pages – great for loyal customers or advocates, who are keen to explore your offerings in more detail.

Landing pages are usually shorter than pillar pages. When someone sees one of your ads, you want them to click through to a landing page – and then act. A landing page usually has only one or two brief sections: a main heading, perhaps one or two sub-heads and a call to action. You'll usually include informational copy only if the product needs some more detailed explanation.

The heading on a landing page must do two things: it must grab your reader's attention and it must include your central keyword.

A landing page should probably have a very strong visual. Include images – or, better, a single image – that relate closely to the offer and illustrate the value proposition you're making.

On a landing page, the call to action is critical. If it fails, you've lost the sale. Don't be shy. Tell the reader exactly what you expect them to do at this point.

Download now

Click here

Read more

Get yours

See more

Contact us

A neat trick on landing pages is to phrase the call to action in the visitor's words.

Yes! Rush me my first consignment of Nordic socks now.

I want to go to Madeira. Tell me how.

Book my tickets.

The CTA must stop the reader in their tracks and make them do something. Now.

On some landing pages, you'll write only a small amount of copy: maybe a couple of sentences; maybe only a short sub-heading. Every word counts. Don't be afraid to use imperative verbs – verbs that give an order.

Book your dream holiday now.

Choose your free gift.

Make a difference to a child's life today.

If you're writing a landing page where you're asking for a large commitment, you might want to make the page considerably longer. It might look rather like a long sales letter. You're making a direct and very personal appeal to the visitor, so you need to build a relationship that will engender trust – both in you and in what you're offering. You could include:

- all the benefits of your offer, in detail;
- examples and testimonials;
- pictures of the product in use;
- a Q&A section.

These pages can look surprisingly old-fashioned: underlining, highlighting, multiple call-to-action buttons, handwritten margin notes and all the other old-school sales tricks. Surprisingly, this kind of copy still works.

STUDYING LONG COPY

Find a landing page with long copy. Use the phrase 'long copy landing page' or 'long form landing page' in a search engine. What makes it work? How is it structured? How has the copywriter created a persuasive *sequence* as the page progresses?

What could you do better? And how could you use any of the techniques on that page in your own landing pages?

E-commerce copy

Product description copy is essentially catalogue copy. It describes and explains a product concisely and attractively, without succumbing to cliché or generalized waffle.

Pull out both the key features and the key benefits. Use as few words as possible: maybe no more than 50 or 60. You might be able to include a testimonial. You'll certainly want to leave room for the all-important 'Add to cart' button.

Around this very tight product description copy, you might find yourself producing broader e-commerce copy. At every stage of the buying process – from adding items to a basket to completing the online order form, confirming payment details and receiving confirmation of the order – the reader must know that you haven't lost them and that you can answer any 'What if?' questions that might arise. Maintain your brand voice throughout this process; don't let the mechanics of the sale destroy your hard-earned relationship with the customer.

The F-pattern: dispelling the myth

The F-pattern is the shape made as readers' eyes scan a web page. This pattern was first identified by the Nielsen Norman Group back in 2006. (And this section is indebted to material from its website.)

In the F-pattern, users first read horizontally, usually across the upper part of a content area. They then move down the page a little and read horizontally again – typically covering a shorter area. Finally, they scan the left side of the content vertically. These three movements create the shape of a letter *F.* Users look more at the first lines of text than at subsequent lines. And they fixate more on the first words of those lines than on subsequent words.

The F-pattern has been much misunderstood. For a start, it applies *only* to a web page's content area. It doesn't apply when users arrive in a new section and inspect navigation aids, which are typically at the top or on the left of the page. But the greatest myth about the F-pattern is that it's a normal way of scanning a web page. It's not.

In fact, the F-pattern is bad news. Users resort to the pattern *only* when a page or a section of a page is poorly formatted. When users follow the F-pattern, they miss big chunks of content. The words and phrases that they skip are often as important as – or more important than –the copy they read. Users default to the F-pattern because they've learned that it helps them navigate the web *as a whole.*

If you want users to stay on your web page, you need to *stop* them defaulting to the F-pattern. Format the page so that users can see what you want them to see – and what they want to see.

- Put your most important points in the first two paragraphs.

- Use headings and subheadings. Design them to stand out.

- Start headings and sub-headings with information-rich words. The first two words of any heading or sub-heading should offer the gist of a section or sub-section.

- Group small amounts of related content visually, using borders or different backgrounds.

- Use bold to highlight important words and phrases. Avoid random bolding, however. Bold works best when it highlights complete sentences – or at least phrases with a complete, summarizing meaning (as I've done here). Putting individual words in bold is more or less ineffectual.

- Format links in different ways and give those links information-bearing words and phrases rather than generic *click here* or *more*. Doing so also improves accessibility for users listening to content rather than looking at it.
- Use bullets and numbers: bullets for lists, numbers for processes. Use bullets and numbers *only* for these kinds of content.
- Cut unnecessary content.

You might not be able to control your user's motivation or goals, especially when they're browsing. But you can optimize your content so that users can find something interesting – or what they're looking for – more easily.

SUMMARY

You could be involved in website development in two ways: to create a new site or to upgrade an existing one.

Think about how you will work with the designer. Leading with the copy has three advantages:

- A site is only as good as the ideas it communicates.
- Well-written copy will suggest the nature of the design.
- Leading with the copy makes for a more efficient project.

A website should:

- generate sales (directly or otherwise)
- present a brand to the world
- reinforce, link to and complement other communication channels.

Websites are familiar, flexible and efficient. They can carry authority and help build rapport with users.

Websites are not easy to find. Promoting a website can be costly. Navigating a website can be difficult. Websites are very easy to leave.

When designing a website, ask:

- What are you trying to achieve?
- What ideas and information do you want to include?

Decide what sections to include.

Your website should speak consistently with your brand voice.

To maximize SEO:

- create content that your readers will find valuable

- do whatever you can to hold readers on pages for longer
- use your readers' language

How to create a homepage:

- Create a compelling headline.
- Write a clear sub-heading.
- Include primary calls-to-action.
- Stay above the fold.
- Include testimonials if you've got room.
- Make the navigation clear.
- Use striking imagery.

Create pillar pages to present your content pillars and the topic clusters that surround the content. Pillar pages are usually a few thousand words long. Structure the pillar pages as pyramids.

A landing page seeks to sell something. Landing pages can work at any stage of the customer journey. Landing pages are usually shorter than pillar pages. The heading on a landing page must grab your reader's attention and it must include your central keyword. A landing page should probably have a very strong visual.

On a landing page, the call to action is critical.

Some landing pages can include long-form copy.

Product description copy is essentially catalogue copy.

Do everything you can to stop users scanning pages using the F-pattern:

- Put your most important points in the first two paragraphs.
- Use headings and sub-headings.
- Start headings and sub-headings with information-rich words.
- Group small amounts of related content visually.
- Use bold to highlight important words and phrases.
- Format links in different ways.
- Use bullets and numbers.
- Cut unnecessary content.

14

Email marketing

In the time that it takes you to read this sentence, 20,000 emails have been written.

According to market data analyst Yaguara, 2024 saw 347.3 billion emails being sent and received globally: a 4.3 per cent increase over 2023. And that, you might think, makes email a major marketing tool.

But beware. Yaguara estimates the average open rate for emails worldwide at just 18 per cent. And click-through rates, across all industries, averages a depressing 1.33 per cent.

So, should we be sceptical about email marketing? Not at all. Real people – people who don't work in marketing – use email as an everyday communication tool. You can tap into that mindset. Email can help you stay in your customers' eyeline and even assemble them into a community.

But you have to use it properly.

The trouble with email

Email is full of paradoxes. We think of it as private, but an email is more public than a picture postcard. Emails take time to write, yet they're surrounded by a culture of urgency. And – the most serious paradox of all – we think of email as a conversation, but it lacks what psychologists call paralinguistic information: facial expressions, gestures and tone of voice.

When we write an email, we often assume that we're using those non-verbal elements, and that our reader can see and hear them. Professor Justin Kruger and his colleagues at New York University found that these assumptions have three consistent effects.

- First, we're significantly worse at conveying meaning in email compared with when we hold a real conversation.

- Second, we generally overestimate how well we convey our meaning in emails.
- And third, we consistently overestimate how well we understand the emails we read.

Professor Kruger found that these problems are greatest when we try to convey double meanings: irony, for example, or sarcasm.

Research by Professor Kristin Byron of Syracuse University takes these findings further. Byron found that we tend to read emails as more emotionally negative than the writer intended. We interpret positive expressions as neutral; we interpret neutral expressions as more emotionally negative. These effects are amplified in certain conditions: if, for example, we perceive the email writer to be older than us, of higher status, or – interestingly – male.

What causes this negative bias? Perhaps the lack of paralinguistic information creates a sense of threat. The effect may be super-subtle, but it's almost always there. And it will influence all your email marketing. Your reader will almost certainly approach your email warily – if not suspiciously.

The email frame of mind

We treat our inboxes as intensely personal spaces. And we don't want that privacy invaded or violated.

OPENING THE INBOX

Before you read on, take a moment to reflect on what goes through your mind when you open your email inbox. Write down your thoughts as complete sentences, as if you were talking to yourself.

- How would you describe your feelings about your email inbox?
- What's the very first thing you look for when you open the inbox?
- How do you decide what emails to look at first?
- What do you read or look at as you scan the emails in front of you?

- Compare your notes with a friend or colleague. How do your thoughts differ? Where are they very similar?

- How different or similar do you think your reader's thoughts would be? If you've already created a reader persona, let them speak to you about their attitudes to email.

- How do all the answers to these questions influence the way you think about creating marketing emails?

Here are some examples of common thoughts people have about email.

- *I'm busy. I want to read only what interests me.* Email from relatives and very close friends will take priority. I welcome emails from people and organizations I like.

- *I like to keep my inbox neat and tidy.* I delete junk email before doing anything else. I keep all deleted emails in a trash folder for three months and do a mass deletion when it reaches 2000 emails.

- *Ok. Who sent me email today?* I need to know what's going on here. I can't resist checking my emails, at least every 30 minutes.

Your copy should work with these mental habits, not against them.

It's a privilege to enter your reader's inbox. How do you earn that privilege and maintain it? In this chapter, we'll answer those questions.

How to write a great subject line

After the sender's name (more about this later in the chapter), the strongest influence on opening an email is its subject line. Here are various ways to make your subject lines work for you.

Deliver a message, not a subject

The **subject line** is misnamed. The subject is whatever your email is about. It's like a label on a box or the name of a folder on your computer. But it doesn't say anything. Put a subject into the subject line and you are immediately losing a huge opportunity.

Instead, think of the subject line as a 'message line'. Imagine that it's a headline in a newspaper: your subject line should attract your reader's attention in exactly the same way.

To find out more about headlines, go to Chapter 6.

Keep it brief

Long subject lines will get cut off, especially on mobile devices. Advice on word or character count varies. Campaign Monitor suggests optimizing subject line length to between 41 and 70 characters. A report by Retention Science found that subject lines with 6 to 10 words deliver the highest open rate. Mailchimp recommends no more than 9 words and 60 characters. It also suggests limiting punctuation to three marks per subject line.

Personalize when possible

Personalized emails – and subject lines – tend to perform better than non-personalized ones. We're not talking here about simply inserting a first name into the subject line. The mail merge function used to be impressive, but these days nobody is fooled. True personalization depends on having a segmented database. The more segmented your list, the better you can personalize the subject line and provide relevant content to each email recipient.

To find out more about personalizing, go to Chapter 3.

Align your subject line copy and email copy

This might seem obvious, but your subject line should promise what the body copy of the email delivers. And the body copy should deliver it. If your reader fails to find what you've promised them, they'll get irritated.

Making the most of the preview pane or preheader

The **preview pane** is the line or lines of text that normally appear below the subject line in the reader's inbox. In an ordinary email, it will be the first line or so of the email body copy. Your reader can set the number of lines appearing in the preview pane: typically, they will see just the first line. Preview text will also look different on a mobile.

Preheader text is an extra, small line of text that appears after the subject line in an email inbox but doesn't appear in the body of the email. Preheaders on mobiles can be almost as prominent as the subject line. You can add preheaders in two ways: either using code – typically, HTML or CSS – or by choosing email software that lets you customize your preheader text without using code.

Here are four principles that apply equally to preview pane text and preheaders.

1 Add a call to action.

2 Don't repeat the subject line.

3 Make your subject line and preheader text work together.

4 Excite curiosity.

Add a call to action

And yes, I mean *in the preheader*. Not just in the body of the email itself. Sometimes all you need to do is ask. Imagine this subject line.

> Don't miss out on the Rolling Stones' final tour!

The preheader might look like this.

> Here's how you get to the top of the queue

A preheader CTA follows the same rules as any other CTA. Promise a benefit. Keep it short. (You're severely limited for space anyway.) And make it easy. The call to action in the preheader might be no more than a call to open the email itself.

> Open this if you want to grab tickets.

Don't repeat the subject line

Why say the same thing twice? The preheader is a chance to build on your subject line by adding detail and exciting curiosity.

Make your subject line and preheader text work together

You can use the preheader to build on a great subject line – and to get more people to open your email.

Use the preheader to build curiosity

You can use any of these five ways to generate curiosity in your preview text or preheader.

- Ask a curiosity-inducing question.
- Start a sequence of events but don't finish (for instance, an unfinished story).
- Disrupt the reader's expectations.
- Imply that you have information that the reader needs but lacks.
- Imply that the reader used to know something but has since forgotten it.

Use this as a checklist for your preheader – and, indeed, for the subject line itself. Can you use more than one of these techniques at once?

> *To find out more about stimulating curiosity, go to Chapter 2.*

How to write the email

Now that you've crafted a stellar email subject line and an exciting preheader, you've enticed the reader to open the email. So, what do you write in the email itself?

1 Organize your material.
2 You need to get to the point *and* establish a relationship with your reader – in the same sentence. Signal what's coming and then deliver it.
3 If you have a number of points to make, arrange them in some kind of rational order. AIDCA is a great structure to hang your material on. If you're giving instructions, number them.

To find out more about AIDCA, go to Chapter 7.

Start with the most important information and work your way down. Use headings, bullet points or numbered lists. But be aware that this fancy formatting might not come out clean in your reader's email reader.

1 **Avoid large blocks of text.** Use subheadings, perhaps in bold, and clear paragraph breaks. If the material demands more complicated formatting, create an attachment and use the email to deliver it.

2 **Focus on benefits.**

3 **Don't try to be clever.** Focus on your offer. Remember: *value equals benefit minus cost.* All three elements will be in your reader's mind. Respond to all three.

To find out more about the definition of value, go to Chapter 4.

An email arrived in my inbox the other day. This was the subject line.

Get your contact lenses delivered before the weekend.

Then I noticed the preheader.

And enjoy free shipping.

And then the text.

The weekend is coming. Are your contact lenses on their way? With fast, free shipping, you'll have them – just when you need them.

Keep your weekend in focus!

[*Button copy:*] Reorder now

Imagine if that punning last line – *keep your weekend in focus* – had opened the email. Why would I want to keep my weekend in focus? Why are you writing to me about the weekend? Far better to focus first on the specific benefit and the action needed to realize it. The (slightly) witty line then becomes an acceptable throwaway extra.

Write in the second person

Use *you, your* and *yours.*

> Hi Josie
>
> We're delighted that you've registered with Guppy.com. We look forward to providing you with many superb shopping opportunities. As a Guppy.com customer, you now have access to these benefits:
>
> - A 60-day money-back guarantee
> - Super-easy returns if your choice is not exactly right
> - Award-winning customer service
> - And a great selection of top-quality products
>
> Your account page is now ready for you to customize.
>
> - View your order history
> - Track your orders online
> - Store your billing and shipping information
>
> We're proud that you registered with us.

That second-person language keeps the focus on the customer, not the brand. This subtle tactic also helps you stay focused on value.

Be brief

Focus on one message for the whole email. Ditto with calls to action: stay focused on just one action – emails with single calls to action have higher click-through rates.

Number of words? In a recent survey by AWeber, marketing emails contained an average of 434.48 words. But more than half contained 300 words or fewer. So, aim for no more than 300. Usually. But don't dismiss longform email: 24.1 per cent of the emails in AWeber's survey contained 601 words or more and 11.4 per cent of them had more than 901 words.

In short, offer value. People will read longer emails if the topic matters to them.

Be personable

Which doesn't mean 'get personal'. Remember Kristin Byron's thoughts on negative bias: your reader will probably read your email more negatively than you intend. Raise the emotional temperature – a little. But don't go too far. Focus on creating rapport rather than trying to be overly nice.

Rapport works in two directions. Of course, you want your reader to like you. But they will trust you even more if you can show that you like them. You could begin by demonstrating that you understand their situation. As I was working on this chapter, I read this great example in an email.

> I know how busy things can get, so please don't put this offer aside for later. Before you know it, your subscription will expire and you'll miss out on the savings.

Steer clear of capital letters and exclamation marks. Clear and cool, remember? Focus on the offer, the solution and the relationship.

COLLECTING EMAILS

Start a collection of marketing emails that you receive and like. Copy them into a swipe file or dedicated folder. Note down what you like about them. Think about how you can use some of the same ideas in your own emails.

Getting the email delivered

Of course, there's no point in writing an email without an address to send it to. How do you gain access to those all-important addresses? Here are four golden rules.

1 Never use cold emailing.
2 Take time to build up a good email list.
3 Modulate the frequency with which you email.
4 Provide readers with an easy and highly visible means of unsubscribing.

Never use cold emailing

However tempting it may be, cold emailing – the equivalent of cold calling on the phone – is absolutely unacceptable. First, you could be breaking the law. Second, it doesn't work. Your reader will almost certainly consider your email as spam. They'll delete it without reading it. And third, it damages your reputation. Worst-case scenario: if you consistently send emails to people who haven't asked for them, you could end up on an email blacklist: a list of IP addresses or domains that are known spammers.

Take time to build up a good email list

That list forms the foundation of a brand community. Find people who are genuinely interested in what you provide. Offer them something useful that makes it worthwhile for them to give you their email address. Then, build into the list all the qualities of a supportive, creative community.

Here are five suggestions for starters.

- **Create a sign-up form on your website.** You can use different kinds of opt-in or subscription forms in different places on the site. Embed them within content or use sidebars or pop-ups.

- **Create personalized landing pages with opt-in invitations.** Do your visitors have specific interests that you could exploit? Maybe you could create multiple landing pages with tailored opt-in forms and messaging.

- **Use face-to-face connections.** Linking your business to a real person – in a store, at an event or during a conference – can be the first step in creating a community. You could collect the information on a clipboard or an iPad.

- **Add a sign-up button on social media.** Most social media platforms allow you to add buttons. With less link-friendly platforms like Instagram, you could include multiple links in your Instagram biography, sending people to your website or elsewhere.

- **Don't forget the checkout.** Your customer's purchase is just the start of a new journey as part of your community. Encourage them to sign up to your email list as they check out. As ever, specify the value they will enjoy in return: email-exclusive discounts, product updates or instructional content.

Use email hooks

To build your mailing list, offer 'opt-in email hooks' or 'lead magnets'. Here are four examples.

- **Discount.** This is one of the most common and effective opt-in offers and it's particularly good for winning new customers.
- **Free shipping.** Many prospects are put off purchasing when they see the cost of shipping. Capture them by offering free dispatch.
- **Priority access.** Customers love to be first in the queue. Encourage people to sign up to your mailing list by offering to tell them in advance about discounts and product launches.
- **Informational content.** Use newsletters, videos or ebooks. A series of videos or a vlog can be highly effective. You could offer these resources behind a firewall: in other words, only subscribers – who have, of course, given you their contact details – will have access.

To find out more about email newsletters, go to Chapter 15.

Modulate the frequency with which you email

Most customers want fewer emails. An opt-in is an invitation to hold a conversation, not an opportunity to pester people. Sending emails about twice or three times a week seems to be the optimum. Monitor customer engagement. Are subscribers staying subscribed? Or are they falling away? One thing is certain: if you send too many emails, people will unsubscribe.

Provide readers with an easy and highly visible means of unsubscribing

Do you have to have an unsubscribe button? Yes, you do. The law in the country in which you're operating will almost certainly require you to give your subscribers this option. Indeed, you might be able to use unsubscribing to help you draft better emails.

- **Make it easy to unsubscribe.** It should be a matter of one or two clicks. Your unsubscribe button or link should be visually accessible. You could be fined for making your unsubscribe button hard to find. No pale colours or tiny fonts, please.

- **Use clear language on the unsubscribe button.** Confusing or complicated language here might violate the law.
- **Offer the option to update email preferences.** A subscriber might not want to opt out of all communication from you. Asking them about their preferences can sometimes save subscribers and foster trust.
- **Avoid using negative language.** Honour the decision to unsubscribe. Thank the customer for subscribing. *We're sorry to see you go* sits rather well, in my experience.
- **Include links to your company's social media profiles.** Unsubscribing might not mean losing a customer completely. Always include social media links on your emails so that customers can follow you easily if they want to.

Increasing your open rates

Once you're delivered your email, the next goal must be to get the reader to open it. Here are three things you can do to begin with.

Choose the right time to send

Research has not found any specific day of the week that works better than any other. Apparently, the highest open and click-through rates happen on Tuesdays, but the difference with other days of the week is minimal. Metrics tend to drop at the weekend. No surprise there.

As for the time of day, Yaguara suggests that emails sent at 4am apparently have the highest open rates, at 24.31 per cent. (Next highest are emails sent at 9am, followed by 11am.) You might want to consider two slots: early in the morning (04:00–06:00) and late in the afternoon (17:00–19:00). Arguably, inboxes are less cluttered at these times.

Optimize for mobile

According to research by CRM expert SuperOffice, email open rates on mobile devices have grown by 100 per cent since 2011. In 2023, 81 per cent of emails were being opened on mobiles or tablets. And if those emails weren't optimized for mobile, they got deleted. (Specifically, 80 per cent of readers deleted them immediately.)

But according to SuperOffice, only 20 per cent of email campaigns are currently optimized for mobile. So, check out how your marketing emails look on your mobile.

Use a personal sender name

The most important factor in deciding whether to open an email is the sender's name. Forty-five per cent of respondents to SuperOffice's research said that they were likely to open an email based on who it's from.

Use a human name. You're developing a relationship with your reader: unsurprisingly, we prefer to make relationships with people rather than companies or organizations. Research from Pinpointe Marketing suggests that using a personal name rather than a company name could increase open rates by as much as 35 per cent. Yet companies have seemingly not woken up to this simple fact. SuperOffice claims to have discovered that 89 per cent of email marketing campaigns continue to be sent from company names.

Use actionable language in your call-to-action

The CTA in the email should be super-easy to find. People scan their emails; if there's one thing you don't want them to miss, it's the CTA.

If you're sending an HTML email, you'll probably decide to add a button. Two qualities will make this CTA button effective.

1 **Great design:** Choose a size and colour that stand out from the overall design of the email.

2 **Great copy:** Don't ignore the copy on the button. It should specify the action you want the reader to take, not just say click here.

You can also create powerful buttons using text – or a text box – with a link attached. If the email overall has a quiet design, a simple hyperlinked CTA can attract just as much attention as the fanciest coded button.

Email in the customer journey

Finally, let's look at how we can use email as part of our content strategy, at various points in the customer journey.

To find out more about the customer journey, go to Chapter 12.

Awareness

Who was it that said you never get a second chance to make a first impression?

WELCOME EMAILS

Send a welcome email to every new subscriber, the moment they sign up. Make the most of these emails: they're your first opportunity to introduce your brand. Welcome emails have high open rates and can generate lots of click-throughs.

Stay cool. Offer useful information in exchange for the gift of their subscription.

GUIDES AND LINKS TO BLOG POSTS

The more you can help your customers learn, the more loyal they'll become. Keep each email focused on one topic and use it to link to other content that can provide more information more easily: web pages or blog posts.

To find out more about articles and blog posts, go to Chapter 17.

Consideration

At this stage, use email to convert subscribers into buyers.

ANNOUNCEMENTS

Use this content to promote new features, products or services. Announce limited editions or events. Emphasize urgency and limited availability. Include promo codes to underline exclusivity.

ABANDONED PURCHASE

According to Mailchimp, 69 per cent of customers abandon their baskets or carts before checking out. Automated abandoned cart emails can bring them back. Create personalized product recommendations based on past behaviour. If items in the basket are going out of stock, create a sense of urgency by telling the customer that there are only a few of the items left, or include customer reviews to convince them. These emails will almost always be automated, so pay close attention to the copy you create for them. Make it as conversational as possible and review it regularly.

Decision

The moment of sale might be the only time your customer – for now they are a customer! – will actively search their inbox for an email.

ORDER CONFIRMATION

That email confirming the order, with the all-important reference numbers and details of delivery, must maintain the brand personality you've worked hard at elsewhere. Use this moment, also, to thank the customer and reassert their membership of the brand community.

PROMOTIONAL EMAILS

Offer new deals, sales info and other offers that are time-limited or restricted to subscribers.

Retention

Use email to build loyalty. You can offer discounts, remind them of offers that are about to expire, ask for feedback – even send birthday greetings. Offer exclusive content.

TESTIMONIALS AND REVIEWS

If you managed to gather meaningful feedback during a survey, put it to good use with testimonials and reviews. They provide a subtle yet powerful way to nurture loyalty. Customers often love seeing their comments broadcast.

SNEAK PREVIEWS

Expand your content offering by giving loyal customers exclusive insights into upcoming promotions or initiatives.

RE-ENGAGING CUSTOMERS

Even inactivity can be a touchpoint on a customer's journey. Send an email highlighting the anniversary of a subscription; send them a special offer. Find ways to connect them to the community you're building.

ADVOCACY

Email is social and conversational, so it can be one of the most important ways to help build your brand community.

REFERRAL PROGRAMME ANNOUNCEMENTS

The most obvious way to create brand advocates is to use a referral programme. And the most obvious way to spread the referral link, of course, is via email.

A referral programme will be more effective if you offer a benefit or incentive, both for your advocate and for the new customer. Most referral programmes offer a one-time discount as an incentive, but you can make the whole referral experience more interesting and entertaining by layering the programme and offering different benefits for different levels.

Surveys

Surveys can generate useful conversations within your community. They can help your advocates to feel valued. And they help you see your brand through your customers' eyes.

Surveys ask a lot of a reader. Keep the topic simple and keep your voice collaborative and polite. Of course, you can also offer something in return for your reader's involvement: a discount or a free gift perhaps.

SUMMARY

Email brings significant communication challenges.

- We're significantly worse at conveying meaning in email compared with when we hold a real conversation.
- We generally overestimate how well we convey our meaning in emails.
- We consistently overestimate how well we understand the emails we read.
- We tend to read emails as more emotionally negative than the writer intended.

All of which has implications for email as a marketing tool.

We treat our inboxes as intensely personal spaces. It's a privilege to enter your reader's inbox.

After the sender's name (more about this later), the strongest influence on opening an email is its subject line.

- In the subject line, deliver a message, not a subject.
- Keep it brief.
- Personalize when possible.
- Align your subject line copy and email copy.
- In the preview pane or pre-reader:
  - add a call to action
  - don't repeat the subject line
  - make your subject line and preheader text work together
  - excite curiosity

To write the email:

- organize your material
- focus on benefits
- write in the second person
- be brief
- be personable

Four golden rules for sending emails:

- Never use cold emailing
- Take time to build up a good email list
- Modulate the frequency with which you email
- Provide readers with an easy and highly visible means of unsubscribing

Increase your open rates.
  Choose the right time to send.
  Optimize for mobile.
  Use a personal sender name.
  Use actionable language in your call-to-action.

At different stages of the customer journey, use emails in these ways:

- Awareness:
  - Welcome emails
  - Guides and links to blog posts

- Consideration:
  - Announcements
  - Abandoned purchase
- Decision:
  - Order confirmation
  - Promotional emails
- Retention:
  - Testimonials and reviews
  - Sneak previews
  - Re-engaging customers
- Advocacy:
  - Referral programme announcements
  - Surveys

15

Producing an email newsletter

Newsletters are fast becoming one of the most popular marketing tools. If it's well done, a newsletter can increase traffic to your website and sales and transform customers into a brand community.

But producing an effective newsletter is a major commitment. And for copywriters, it demands a shift of focus. You have to start to think like a journalist. The clue's in the name: this is both news *and* a letter! What counts as news for your reader? It might not be the same as what *you* think of as news.

Why produce a newsletter?

The benefits of newsletters far outweigh the weaknesses. If you exploit the benefits and mitigate the weaknesses, your newsletter stands a good chance of success.

You can reach people anywhere and any time

A newsletter will reach the reader wherever they are. (It must be optimized for mobile, of course.) And if you choose the right moment to distribute it, you maximize its chances of being read.

You can tailor a newsletter to different segments

Newsletters allow you to tailor your marketing. If you segment your email lists, you can then personalize your newsletters. Good email service providers (let's call them ESPs) offer personalization tools to help you.

Newsletters create a regular source of traffic

A newsletter is more or less guaranteed to generate traffic. If it reaches the reader's inbox, the reader will at least notice it. If they recognize the sender as someone they have already subscribed to – and if the subject line is appealing – they might open it. And if the newsletter contains content that's useful and valuable, they will open it regularly. All of which makes your reader more likely to respond to your calls to action. They'll also remain within your sphere of influence and maybe use *their* influence to expand yours.

Newsletters can save you money (but they also cost money to produce)

Newsletters arguably save money compared with other marketing tools like paid ads or influencer marketing. Newsletter software and ESPs are also relatively low-cost and design aspects can be low if you use templates. But don't underestimate the cost of generating content, regularly and to a high standard.

You can measure success

If you choose a high-quality service provider, they'll give you open rates, click rates, unsubscribe rates, bounces and all the other key performance indicators (KPIs to those of us in the know) – at the click of a button.

You have control of messaging

You have complete control over your newsletter's content. You're independent of external publishers and influencers, social media platforms and search engines.

You can link to other marketing channels

You can combine and link newsletter content with content on other platforms to boost your messaging and build your contacts list. With most email builders, you can add social media elements to headers and footers.

The problems with newsletters

There are a few shortcomings. Consider them carefully.

1 **List-building takes time.** Effective newsletters depend on a healthy contacts list and that takes time and effort to build. On the upside, your contact list has the potential to grow.

2 **They're not physical.** Unlike analogue advertising media – brochures, flyers, letters or magazines – email newsletters remain transient. They have, in technical terms, no haptic presence: you can't touch them or pick them up (although I've printed off a newsletter occasionally). And they don't last. A desk calendar is there for 365 days; a business card may stay in your customer's wallet. An email newsletter will disappear into the labyrinth of an archive – if it's not simply deleted.

3 **They can be easily deleted.** Oh yes. As I just said: like all emails, newsletters are likely to be deleted. You could encourage your reader to set up a folder for your newsletters – in much the same way that old-style magazines sold physical folders to hold back issues.

What do you want the newsletter to do?

The more clearly you know *why* you're producing this newsletter, the more successful it will be. The goals you choose will, of course, derive from your content strategy.

Identify the need

Three questions to ask.

- What's the function of the newsletter as part of your marketing strategy?
- What key performance indicators will measure the newsletter's success?
- How will you produce and distribute the newsletter?

Can you resource a regular newsletter? Do you have the budget, time, people and support at your command? Indeed, are you in charge of the project? Some newsletters start life as vanity projects or ill-thought-out whims of senior managers. The practicalities must be thought through.

Gather the data. Create a plan of action. Talk it through with your colleagues and your manager. If newsletters don't fit the culture of your organization or your industry – or if your business goals don't align with the way newsletters work – then your time might be better spent creating content for a blog or improving your website content.

Review examples of successful newsletters

Look at some examples in (and outside) your industry. Some newsletters look very like personal letters: the writer addresses the reader person to person; the copy is brief and simply presented. That style can work, even if the newsletter is being published by an organization. Other newsletters are more like news bulletins. The reader finds multiple stories, broken into sections, maybe with headlines and standfirsts; the copy might include links to a website or a blog; the design elements reflect the visual personality of the brand.

COLLECTING NEWSLETTERS

Subscribe to a clutch of newsletters, both in your sector and beyond. Indeed, look for some examples in a sector as far from your own as you can imagine.

Add them to your swipe file or create a dedicated folder for these examples.

Pick out and note down ideas for content and approach that you could use in your own work.

Identify the newsletter's function

What do you want your newsletter to *do*? We're back to KPIs. Are you trying to increase the number of leads or customers? Are you seeking to build loyalty among recently won customers? Or encourage them to recommend you to new prospects? Which of these returns can you measure?

Every newsletter should have a clear focus. Many try to support every aspect of the business. Product news jostles against PR stories; links to blog posts go head to head with event details.... Think instead of your newsletter as a tool to help your reader solve specific problems: a regular update that will offer them predictable help, advice and news.

'Offer value,' advises Matthew Stafford of Build Grow Scale. 'The key to marketing and selling is giving away free content that your audience cares about. Give so much that they start perceiving you as their trusted adviser and an expert in your field.'

Be consistent. Your newsletter needs a common thread – something to hold it together, day after day, week after week. That thread might be a single function: dates for your diary, upcoming campaigns, answering customer questions… And it might be a specific topic: something tapping into your customers' interests and needs.

How often do you want to publish?

Are you publishing monthly, fortnightly, weekly – daily, maybe? Your reputation depends, to some extent, on your ability to keep your delivery promise.

Test to see what kind of publishing rhythm works for your customers. 'You need to strike the right balance between familiarity and curiosity for your targets,' says Ellen Sluder of the Forbes Communication Council. 'If you send it too frequently, they won't be curious; if your newsletters are spaced out too much, they won't remember you.'

And don't underestimate the work involved in creating new content.

Choose your software

You almost certainly need to use professional software, provided by a reputable ESP.

Any ESP you choose should offer easy set-up and both a suite of useful tools and dedicated support. You can use free service providers, but they're likely to offer limited tools and sending restrictions. They may have tricky configurations for mail merging. Most importantly, you probably won't be able to set up email authentication: you might be identified as a phisher and sent straight to the spam folder.

FUNCTIONALITY TO LOOK FOR IN AN ESP

Mailjet offers this comprehensive list of features that any professional ESP should offer:

- A drag-and-drop email editor to create newsletters in minutes
- A selection of pre-made, customizable and responsive newsletter templates
- Personalization, to help create targeted email content
- Email segmentation options to divide contact lists
- Integrated image editing for easy image enhancements and adjustments

- Responsive subscription widget to build legally compliant newsletter subscriber lists

- Intelligent contact management for efficiently dealing with contacts' data

- Optimal deliverability to ensure emails reach inboxes

- A/B testing, to help you try out new ideas

- Detailed statistics, to help you analyse success factors and adjust content

- A free trial

- Integration with other systems and services

- GDPR compliance and other certifications

Get the content right

Customers usually sign up to a newsletter because they're looking for valuable information and ideas: insights they can implement at home or at work. They will be wary of content that is simply selling.

Balance your content: 90 per cent informative, 10 per cent promotional

Your newsletter should focus on providing information that's educational, relevant and timely. Unless you have an exciting piece of news about a new product or service, limit the promotional material.

'No one wants to feel like they've been slapped around the face with a sales brochure,' says consultant Kim Arnold. 'You need to balance value and selling. Give your readers things to think about, that might make them smile, or just genuinely brighten their day. *Then* you can sell.'

Newsletters are bottomless pits: you should be confident that you can fill every new edition. If you're struggling to find ideas for content, look around. Every department in your company will probably have something worth sharing. Talk to key stakeholders, content marketers and product managers. What are your competitors doing? What about brands in different sectors?

There's no reason why your newsletter should be a one-way communication channel. Engage your subscriber list to create new content. Include surveys and other kinds of customer comments: by including content from your customers, you make them active participants in the conversation, which has the potential to multiply your readership – and, hopefully, your customer base.

Vary, too, the type of content.

- **GIFs,** for example, can consolidate multiple images into one location. If you're featuring several products, for instance, a GIF can help you.

- **Video** could increase your click-through rate by as much as 80 per cent. It allows you to tell a more dynamic story and it works well on mobiles. Check that your ESP will accept video files.

- What about **curated news**? Think about including content from *outside* your company. If the content matches your customers' values or interests, it could be delivering something of high value. You're showing that you care about your reader, not just bragging about yourself. And you might find yourself being paid the same compliment by those other organizations.

Bottom of the list is company news and announcements. Your managers and colleagues might be keen to shout out the latest staff promotions and appointments; your customers might not be nearly so interested. If, however, you can turn the company announcement into news that genuinely adds value to your readers' lives, then do so.

CREATING DYNAMIC CONTENT

Look at your own brand and use this checklist to generate ideas for newsletter content. Rather than thinking about subjects to write about, ask what you want the content to *do*: how it might influence the reader.

- Highlighting new podcasts
- Linking to guides, white papers or research
- Inviting the reader to a seminar, conference or webinar
- Offering early access to product launches
- Trailing longer form content: blog posts or articles
- Messages from business leaders
- Personalising recommendations of linked content
- Curating material from other sources

A content calendar will help keep the content flowing. Plan ahead and save great content for future newsletters. A good content calendar will also include key dates throughout the year – Valentine's Day, Halloween, Thanksgiving – that could create a theme for a newsletter.

Invite the reader into the newsletter

As with any other email, you've got three opportunities to invite your reader to open the newsletter: the sender name, the subject line and the pre-header.

- Personalize the sender's name. Use the same sender name consistently: readers will come to associate that name with a conversational, useful and entertaining newsletter.
- As with all email subject lines, your newsletter's subject line should offer a specific and enticing message. It should match your brand voice, of course, but don't be afraid to try out new ideas.
- The pre-header is a third opportunity to summarize the newsletter's content. Make good use of it.

Keep your copy concise

Once you have your reader's attention, you have about eight seconds before they lose interest. At an average reading speed (200 words a minute, very roughly), that equates to about 30 words.

One of the most important figures in fashion, Wilma Annerton, has been at the forefront of emerging fashion trends for three decades. Learn how she leads her creative team.

Join her class.

Health savings accounts are for more than routine medical expenses. By investing a portion of your account, you can potentially grow your funds tax-fee.

Find out how.

Our supporters do crazy, heartwarming and hilarious things to raise money for clean water. Their stories inspire laughter, tears, and even donations from our staff.

Here are some of them...

Think about it: you don't *want* your reader to spend ages reading your email newsletter. You want to encourage them to do something else: go to your website; read a blog post; check out your latest offer… The copy in the newsletter should make them click through.

Manage your calls to action

Newsletters contain multiple pieces of content, perhaps with multiple calls to action. But the CTAs need not have equal prominence. Instead, consider leading with one CTA, with the others as 'in-case-you-have-time' options. Place the leading CTA at the head of the newsletter and your reader will be in no doubt about the big story of the week.

And don't forget the footer

It's where you place email preferences, contact information, a *view in browser* link – and the all-important unsubscribe link. You can also use it as an opportunity for the reader to go elsewhere: *Liked this? You might also like…* – with a list of links.

Get the design right

You might not be a trained designer. Don't worry. Good design should be simple: your copy should be readable, not pretty. All the design elements should support your copy.

Make your newsletter mobile friendly

The technical term here is 'responsive design': design that works well over a range of different devices. If your newsletter looks clunky on a smartphone, check out responsive design. If you're using a pre-formed template, make sure it's responsive.

Use your brand kit

To develop rapport with your reader, use all your branding elements. The moment they open your newsletter, the reader should feel a sense of familiarity with your logos, colours and typography. These elements also give your newsletter – and your content – added authority.

Use white space

White space alleviates any sense of clutter. It's especially useful when the email's read on a mobile, making it much easier to click the right link.

Here's a super-simple design idea: use one thumbnail image beside one paragraph of copy, leading to a link. Job done.

Going a step further, you may have visual guidelines to help you choose the right format, images and colour scheme. Within those guidelines, you can apply three more simple techniques to align design with copy.

Don't go too wide

Keep the width of the newsletter within 600 pixels. If your reader needs to scroll sideways to read the copy, they probably won't bother. And avoid multiple columns.

Make it scannable

Break the copy into sections. Use descriptive headlines and bullet lists to help the reader navigate the copy.

Create a visual hierarchy

Most newsletters have three main sections: headline, body copy and CTA. The headline delivers your message; the body copy supports the message with essential information; and the CTA seals the deal.

Those three elements – headline, body copy, CTA – must be easy to find. Create a hierarchy of ideas that allows your reader to see the main points at a glance. It's a variation of the 'make your point, then support it' principle.

1 Identify the take-away points.

2 Put visual weight on those points using colour, contrast, point size and positioning.

3 Use large point sizes up front and reduce the point size for supporting information.

To find out more about the 'make your point, then support it' principle, go to Chapter 9.

Complement the visual hierarchy with a copy hierarchy. Use bold titles, sub-headers, quotes and italics to show the hierarchy of your ideas. But keep the typography simple. And avoid underlining: it makes reading more difficult and looks old-fashioned.

TYPOGRAPHIC QUICK-HITS

- Clearly separate the header, main body and footer of your newsletter.
- In order to avoid erroneous clicks, ensure that the embedded links have sufficient space between them.
- Use only two fonts. Body copy should be at 16–18pt, with titles no bigger than 26pt.

Use directional cues

Directional cues are graphics that point the reader in a specific direction. They're especially helpful to emphasize a click button or a call to action. Check out arrows, pointing fingers or even an image to act as directional cues. Don't overuse them. And apply the techniques for dispelling the F-pattern that we discussed at the very end of Chapter 13.

To find out more about the F-pattern, go to Chapter 13.

Use colour carefully

You may be using a pre-determined colour scheme. If you have any choice in the matter, choose colours based on their communicative effect. They say that red suggests passion, yellow communicates warmth and green usually signifies health, nature or peace. You'll find plenty of colour charts online to help you. Limit yourself to two colours, or three at the very most. Choose compatible colours and don't use colours that some users might find difficult to distinguish – or that might make reading the copy more difficult.

You can also use colour to draw the reader's eye to particular pieces of content: use highlighted blocks of colour, for example, to make content stand out.

Background patterns could help your content to pop, especially if you don't have any useful images or your brand is not especially visual. Experiment and test to find a background that works for you. As ever, simplicity rules.

Choose good images

They say that a picture is worth a thousand words. I don't believe it. An image should complement the copy: it must inform or persuade. Any image you choose for your newsletter must illustrate *an idea* – and you can communicate that idea *only* in words. (But not in a thousand words, obviously.)

DON'T FORGET ALT TEXT

Alt text (alternative text) describes an image on a page. (Unlike an image caption, which appears on the page itself.) Alt text will appear on a page when an image fails to load.

Alt text helps visually impaired people understand what the image shows and helps search engine bots understand the content of images – which can positively impact your ranking.

Alt text is sometimes known as the 'alt attribute' or 'alt tag' because it can be added via the 'alt attribute' in the HTML code of an image. Most content management systems have a dedicated field for alt text so that you don't need to edit the HTML directly.

Here – with thanks to online research tool Semrush – are three pointers to creating effective alt text.

1. Add alt text to the right kinds of images

Don't write alt text for images that are simply decorative. Add it to images that offer meaning to the reader. For example:

- images of useful text (for example, screenshots of social media posts)
- icons that denote functionality (for example, shopping cart icons)
- photos that provide supplementary information (for example, a smartphone size comparison)

- charts that illustrate otherwise unmentioned data
- graphics that demonstrate processes (for example, how to hold chopsticks)

2. Be descriptive yet concise

According to the Web Accessibility Initiative (WAI), alt text should be 'the most concise description possible of the image's purpose'. When writing alt text, think about how you'd describe an image to someone in a phone conversation. Don't include:

- photo credits and copyright information (include these in the image caption instead)
- redundant phrases like image of or photo of (unless the format is relevant)
- information that all your readers need (include this in the caption or copy) or
- information that's already provided via the image caption or copy

3. Include a keyword

Adding relevant keywords to alt text can improve your ranking in Google image results.

Test, test, test

Test each newsletter. It's embarrassing when a link doesn't work or when a design aspect looks wonky. Check it on both a computer and a smartphone. If you can, do A/B testing. It will show you what your readers prefer and whether your placement of CTAs is working.

Develop your KPIs

KPIs are the statistics and metrics that tell you, to some extent, how well your newsletter is performing and how you might improve it. KPIs include:

- open rate;
- delivery rate;
- unsubscribe rate;
- click-through rate;
- bounce rate;
- spam rate;
- conversion rate.

The KPIs you choose will depend on your content strategy. If you want the newsletter to increase sales, then conversion rates will be of primary importance. If you want to offer your customer community useful and valuable information, then clickthroughs and unsubscribe rates may matter more.

Find the optimal sending time

You can also use metrics to determine the best time to send your newsletter. Your ESP can probably also tell you the times when readers opened your specific newsletter. Tools like Google Analytics can show when your readers are most active on other channels, like your website.

SUMMARY

Newsletters offer a range of benefits as marketing tools:

- Ability to reach people anywhere and any time
- Tailored customer communications
- Regular source of traffic
- Cost savings
- Easy performance measurement
- Control of messaging and costs
- Easy links to other online marketing channels

But they also carry potential problems and risks:

- List-building takes time.
- They're not physical.
- They can be easily deleted.

Identify the newsletter's function. Align that function with your content strategy:

- Identify the need.
- Review examples of successful newsletters.

Decide how often you want to publish.
    Consider whether to use professional software provided by an ESP.
    Manage the content:

- Balance your content: 90 per cent informative, 10 per cent promotional.

- Invite the reader into the newsletter.
- Keep your copy concise.
- Manage your calls to action
- And don't forget the footer.

Get the design right:

- Make your newsletter mobile friendly.
- Use your brand kit.
- Use white space.
- Don't go too wide.
- Make it scannable.
- Create a visual hierarchy.
- Use directional cues.
- Use colour carefully.
- Choose good images.

Test each newsletter. Develop your KPIs. Find the optimal sending time.

16

Writing a press release

Press releases have their roots in journalism. If you're writing one, you're moving from marketing into public relations, or PR. Any sub-editor who smells a whiff of marketing – or, heaven forbid, advertising – in a press release will chuck it unceremoniously into the bin.

Why write press releases?

That's not to say that press releases aren't useful as marketing tools. Here are three ways they can help you win customers.

Newsletters build brand awareness and credibility

If you're a new business or looking for new markets, press coverage can be useful. It might also improve your search engine rankings: if you include relevant keywords and links in your releases, you might boost your brand's online visibility.

They help you reach new audiences

Because media coverage is fast, press releases can help you access wider audiences quickly. That advantage of speed has increased exponentially with the development of online media like blogs, social platforms, online magazines and livestreams.

They help you establish productive relationships with the media

Once connected to media outlets, press releases can help you develop your relationship with them. PR professionals nurture relationships with journalists over time, and good releases are a vital element in that process. Those long-term relationships can prove particularly valuable in a crisis.

Think like a journalist

As with any other copy, your release needs to attract your reader's attention.

- It must stimulate their curiosity.
- It must offer something new.
- It must meet a need in the reader.

The difference is that your reader is not a customer, they're a journalist.

To find out more about attracting your reader's attention, go to Chapter 2.

Most releases fail because they contain information that's of no interest to journalists. You might consider a company development big news; most members of the public couldn't care less.

Your release must match, pretty exactly, the structure and style of the publication you're aiming at. Press releases follow a fairly rigid formula; wander from that formula and your release will probably be binned. And, of course, poor grammar and punctuation will condemn your release to instant oblivion.

The good news is that if you get it right, your release can appear, almost unchanged, in your target media. As a result, you'll stay in control of your message.

WHAT TO AVOID

- **Overly promotional content:** the aim is not to promote your product or service. The aim is to create a story that somehow involves your product or service.

- **Sales language:** never use phrases like *buy now, limited time offer*, or *don't miss out*. You're not writing an advertisement, you're writing a news story.

- **Excessive branding:** don't plaster your brand name all over the release. Avoid logos, slogans or any other overtly brand-related content.

- **Superlatives:** we've said this before but it's worth repeating. Jumpy, vague adjectives like *amazing, incredible* or *unbelievable* have no place in a press release.

Find a newsworthy story

Making your story newsworthy demands mental mobility. You're looking for what journalists call 'an angle'. An angle is not unlike a topic. It captures the reader's attention – that is, the *journalist's* reader – and holds it. Different angles serve different purposes.

- For a news outlet, the human interest angle helps to communicate complicated issues or ideas more clearly. Stories about people are easier to relate to than stories about companies, products or ideas.
- In public relations, an effective angle might *incidentally* highlight the key qualities of the brand, the organization or the initiative you're writing about.
- In media relations, angles can also come into play in a direct pitch. Some journalists are better at writing about certain topics; pitch the story with an angle that they find comfortable and they might just pick it up.

To find out more about topics, go to Chapter 9.

So what?

This is by far the most important question to ask. Why should a journalist be interested in what you're telling them? Journalists are curious about news. And news:

- is anything that involves or affects people;
- is about people doing things;
- involves special people: heroes, carers, achievers, victims;
- is whatever is happening now or in the near future;
- is something unusual: a crime, an event, an accident, a tragedy;
- is about conflict;
- is an announcement: research findings, facts and figures;
- is emotional: funny, sad, horrific, annoying, arousing;
- is visual: something you can take a photograph of

Your release should relate to at least one of the items in that list. The more it checks, the better.

Where's the human interest?

Most of us prefer stories about people. Or about entities that *behave* like people. Who is affected by the story? Who embodies the danger, or the benefit, at the heart of your story?

Who is the journalist's audience?

Research the publication's readership as deeply as possible. Opening a new store in a small town might not be newsworthy for a national paper but might be very interesting to local news sources. Creating a new interactive database for job applicants might not be interesting when pitched as an organizational initiative, but pitched to a student magazine as a new opportunity to find alternative careers, it might work.

Most stories originating from corporates or advocacy organizations will be of interest only to a specific sector. Tie that sectoral knowledge to your analysis of impact. The more specific you can make your story, in terms of impact and audience, the easier it will be to pitch to the right outlets or journalists.

Why now?

The story itself might not be new, but you might be offering information that's new to your audience. Check out this headline.

> New Species of Dinosaur Discovered in Africa

You could obviously drop the word 'new' – after all, the species itself was hardly new – but imagine the loss of impact.

Newness might depend on trendiness. Has the time for your story arrived? Are you able to piggy-back on a theme that's currently trending?

Why you?

Why should the journalist believe you? This is Aristotle's *ethos* repackaged. Your authority – your brand's authority, the authority of your organization – is *not* the story. But it must *back up* the story.

To find out more about ethos and Aristotle's modes of appeal, go to Interlude 2.

What's different about this?

What makes this story surprising, or unexpected? You never read about a plane that landed safely. (Unless its landing gear had failed or it was landing in a hurricane…)

Where's the conflict?

Most of us are interested in conflict – especially when it's simple and two-sided. Conflict – or argument – engages our emotions and rewards us when the side we're rooting for wins. Conflict can also clarify a complex issue.

Creating conflict in your story might be tricky. You should aim to avoid kickbacks from disgruntled players. If you can create a hero in the story, you can probably find a villain, but the villain need not be a person or organization. It could be an element in the environment.

Testing newsworthiness

Before you pitch the story, test it with a journalist. If they're not interested, offer them another angle. And then another. 'How about this part of this story? Surely your readers will be interested in this angle?'

Cultivate resilience. Journalists are impatient and busy; they might not take well to having their brains picked. But with practice, you'll sharpen your pitching skills and start producing releases that have a more than average chance of being used.

Create a good headline

Journalists are inundated with pitches. They might make a snap judgement based on the quality of your headline. It will have to do more than summarize the story; it will have to demonstrate its *value* to the journalist's readership.

The headline is usually in a bigger size font and bolded. With digital submissions, an email subject line matters just as much as a headline. (Think about the preview pane or pre-reader as well.) Convince the journalist to open your email in a few words.

Don't try to create a witty headline. That's the sub's job.

To find out more about headlines, go to Chapter 6.

Work on the first paragraph

The first paragraph in a press release summarizes your story. It should be about two sentences long – maybe 50 to 60 words – and give the reader the crux of the story while also creating intrigue to keep them reading.

- **The first paragraph must attract interest.** Reveal the main news or your irresistible angle immediately.
- **Don't get bogged down in detail.** Round up figures, keep titles and descriptions short, deliver your main statement as a punchy summary.
- **Make it self-explanatory.** Your first paragraph should be able to stand on its own.
- **Keep it short.** No more than 40 words and two sentences.

One way to check whether your first paragraph is working is to run the '6Ws' check. Does it answer the questions why, who, when, where, what and how?

Here's an example.

> Tracy Marsden, leading authority on corporate catering, says food at work is becoming healthier, in a survey of British corporate catering published today. The survey, based on an annual questionnaire, supports the view that organizations benefit from healthier, fitter staff.

That paragraph contains 40 words. And here's the 6Ws check.

- **Who?** Tracy Marsden, leading authority on corporate catering,
- **What?** Says food at work is becoming healthier,
- **Where?** In a survey of British corporate catering
- **When?** Published today.
- **How?** The survey, based on an annual questionnaire,
- **Why?** Supports the view that organizations benefit from healthier, fitter staff.

Build an inverted pyramid

For decades, journalists were taught to structure news stories as 'inverted pyramids'. The pyramid is inverted because the 'base' of the pyramid – the core of the story – appears at the top of the piece. Information to support the core story is then presented, in decreasing levels of importance, in the following paragraphs.

So, the headline gives a very short, brilliantly engaging summary of the story. The first paragraph covers the essential facts – the 6Ws – in no more than about 50 words. The following paragraphs *repeat* the story in greater degrees of detail. These middle paragraphs might include a quotation. The final paragraph – sometimes called the 'boilerplate' – gives background information about the organization issuing the release.

The inverted pyramid structure is the product of an old media technology: the telegraph. When journalists sent copy over the wire, it made sense to transmit the most important information first, in case the connection was lost. The inverted pyramid structure also benefited sub-editors: if the story needed to be cut to fit a column, they could simply chop from the bottom, paragraph by paragraph.

TEST THE STRUCTURE OF A PRESS RELEASE

Find a press release issued by your organization (or another one). Remove the paragraphs from the bottom up, one by one. As you do so, check: does the release still make complete sense?

Some say that the inverted pyramid has had its day. Some say that it's contributed to a decline in newspaper readership by giving away the ending of the story at the beginning. Some say that it offends the very fundamentals of narrative. Whatever. The inverted pyramid has not gone away. If your release is 'newsy' – and if it isn't, it probably isn't a press release – then use the inverted pyramid.

Include credible information

A journalist might be happy to copy-paste your copy from the release direct into their story. And they might want to use your release as reference. In which case, you must give them something to work from.

Data

Any time you can include meaningful numbers, the potential value of your release goes up. Keep the evidence simple: not too many numbers, not too much detail. How many customers will be affected by your latest service upgrade? How many parents are stressed about their baby's eating habits? The numbers add credibility and make the story more newsworthy.

When including original research, you'll need to prove that you aren't just making up your numbers. If you include a link to your company's research report, or describe the process used to get your results, journalists will feel confident about your information.

Quotes

Quotes are the voice of the article and can provide context to a story. Give a quote from someone who's relevant to the story and can vouch for it. If you simply quote the CEO talking about how wonderful this new initiative is, your reader is unlikely to be convinced. Quote someone whose life has been transformed by that initiative, however, and the quotation gains immediate weight.

If you manufacture a quotation for someone (it happens, often), ask them to authorize it before the journalists get to them.

Get the language right

An editor will be more likely to use your press release if it needs minimal edits. Of course, your spelling, grammar and punctuation must be spot on. Seek out unnecessary words, passive verbs and abstract nouns. Find the strongest verbs that you can. Follow the advice of the great journalist and editor Harold Evans, who said: 'Sentences should be full of bricks, beds, houses, cars, cows, men and women.'

To find out more about passive verbs and abstract nouns, go to Chapter 11.

Work hard on the style of the release. As a general rule, aim to mirror the style of the publication you're pitching at.

- **Watch the hype.** What is amazing or unique to you will be deadly boring to a cynical press hound.

- **Avoid jargon.** Stick to common language. Explain technical terms.

- **Use short words and phrases.** The guidelines of plain English will help here. Prefer short words to long ones and one word to a dozen. But avoid tabloid language, in which *disagreement* becomes *clash* and *reduce* becomes *slash*.

- **Cut all the adjectives and adverbs.** Then see which you (really) need.

- **Beware of abbreviations.** If you must use them, explain them first. Avoid more than one abbreviation in any one sentence.

Keep it short and simple

The KISS principle is critical. One page of A4 is ideal. Keep your paragraphs to no more than 40–50 words. If you must go onto a second page, put *More follows* at the bottom of the first page. At the end, put *Ends* or *End* or three hashtags (###). If your release is getting too long, you could be losing the essence of the story. You might be trying to target too many publications. Consider writing a number of releases, one for each target publication or type.

Use signifiers

The release should be written on the company letterhead, with the words *Press Release* or *News Release* at the top left corner of the page. Below this, indicate when the information is available for publication.

FOR IMMEDIATE RELEASE

or

NOT TO BE USED BEFORE 1100 HOURS, 5 MAY 2003

or

EMBARGOED TILL 0100 HOURS, 12 DECEMBER

Put the release date below the *immediate release* or *under embargo until* statement. Always include contact information, preferably in the top right-hand corner.

Don't embargo unless you have to. Occasionally, you might want more time to gather other information or would prefer that the journalist publish the announcement at a later date. Usually, embargoes make sense for the release of financial figures or for a speech (in which case, add *Check against delivery*). Otherwise, embargoes are an annoyance to journalists.

Add a boilerplate

A boilerplate is a brief paragraph at the end of a press release identifying the issuing company and its core business information. It's standardized copy, but the succinct nature of boilerplates means the writer has to think creatively about how to describe the company best.

Why is a boilerplate important?

The boilerplate is crucial public relations. It tells journalists who you are. But boilerplates can do more.

- **It adds credibility.** Journalists are more likely to take notice of an organization with a strong reputation or recognized authority.
- **It helps to build brand recognition.** If the boilerplate highlights key elements of your culture or values, it will serve to underline your brand's profile.
- **It can be reused.** Your colleagues can use it over and over.
- **It conveys your vision.** The boilerplate is a great place to show your commitment to excellence, sustainability or other core values.
- **It can highlight your company's accomplishments.** If you've won awards or garnered accolades, the boilerplate is a great place to flaunt them.

How to write the boilerplate

Start by writing a brief, one-sentence summary describing what your business does. Add compelling details about your business's impact, revenue, growth and relevance. Then pull together some more material to play with. Answers to these questions will help.

- What industry is your business in?
- What does your business do?
- Who does your business work with?
- Where is your business located?
- When was your company founded?
- What size is your company (such as in terms of employees, revenue and regions served)?
- Have you received any awards, commendations or recognition?
- What is your market share?
- What are the biggest challenges faced by your ideal customers?
- What is your mission or vision statement?
- Who are your company's founders or chief operating officers?

A good boilerplate should sound confident. It should also be up to date.

Use all the material you've gathered and construct a short paragraph: no more than 100 words.

1. USE YOUR BRAND VOICE...

Most boilerplates unfortunately are written in a voice completely unlike that of the brand itself. Be bold: don't be tempted to collapse into faceless corporate jargon just because this is the official brand or company definition. Boilerplates written strongly in the brand voice will stand out.

2.... BUT DON'T MARKET

Make the boilerplate as objective and as cool as possible. Consider highlighting aspects such as financial growth and the organization's place in the market.

3. OFFER BUSINESS-TO-CONSUMER COMMUNICATION

Include all the most important contact information to allow people to find and communicate with you.

COLLECTING BOILERPLATES

Take a look at press releases from different companies and organizations. Create a collection of boilerplates that you like. Try to find some that are unusual or that avoid run-of-the-mill presentation.

Distribute with care

Finally, of course, you will issue the release. You can build a media contact list and send releases to journalists via email for free. You can also contact social media influencers who might want to break your story, send it to trade publications within your industry and submit it to local media outlets.

Target journalists individually, if you can. 'Spray and pray' doesn't work. Scour the media – and social media – for relevant journalists: look in their biogs or portfolios for contact details. Once you know who you want to cover your news, send them personalized emails with your press release. Send it to a named person if you can. Second best is to address it to 'The Health Correspondent' or 'The Business Page'. If it's real news, send it to the News Editor.

Don't be afraid to pitch a story more than once. You'll find plenty of PR experts who will tell you that pitching more than once will risk annoying and upsetting journalists; I think that it does no harm to remind them about a story once or twice.

And don't be tempted to add attachments. Journalists dislike PDFs: they're not easy to preview, it's a hassle to download them and they can't use the images.

Be ready to follow up on any release you send. Get more facts ready. Have a quotable person on standby. Anticipate photo-calls. Send your release to the relevant people in your own organization and if you expect a big response, alert your switchboard. All of this becomes doubly important if you are handling a controversial story.

But don't instigate the follow-up yourself. It makes little sense to follow up a release with a phone call. Journalists don't have the time. If they like the release, they'll contact you.

Put it on the wire

In addition to reaching out to journalists, you may want to put your news announcement on the wire. We're talking about newswires, otherwise known as wire services or news agencies, which distribute syndicated news copy to subscribers.

There are essentially two types of newswire service. News agencies like Reuters, Bloomberg and Associated Press hire journalists to write original articles that are published on the wire and picked up by a variety of subscribing news outlets. These articles will always include the journalist's name and the news agency they work with.

Pitching successfully to a news agency journalist is striking PR gold. To call it a tough sell is understating the case; these journalists are swamped with material.

The second type of service is a press release feed. When a PR professional refers to 'the wire', they're usually referring to this type of wire service. It will post releases (usually for a fee) that subscribing journalists and news outlets can access. Examples include Agility PR Solutions' service and Cision's PR Newswire.

According to an insightful 2015 study by Vitis Business Consulting, 67 per cent of journalists use newswires and 37 per cent of journalists check them daily. The Vitis study also makes three further points worth noting.

- **Relevance is a major issue.** Journalists understandably refuse to wade through a newswire clogged with irrelevant rubbish. Find a newswire specializing in your sector and subscribe to it.

- **You get what you pay for.** The newswires ranked the most valuable tend to be the most expensive ones.

- **Journalists use newswires as much for reference as for stories.** Monitoring industry trends and checking facts are popular uses.

Don't expect too much from the wire. The best way to get your story noticed is to target a journalist, follow them, understand what interests them, and pitch a story exclusively to them. In other words: just like every other type of copy, press releases should form part of a conversation with an interested individual.

Create a newsroom

For some time now, organizations of any size have had a news page on their website. For many, it's little more than an archive of releases. But times are changing: as comms channels proliferate, companies are starting to create online newsrooms.

An online newsroom is the public-facing heart of your brand, the place where you can control your own narrative. It can become a key resource for journalists. They can use it to research your company and find credible, authoritative information. It's a conversation starter: a window into company life and a unique opportunity for you to speak to the press, trade publications, bloggers and influencers. You can also use the newsroom to communicate directly with investors and stakeholders, your customers and sometimes the general public.

As newsrooms develop, press releases will change. The traditional format may give way to different kinds of copy: for example, an in-depth piece in the newsroom archive, linked to short teaser-style emails or social posts. In the newsroom, your versatility comes powerfully into play, not just as crafter of press releases but as storyteller and blogger – hopefully as part of a multi-functional team of photographers, videographers and social media wizards.

As a copywriter, you need to be ready for the challenge.

SUMMARY

Press releases can:

- build brand awareness and credibility
- reach new audiences
- establish media relations

As with any other copy, your release needs to attract your reader's attention:

- It must stimulate their curiosity.
- It must offer something new.
- It must meet a need in the reader.

The difference is that your reader is not a customer, they're a journalist. Most press releases fail because they contain information that's of no interest to journalists. Avoid:

- overly promotional content
- sales language
- excessive branding and
- empty superlatives

Find an angle, which is not unlike a topic:

- Why should a journalist be interested in what you're telling them?
- Where's the human interest?
- Who is the journalist's audience?
- Why now?
- Why you?
- What's different about this?
- Where's the conflict?

Before you pitch the story, test it with a journalist.

Create a good headline. But don't try to create a witty headline. That's the sub's job.

The first paragraph should be about two sentences long. It should cover all the 6Ws of your story: why, who, when, where, what and how?

- The first paragraph must attract interest.
- Don't get bogged down in detail.
- Make it self-explanatory.
- Keep it short.

Structure the release using an inverted pyramid. The core of the story appears in the first paragraph. Information to support the core story is then presented, in decreasing levels of importance, in the following paragraphs.

The final paragraph is a boilerplate.

Include credible information: data and quotes in particular.

Get the language right. Eliminate errors, unnecessary words, passive verbs and abstract nouns. Find strong verbs.

Work hard on the style of the release:

- Watch the hype.
- Avoid jargon.
- Use short words and phrases.
- Cut all the adjectives and adverbs you don't need.
- Beware of abbreviations.

One side of A4 is an ideal length.

The release should be written on the company letterhead, with the words *Press Release* or *News Release* at the top left corner of the page.

Don't embargo unless you have to.

Work on the boilerplate:

- It adds credibility.

- It helps to build brand recognition.

- It can be reused.

- It conveys your vision.

- It can highlight your company's accomplishments.

Start by writing a brief, one-sentence summary describing what your business does. Add compelling details about your business's impact, revenue, growth and relevance.

Target journalists individually, if you can.

Don't be afraid to pitch a story more than once.

Don't add attachments.

There are essentially two types of newswire service: news agencies and press release feeds. Don't expect too much from using a wire:

- Relevance is a major issue.

- You get what you pay for.

- Journalists use newswires as much for reference as for stories.

Create or develop your company newsroom.

17

Writing articles and blog posts

With articles, your copywriting can take flight. You have 500 words, or more, to develop a topic and deliver it with all the style you can muster. You can post the article in a magazine, in a blog – internal or external – or on social sites like LinkedIn. It could become a white paper or thought leadership piece. This content can do anything from giving instructions to promoting initiatives, from answering customer questions to providing powerful thought leadership. But whatever an article or blog post does, it must also entertain. Somehow, you must find a way to maintain your reader's attention from start to finish.

In this chapter, I'll continue to use the word 'article'. Everything here refers equally to blog posts and other kinds of long-form content.

Finding an idea

The value of any article lies in the idea it offers. No amount of stylish writing can hide a weak idea.

To find out more about finding topics, go to Chapter 9.

To find out more about newsworthy topics, go to Chapter 16.

From subject to topic

The subject of your article is what the article is about. The topic of the article is your point of view on the subject.

Suppose you run a company that helps authors self-publish books. The obvious subject for an article would be 'self-publishing'. To create a topic, think about *how* or *why* you want to talk about self-publishing. For instance:

How to self-publish in three easy steps

Why self-publishing is a viable way to produce your book

Before long, you'll find yourself generating lots of ideas for topics.

How to tell a good story

How to promote your book

How to start as a self-published author

How to avoid the pitfalls in self-publishing

How to prepare your manuscript for publication

How we can help you publish your book

How to find the best title for your book

And so on. With a rich list of potential topics, you can now research the ones that are likely to interest your reader.

FROM SUBJECT TO TOPIC

Pick a subject that you think you could write an article about. Write down the subject.

Now create a series of topic phrases, beginning with the word *how* or the word *why*.

Write as many as you can.

Which topics align best with your content strategy?

Which could you develop?

What's the unique angle of this article?

How will this article help your reader?

What can you say that's different from what everyone else is saying?

You can also find topics by doing market research. What do your customers need to know? Where do they need help? Use tools like AnswerThePublic. Lurk in forums, social media groups and online communities.

Then, check out what content is currently available. Do top-ranking articles have similar titles? How do these articles deal with the topic? Are any of these articles worth linking to? Most importantly, where are the gaps? Where can you see an opportunity to add something unique?

Once you've found a promising topic, research it. Balance breadth and depth. Your content should provide something new, something beyond the obvious or superficial: evidence that demonstrates expertise and experience. Explore different angles and viewpoints, but don't dilute your argument. A clear point of view is essential. Reference trends and recent events to show that you're up to date. Include testimonials, quotes, industry data (but not too much) and expert opinion. Use reliable sources; check your facts; attribute and cite sources accurately.

Include links. Internal linking, in particular, allows search engines to find and rank your pages more easily; it also allows human users to navigate more efficiently around your website. You can also link outside your own site. Your reader will appreciate being guided to more of what they're looking for, and you will gain a little more of their trust.

From topic to message

Now, step away from all the material you've researched. Take a deep breath. Remind yourself of the topic you're working on. Write down a sentence that delivers your article's message. That message is the article's governing idea. Everything in the article will support or expand upon that message sentence.

Let's go back to the example of self-publishing. The topics we listed earlier in this chapter might generate message sentences like these.

Self-publishing is now a completely viable way to produce a book.

We can help you promote your book.

To tell a good story, you need three things.

CREATING A MESSAGE SENTENCE

Go back to the last exercises in this chapter. Pick a topic and generate a message sentence from it. The message sentence must:

- express one idea
- be self-explanatory to your reader and
- prompt a question in their mind

Write down the message sentence and the question it provokes.

Finding the core structure

At the heart of your article will be a core structure. This is not the structure of the article itself; we'll come to that shortly. The core structure creates the essential focus of the article and stops it from rambling.

The article's core structure is determined by the message sentence you've just created. What question does that message sentence provoke? The core structure of the article should contain the answers to that question. Your article is likely to be either arguing a case or explaining something. The core structure will be the structure of that argument or explanation.

Constructing an argument

The core structure of an argument is made up of a claim – the point you're arguing – and at least one reason that supports that claim. Reasons are connected to claims through the word *because* – *X is true because Y is true* – or *therefore* – *Y is true; therefore, X is true.*

To find out more about constructing arguments, go to Chapter 4.

Patterns of explanation

If your core structure is an argument, you'll find that the reasons supporting the claim will often be explanations. For example:

[X] is a [Y].	{Define [Y]}
[X] will cause [Y].	{How does [X] cause [Y]?}
[X] has desirable consequence [Y].	{What sort of consequences?}
[X] is like [Y].	{In what way?}

If your article is explaining something, then you must decide how you want to explain. We can explain in six ways.

- Example
- Definition
- Categorizing
- Comparison and contrast
- Cause and effect
- Process analysis

(This is not exactly true. But it's a useful model. Take it from me, most explanations will fall into one of these six types.)

EXAMPLE

We can explain by listing or by giving specific instances of a broader idea.

Our waterproof fairy lights have three features that make them unique.

We see three drivers of improved share performance.

Here are six simple ways to force yourself to save money.

DEFINITION

A definition identifies something uniquely: an object, a procedure, a term or a concept. A definition is essentially made up of two elements:

- the *class* of things to which the object belongs and
- the *unique features* that mark out the object from all other members of its class.

Account-based marketing is a marketing strategy that targets specific prospects or clients rather than market segments.

Poaching is a form of cooking using very low heat in barely simmering liquid.

An all-terrain tyre is a tyre designed to function well in varied types of terrains.

CATEGORIZING

We create categories by assembling items into groups or by breaking down a large dataset into smaller segments. Categories should be mutually exclusive and collectively exhaustive.

- **Mutually exclusive:** Items should fit into only one category. If you cannot decide where to put something, ask if it can be eliminated as irrelevant or whether it needs a category to itself.
- **Collectively exhaustive:** Every item under consideration should fit into one of your categories; if you have items left over, add other categories or rework your existing categories.

Give each category a clear name. Sub-categories will come under larger categories with more general names. Here's an example.

Seven types of digital marketing happen only online.

- Inbound marketing brings customers to you instead of sending you out to them.
- Search engine marketing uses a range of search techniques.
- Content marketing uses detailed content to encourage customer engagement. Affiliate marketing uses a range of techniques provided by a third party.
- Social media marketing covers the full range of social channels, and email marketing employs email in a range of ways to maintain close contact with customers.
- Finally, mobile marketing exploits the technology of mobile devices in a host of ways to deliver marketing messages.

COMPARISON AND CONTRAST

Comparisons display the similarities between things; contrasts show the differences. You can use them separately or together: comparison before contrast.

The items under consideration must be comparable. You wouldn't compare the costs of freight haulage by rail in the UK to container haulage to Australia by ship. Establish the criteria by which you are comparing and contrasting. Here's an example.

Comparative advertising has both important advantages as a strategy and even more important risks. On the one hand, it creates a clear focus on a single brand or product and, done well, educates customers about an important element of your value proposition. On the other hand, it can create confusion between brands and may create a bad impression with your customers. It can also result in legal action if done carelessly.

CAUSE AND EFFECT

This pattern explains why something happened. The difficulty, of course, is in deciding which is cause and which is effect. A cause is so often the effect of another cause, which may be harder to determine or control. Look for the immediate cause, the underlying cause and the ultimate cause. Your analysis will be circumscribed by the areas of responsibility involved.

Cause and effect is a technique fraught with danger. Determine which type of cause you are searching for: immediate, underlying or ultimate. What is your purpose in identifying these causes? Be open-minded. Try not to rush to conclusions or to allocate blame. Be as logical as you can. Eliminate coincidence. Take all factors into account. Is there more than one cause? Are there other effects that you have not considered? Trace all the links. Can you identify an ultimate cause? Here's an example of cause-and-effect explanation.

Robust advertising growth will be largely driven by demand from both local and multinational advertisers, buoyed by deregulation and relatively stable economic conditions.

PROCESS ANALYSIS

A process analysis lists all the steps necessary to carry out an operation. It may take the form of a set of instructions (like a recipe or a checkout process), a quality procedure or a technical product specification. This pattern of explanation proceeds step by step. The steps must occur in a particular order: if the order is wrong, the operation will fail. (Be careful to distinguish between a process – in which operations must be carried out in a specific order – and a list of actions which could occur in any order or simultaneously.)

If you're explaining more than about ten steps, group the steps into a smaller number of larger steps. Aim for a maximum of six or seven steps overall. Here's an example.

To create a simple marketing plan:

1 Identify your marketing objectives.

2 Identify demographics of your target market.

3 Identify your competition.

4 Describe your product/service.

5 Define your distribution strategy.

6 Choose your promotion strategy.

7 Develop a pricing strategy.

8 Create a marketing budget.

Creating an outline: Monroe's Motivated Sequence

The outline sets your core structure within an external structure that maps out the article from beginning to end. In this outer structure, you must arouse your reader's interest and curiosity, and then deliver content that fulfils that interest. Monroe's Motivated Sequence will help you to do just that.

To find out more about 'arouse and fulfil', go to Chapter 7.

Alan Houston Monroe was an American psychologist, author and pioneer in the field of effective communication. In the 1930s, he developed a structure that developed the idea of arousal and fulfilment. 'When confronted with a problem that disturbs their normal orientation,' he wrote, 'people look for a solution.' When they feel a need, they want to satisfy it. Each stage in this sequence, then, sets up a need that the next step in the sequence satisfies. That's how the sequence holds the audience's attention from start to finish.

Here's the full sequence.

Step one: capture attention

Create a sparkling introduction that capture's your reader's attention immediately. Ask a question. Say something unexpected. Tell a story (very briefly).

Make a claim (an outrageous one will be most effective). Paint a picture. Present a surprising statistic.

Your reader – curiosity aroused – is now asking, 'What's going on here?'

Step two: state a need

Explain a need that the reader will be concerned about. Show how serious the issue is by presenting relevant evidence. Refer to statistics or research. Combine evidence demonstrating the seriousness of the need with a vivid picture of how the problem looks in concrete terms.

The reader is now asking. 'How do we solve this problem?'

Step three: satisfy the need

This is where your core structure sits. Your argument or explanation is now presented as the solution to the reader's problem. Illustrate the core argument or explanation, again, with vivid examples.

The reader is now asking, 'Is this solution feasible?'

Step four: visualize the future

At this stage, you must develop your core idea and show that it's realistic. The most powerful way to do that would be to show how you have already made it work. Bring in the subject matter expert or the satisfied customer. This is subtle content marketing; avoid the temptation to sell overtly.

Aim to have the reader asking, 'So what can *I* do?'

Step five: inspire action

Finally, prompt your reader to act. Point the way forward. Has your company committed to an initiative that you want your reader to join? Are you setting up a campaign? Are you publishing an important report? You could also provide links to other content or ask your reader to share your article or add comments.

Creating the headline and standfirst

Your article will often have both a headline and a standfirst to attract the reader's attention. The **headline** could ask a question (*Do you need to put* *your camera on during a virtual meeting?*), suggest a controversial proposition (*Why groceries should cost more*) or make an announcement (*Why we're putting sustainability at the heart of our strategy this year*).

To find out more about headlines, go to Chapter 6.

The **standfirst** sits between the headline and the body copy. It's often typographically distinct from the rest of the copy: it might be presented in bold, in italics, in a different font or in a larger point size. It can act as a summary or an introduction to the article, enticing the reader to read the body copy. It might also indicate the article's structure. It might indicate your approach; it might even mention your name.

STANDFIRST ANALYSIS

Find three articles with standfirsts, in three different sectors – just one of them should be from your own field.

- How do the standfirsts connect their headlines to the body of the article?

- How well do they do so?

- Could you improve any of the standfirsts you've chosen? Could you expand them to make them more informative or condense them to make them more efficient?

- Which standfirst is closest in style to the kind of standfirst you might write?

- What ideas can you take into your own work?

Writing the article

Draft your copy before editing it. As you edit, think about these key points. If you're reading this book from beginning to end, you've heard about them before.

Speak to your reader

Profile your reader. Imagine speaking to them and write down what you would say – word for word.

To find out more about profiling your reader, go to Chapter 3.

Edit paragraphs, sentences and words

Manage paragraph length. Work on the number of sentences rather than the number of words. Most paragraphs work well with a minimum of three sentences and a maximum of about six. Create strong, simple topic sentences.

To find out more about paragraphs and topic sentences, go to Chapter 9.

Vary sentence length. One great way to do that is to alternate long and short sentences.

Use words that are familiar to your reader. Balance nouns and verbs. Use your reader's language.

To find out more about sentence construction, go to Chapter 10.

To find out more about how verbs and nouns work together, go to Chapter 11.

Using images

Choosing images shouldn't be an afterthought. An irrelevant or poor-quality image can undermine the whole article. The best images convey clear ideas. Find an image that relates to the idea you want to convey. Captions are another opportunity to hit your reader with a kind of headline, summarizing your point. Attribute the image properly and add alt text.

To find out more about alt text, go to Chapter 15.

How long should an article be?

It depends. Many consultancies will tell you that search engines rank longer articles higher than shorter ones. They also tend to get more shares. And shares can lead to backlinks: links from other sites *back* to your article, which can boost your search rankings still further.

But long-form articles bring their own challenges. They take longer to produce. They require more careful planning. All of which means that they can be more expensive to produce.

It's a question of ROI. Are you likely to get a high return on your investment? To help answer that question, think about these issues.

- **The reader persona.** Are they focused on detail or interested in more anecdotal material? Are they keen readers?

- **Where your reader is in the customer journey.** At the awareness stage, your reader might need carefully structured explanations of decision-making factors; at the consideration stage, you might want to lay out product comparisons relatively briefly. At the decision stage, long-form explanation might just tip the balance in favour of buying.

- **The reader's search intent.** What are they looking for?

  o At the awareness stage, the intent might be informational: the reader is trying to understand what they need.

  o At the consideration stage, intent might be navigational: the reader is looking for product- or company-specific information and needs a short cut to get there.

  o At the conversion stage, intent is likely to be transactional: the reader needs to find the information to clinch their decision to buy.

- **Your niche or industry.** Either the one you're working in or the one you're targeting. Some industries will require detailed – often technical – information; others will rely on narrative-shaped anecdotal material.

500 WORDS

500-word articles are best for answering direct, simple questions. They can be useful for emerging businesses and brands. Some companies use a 500-word article to highlight their brand's history, mission and goals. Others might highlight very specific keywords.

1000 WORDS

With 1000 words, you can go into more detail. You can also adapt technical content to specific user segments or reader personas.

2000+ WORDS

With 2000 words, you can demonstrate your expertise and experience. Content at this length should offer high value in the form of research, data and analysis. A reader looking for reliable information will respond positively to a long-form article – *if* it's well written.

Make the structure highly visible and easy to navigate. Your reader doesn't want to work too hard: they will welcome signposts showing them what they can expect to find and where to find it. Create summaries, section headings and a linked menu for easy navigation.

And make the content easy to read. Use all the techniques you've explored so far in this book: pyramid-style paragraphs, narrative introductions, well-shaped sentences, short lists...

MAPPING OUT AN ARTICLE

Source some recent research conducted by your organization or a case study produced by your marketing department. Map out an article based on this material. Work quickly and see how much you can achieve in a short period of time.

- Decide what will interest your reader.
- Pick a topic.
- Create a core structure: either persuading or explaining.
- Break the topic into sections.
- Write an introduction: no more than 90 words.
- Write a headline and standfirst.

Put your work to one side and do something else. Come back after a few hours and assess how promising this material is. And if you like what you see – write the article!

SUMMARY

Articles and other forms of long-form content can argue a case or explain something. But they must also entertain and absorb the reader. Find the article's governing idea by pulling focus from a broad subject, through a topic, to a concise sentence.

Create possible topics by generating phrases beginning *How* or *Why*:

- Which topics align best with your content strategy?
- Which could you develop?
- What's the unique angle of this article?
- How will this article help your reader?
- What can you say that's different from what everyone else is saying?

Once you've found a promising topic, research it. Write down a sentence that delivers your article's message. The article's core structure will be determined by its function: to argue or explain.

An argument is made up of a claim and at least one reason to support it. The reasons in an argument will often be explanations. If explaining, decide how to explain. There are six patterns of explanation:

- Example
- Definition
- Categorizing
- Comparison and Contrast
- Cause and Effect
- Process analysis

Create an outline using Monroe's Motivated Sequence:

1 Step one: capture attention.
2 Step two: state a need.
3 Step three: satisfy the need.
4 Step four: visualize the future.
5 Step five: inspire action.

Create a headline and a standfirst. The standfirst sits between the headline and the body copy. It can act as a summary or an introduction to the article, enticing the reader to read the body copy.

Follow these principles when editing:

- Speak to your reader.
- Edit paragraphs, sentences and words.

Add images that convey information that supports your ideas. Add alt text.

Long articles might rank higher than short ones and get more shares. When deciding on the length of your article, think about:

- the reader persona
- where the reader is in the customer journey and
- the reader's search intent: informational, navigational or transactional

Think also about norms in your industry or sector:

- 500-word articles are best for answering direct, simple questions.
- With 1000 words, you can go into more detail.
- With 2000 words, you can demonstrate your expertise and experience.

Make the structure highly visible and easy to navigate. And make the content easy to read.

What about AI?

The AI story is developing very quickly. That's why I've devoted no more than an interlude to AI. By the time you read it, my thoughts could be out of date.

The story begins – as far as copywriters are concerned – with the launch of OpenAI's ChatGPT on 30 November 2022. GPT stands for 'generative pre-trained transformer'; a GPT is pre-trained on large datasets of unlabelled text to generate new content that looks – somewhat – as if it's been written by a human being.

ChatGPT's release has spurred the release of competing products, including Microsoft's Copilot in February 2023.

Three responses to AI

At the time of writing (July 2024), copywriters have been dealing with the advent of AI in their work for less than two years. In that very short time, three broad responses have emerged.

The first response is best summarized as blind panic. On 24 January 2023, barely three months after ChatGPT launched, Henry Williams published an article in *The Guardian* with the headline 'I'm a copywriter. I'm pretty sure artificial intelligence is going to take my job'. Plenty of copywriters continue to voice this fear in chat forums and community blogs.

A second response followed hard on the first. It's typified by a post by Joe Friedlein published on Browser Media's blog on 18 January 2023. Friedlein outlines what he sees as the advantages of AI in copywriting: the time and effort it saves and the errors and inconsistencies it eliminates. He then lists the limitations of AI: the algorithms are only as good as the data they're trained on, and they often struggle to understand nuance and context. Friedlein concludes that AI-powered copywriting will probably never entirely replace human copywriters. 'Instead, it will complement and enhance their writing skills, allowing them to produce more high-quality content in less time.'

All of which implies a third response to AI. And, in fact, Henry Williams hinted at that third response at the end of his *Guardian* article. 'Change is coming,' wrote Williams, 'and those who embrace it and adapt will be best placed to thrive.'

In other words, AI tools are like any other tool. We might be able to find them useful if we learn how to use them well.

There is, however, another question. *Should* we be using AI tools to write our copy? I'll address that question shortly.

Using AI to plan content

Lauren Plug, a copywriter working out of Chicago, summarizes some of the ways AI can help you plan content. (I'm paraphrasing somewhat here and adding some of my own ideas. Lauren's post is excellent.)

AI can help you get inside your reader's head. But you have to know who that reader is and you have to understand your objectives in writing the copy. Critically, you need to know that AI is giving you relevant, accurate information. (ChatGPT does *not* understand the words it's using.)

AI can help you generate ideas. It's surprisingly good at outlining and summarizing. It can throw up words and phrases that might resonate with your reader. It's good at generating headlines.

AI can help you push through writer's block. Try AI if you feel you're lacking perspective, inspiration or focus.

AI can substitute for collaborative brainstorming. If you're all alone in your garret, you might be missing the creative buzz of working with colleagues. You can prompt AI to work on the same idea from different perspectives. It can speed up your first-stage thinking and help you flesh out ideas.

A recent HubSpot post by Erica Santiago reported on three AI tools: ChatGPT, Scalenut and HubSpot's own AI content writer.

- ChatGPT, thought Erica, summarized well but lacked detail or excitement. To use it well, you must provide specific and detailed prompts, often over multiple iterations.
- HubSpot's AI content writer is user-friendly, quick and helpful, in Erica's estimation. But, once again, she found the opening summaries more helpful than anything else.
- Scalenut asks you to submit keywords before entering a prompt. Scalenut is more collaborative than the other two tools tested, which suited Erica's way of working.

Erica also tested other AI tools designed to create copy for social media and emails. She particularly liked Hypotenuse AI, partly because, again, it allowed her to put detailed prompts into the tool.

Using AI to edit content

Whenever I've tried ChatGPT, one thing has struck me. However inaccurate or plain wrong the copy might be, it's never – as far as I can remember, *never* – written ungrammatically. By which I mean that the copy it produces always follows the conventions of standard English. In fact, that faultless grammar is often what marks out AI-generated copy as inhuman. You might find AI helpful simply to iron out grammatical problems in your copy.

Of course, Grammarly, Hemingway, Ludwig and other tools also help you improve your style and eliminate mistakes.

What's not so good about AI

Again, these thoughts come with help from Lauren Plug.

AI can't tell stories. In fact, I have asked it, once or twice, to write a story; what emerged was sentimental tosh.

AI has no imagination. Brainstorming in a team can stimulate ideas laterally. Wacky ideas trigger more ideas and new ideas until something feasible begins to emerge. AI can't do that, it simply regurgitates what it's been taught.

AI has no sense of humour. Did you ever read anything AI-generated that made you laugh out loud? AI's humour tends to be slapstick, with emojis thrown in. And it's usually easy to tell that the joke has been generated by AI.

AI can't write from a point of view. That probably isn't exactly true, but it certainly can't understand your client's point of view as well as you can.

AI is only as good as its input. One of the most interesting developments in the last couple of years has been the invention of a new job: the prompt engineer. The internet is now flooded with advice about how to prompt AI to get better results. Not everyone has the time, energy or knowledge to prompt AI well; hence the appearance of a new specialist.

Time spent prompting the AI tool, of course, is time that could be spent producing copy. Why not spend that time prompting and priming yourself?

Finally, AI reduces diverse thinking. Like many other technologies, AI encourages us to stay in our niche, work in our niche and think in our niche. ChatGPT *might* offer you new ideas that you hadn't thought of, but it's unlikely to help you *think like your reader* or take your thinking into completely new realms. Mental mobility? AI will not supply it.

In conclusion – as ChatGPT would say – AI is helpful, but it's only a tool. It can create copy that's bland, generalized and inaccurate. Which means that you will need to put in the hard graft to bring it to life.

What about ethical considerations?

We might find AI helpful in producing copy. But should we be using it? Before you start, think carefully about these issues.

Biased and inaccurate outputs

ChatGPT was trained on a vast number of sources, some of which contain obvious biases. As a result, the tool sometimes produces output that reflects these biases. Such biases can perpetuate harmful stereotypes. The tool has also been criticized for its tendency to produce inaccurate or false information as though it were factual.

At the moment, we don't know what sources the tool was trained on. Some of those sources might be questionable, morally dubious or plain illegal. Any copy that you enter into an AI tool could be used by others to create fake copy that's damaging, offensive or dangerous.

Violations of privacy

AI might generate personal information or sensitive data that could be used to identify or harm individuals. If you input personal details about yourself or someone else, that information could be used maliciously by another user.

Plagiarism and cheating

AI tools can be used to cheat, intentionally or unintentionally. Copywriters could pass off AI-generated work as original or fabricate data to support a claim.

Copyright infringement

Many of the sources on which ChatGPT is trained are protected by copyright. At present, writers or publishers have no recourse to reimbursement for the unauthorized use of copyright material. OpenAI has stated that users are responsible for the content of outputs; in other words, *you* might be liable for copyright infringements that result from your using AI. It's more or less impossible to know whether you are infringing copyright because ChatGPT doesn't provide information about the sources it was trained on.

Lack of oversight

Some companies – Amazon, Apple and Samsung are among the biggest – have forbidden their employees to use AI to write copy. As a result, AI is increasingly going underground: according to a survey published by Salesforce in late 2023, half of those corporate employees using AI were doing so without approval. Some are using it to protect their reputations or cover up shortcomings in their competence; forums are popping up for people to swap ideas for keeping their AI use secret.

It's your call

As a copywriter, you face two important questions.

- Should you be using AI at all to produce copy and content?

- And if you think you should, how should you use it?

Finally, a declaration of interest. I have not used AI to write any part of this book.

PART SIX

Surviving and thriving

Writing copy is just the beginning. As a professional writer, you must find a way to make a living – or at least make money as part of a portfolio career. In this final section, we look at some of the challenges that you will face and how you can meet them.

- **Chapter 18** itemizes the survival skills that will help you thrive.
- **Chapter 19** gathers together resources that can inspire you and take your career to the next level.

18

Survival skills for copywriters

How will you earn money as a copywriter? There are three basic options.

- You'll have a job with a salary.
- You'll work as a contractor to a business.
- You'll become a freelancer with your own business.

Many copywriters work in hybrid versions of these employment patterns. Regardless of which you choose, you'll need three essential survival skills.

- **Time management:** so that you meet deadlines consistently.
- **Self-organization:** to keep on top of a varied workload.
- **Perseverance:** so that you can keep going, even when you're not inspired.

You've nailed those three? Well done. (It's more than I've done.) Now, read on.

Working with others

Copywriting is a collaborative craft. As well as the creative and technical skills any writer needs, copywriters – perhaps more than any other professional writers – need to be able to work with other people.

Cultivating empathy

Are you a natural empath? A talent for empathy will certainly make you more employable. To paraphrase Andy Maslen, your client can easily hire a proofreader, but it's hard to hire an empathizer. If you can see the brief from your client's point of view and from the customer's point of view – and if you can distinguish clearly between the two – you'll produce better copy *and* grow more productive business relationships.

Empathy also includes cultural sensitivity. You'll need to understand the values of diverse audiences so that your copy promotes brands and organizations that respect everyone.

Working in a team

Are you a team player? Organizations are networks of conversations. Even if you're the only writer working in your company, you'll be working with editors, design specialists, marketing executives, account managers, UX designers and others.

All conversations are two-way affairs. You should be able to express your ideas effectively and you should be able to take feedback. You'll often need to explain and defend your choices, and at times you'll need to give way to others' decisions. You might even have to cultivate conflict management skills.

Pick your battles wisely.

BUILDING A COLLABORATIVE ENVIRONMENT

- Surround yourself with other creatives to inspire and support you.
- Embrace diverse perspectives to create well-rounded content.
- Practise stating your case clearly and respectfully.
- Practise responding to feedback honestly and positively.
- Be honest and supportive in your own feedback.

Networking

Copywriting, like all writing, can be lonely. A strong professional network will give you support, advice and opportunities. You'll find plenty of online networks, some of them of high quality. Look beyond the copywriting silo: connect with marketers and industry professionals. Attend events if you can; engage on social media and chat forums. But don't let networking take over your life.

NETWORKING STRATEGIES

- Ask questions and seek connections.
- Engage with those you resonate with and build genuine relationships.
- Be present and contribute to the creative community.

Working with a brief

Most copywriting assignments begin with a brief. At least, they should do. It's unlikely that you'll have no brief at all. But copywriters often find themselves working with a client or manager who says something like, 'I need you to write some copy for the website. Here's the product information. It's all pretty self-explanatory.'

Do not walk away from this conversation. Ask a few questions and note down the answers. Explain that you'd like to be able to write copy that's as near perfect as possible and you don't want to waste your client's time or money.

- What do you want this copy to do?
- Who's the reader? What do we know about them?
- Where's the benefit?
- What do you want the reader to do after reading the copy?
- Do we have brand guidelines? Can I see them?
- What's the deadline? What's the word count?
- Who will be approving this?

Far better, of course, to agree a proper brief.

When copywriting projects go wrong – and I think they go wrong far, far more frequently than any of us might care to admit – it's usually for one of two reasons. Either the client has provided an inadequate brief or the copywriter has brought inappropriate preconceptions to the project. Both client and copywriter have a responsibility: the client to brief properly, and the copywriter to empathize. Like a good actor, you need to take on the characteristics of your role.

The bottom line: with any brief, you must understand the value proposition, the voice and the target audience.

CREATING A BRIEF

For your next project, agree a brief with your client or manager. Use this template to guide you. The more fully you can fill out each section, the better.

Client:

Date:

Briefed by (name and job title/responsibility):

Project description:

Requirement

What do you think you need? Specify the content and channel. (The copywriter might suggest a different or additional approach, based on the information in this form.)

Purpose

Why do you need this? What are your objectives: short-term, long-term? How will you evaluate or measure success?

Target audience

Describe and quantify. Be as detailed as possible. Use socio-economic classifications if appropriate (ABC1, etc.).

Positioning

Where the brand or product currently sits in the market and where you want it to be. SWOT analysis (Strengths, Weaknesses, Opportunities, Threats).

Benefits

What single benefit will most appeal to your target audience?

Proposition

Summarize that key benefit in a single sentence.

Rationale

Why should your target audience believe you? Evidence, arguments, case studies, examples, stories.

Call to action

What do you want the target audience to do as a result of reading this copy? Specify the action, with all relevant contact details.

Content guidelines

Will the information change often? Do we need to adapt the content for different audiences or media? What other elements will be included: booklets, envelopes, samples, click-throughs…

Brand voice

What sort of voice do you want the copy to have? Do we have brand voice guidelines? Do we want to align this copy to existing content? Examples of existing material would be useful, as well as style guidelines.

Tone

What feelings do you want to stimulate in the reader?

Distribution

How will the target audience see this copy? How will they receive it?

Other activity

Will this copy be accompanied by any other promotional activity?

Background

Please supply any information about the company, the product and the brand which you think the copywriter might find useful.

Context

How does this project fit into your business strategy? What is the immediate competition? Is this project similar to or different from previous projects you have engaged in? How does your target audience feel about this product in relation to competing products?

Content

What do you want the target audience to know? Supply all the information you want to communicate. Information in any form is welcome: draft text, notes, bullet lists, pictures...

If you have any information on keywords for SEO, please supply it.

Attachments

List all documents and objects attached to this brief.

Next action

State the first deliverable, the person responsible and the deadline.

Estimate/budget

Please provide a budget, either specific or estimated. Any estimate given is based on present assumptions of the nature of the item at this stage. These costs may be subject to revision once concepts have been developed or if the brief changes substantially. Agree terms and conditions of working.

Timing

Agree a schedule to show stages and dates for each stage: agree brief, initial concepts, detailed design, draft text, artwork, final revisions, to printer, delivery.

Approval process

Who else will be involved in this project? How? Who will authorize or approve the final copy?

Working with thought leaders

At some point, you might be hired to work with a thought leader. They might be a senior manager or CEO with no time to write. They might be an expert who eats, sleeps and breathes everything about their subject but perhaps lacks the talent to communicate that knowledge coherently.

Your task will be to create content that presents your client's ideas and authority. Your content – an article, an advertorial, a blog post – will be what the thought leader themselves would have written, but better: sharper, more engaging – and *written*, rather than remaining in their head.

You're becoming a ghostwriter.

This new role brings you three new responsibilities.

- First, you'll need to help your client generate ideas rather than mountains of information and data. You might need to challenge them to think in new ways about what they know: to disrupt assumptions and ignite discussion.

- Second, you'll need to shape those ideas into an engaging argument, explanation or narrative.

- Lastly, you'll need to write this content in *their* voice – or rather, in the voice they would use if they had your skills.

Getting buy-in

For this section I am much indebted to my colleague, MaryLou Costa, who has ghostwritten for thought leaders for much of her career.

Your first step will be to bring your client on board with the project you're planning. Getting the necessary face time might itself be a problem. But you should clarify, as soon as you can, your pitch for the piece: its purpose and overall message. Share a brief or an outline, together with suggested talking points, input they could provide and a suggested deadline. Agree the brief and sign it off. Without all agreement, your project could be scuppered at quite a late stage. 'I once spent weeks going back and forth on a thought leadership piece,' says MaryLou, 'only to have it cancelled. He wasn't ready to be as open as the piece required.'

HOW TO BRIEF A THOUGHT LEADER

Your content brief can include the following:

- the topic of the piece and its intended message
- why you have chosen them (flattery never did any harm)
- an outline of the content
- the value proposition and intended impact on its audience
- the insights you need from your client
- specific questions for them
- areas best avoided
- how much of their time you need
- how they can review the copy
- deadlines for review, feedback and final edits
- what insights you would like from that leader – perhaps even specific questions so they can prepare (and anything to steer clear of)
- intended distribution

You – and not your client – will be responsible for ensuring that the content aligns with the organization's strategy, mission and values. Your client may be unaware of recent marketing developments; alternatively, they may have views and ideas that could contribute to new strategies. Your content could articulate those ideas.

Some thought leaders are relaxed about this whole process. Others can be very cautious – you may need to reassure them and pay them the (very real) respect of deferring to their views. Communicate your role as ghostwriter with complete transparency.

Finding their voice

The best way to capture your client's voice is to record a conversation with them. Try to create as relaxed an exchange as possible. Then carefully transcribe a few minutes. It's surprising how quickly you can notice habits and patterns of expression that you can imitate.

Examine the sentence structures that your client is using, and the way they branch their sentences left or right. How do they balance verbs and nouns? How do they use adjectives? What turns of phrase do they prefer? What kinds of words? And, of course, you can always take some of what they say and use it, directly or subtly edited, in your piece.

> *To find out more about sentence construction, go to Chapter 10.*
>
> *To find out more about verbs and nouns, go to Chapter 11.*

Alternatively, find a recording that already exists. They might have given a talk at a conference; I prefer media interviews, which can offer a useful insight into the way someone speaks unscripted in public. Printed articles or interviews are a reasonable third choice.

You're aiming to reproduce the *best possible version* of your client's voice. When they review your copy, they should say, 'I wish I'd said that!'

Notes for freelancers

The freelance life is not for everyone. Freelancing requires you to run a business as well as write great copy. You'll have to handle various administrative tasks, generate leads and manage finances. As you grow, your role may shift from writing to consulting.

Finding work

'Business' here might mean finding clients. It might mean resetting a relationship with an old employer – as a contractor, for instance. One thing's certain: if you're not salaried – or even, actually, if you are – it's worth growing your network. Set up an account on LinkedIn, find the business networks in your sector and get stuck in.

If you're looking for potential clients, start where you are. (Where else can you possibly start?) Every relationship – family, friends, work colleagues, social buddies – can create a link to potential work. Be kind and respectful to everyone you meet. Take time to understand a new lead and their requirements. The more you pay them attention, the better they'll like you. If you haven't met them, send a short video with any proposal, so that the prospect can see and hear you responding to their request. If you get as far as signing a contract, consider using an online facility like DocuSign: it looks professional and it saves a lot of complicated scanning, signing and returning.

Maybe you don't fancy working for one company on a retainer. But don't underestimate the benefit of regular work and a regular income, especially if you're starting out. The arrangement carries the downside of becoming dependent on one client. So, keep scanning for new opportunities.

Many copywriters advocate finding a niche. Become known as the copywriter that works in that niche. It will help you generate more business and it will help you network more efficiently with potential clients. That niche should, of course, fit your own interests and expertise.

Charging for your work

According to a ProCopywriters survey, the UK's largest membership organization for commercial writers, copywriters will usually charge in three ways. Which model you choose will depend on what works for you and your client.

PROJECT PRICING

Project pricing is the most popular option. A simple fee covers every element of the job. Sometimes a client will agree to revise a fee if the work develops unexpectedly. Some copywriters ask for 50 per cent of the fee in advance, especially when dealing with a new client.

Unsurprisingly, project fees vary widely. Key features affecting the fee include the nature of the brief, the amount of planning or idea development involved and the profile of the project for the client's business. The fee can also vary depending on complexity, time spent revising and the amount of liaison required: meetings, auxiliary tasks or collaboration with other project members.

Copywriters can charge more if they can demonstrate experience or specialized skills. They might offer discounts to regular clients or to certain types of client: charities, not-for-profits or start-ups, for example.

It's crucial that you agree in detail precisely what the project fee will cover. A written contract is an absolute necessity.

PRICING BY THE HOUR OR DAY

If you or your client aren't keen on project pricing, pricing by the hour or day is the next best option. The fee you charge will have to reflect a timescale that your client will find credible. And that timescale might be considerably shorter than the actual amount of time you spend on the job.

PRICING BY THE WORD

ProCopywriters discourages charging by the word. This business model, they think, positions copywriting as a commodity rather than a professional service. Clients can use pricing by the word to negotiate unfair fees or to negotiate for 'writing only' – ignoring all the other work a copywriting project might involve. This pricing method is also hard to justify in terms of quality: most work is charged by the final number of words or the number of words delivered – and most copy, of course, improves as words are removed.

Personally, I charge a project fee whenever I can. I base that fee on an hourly rate that reflects my experience and expertise. I estimate the number of hours involved in the project and add about 10 per cent to cover contingencies. The final figure is the project fee.

Looking after yourself

Like anyone else, you have needs. Let's remind ourselves of those three key emotional needs: for competence, for autonomy and for relatedness.

To find out more about emotional needs, go to Chapter 3.

First, you want to feel that your competence is being stretched healthily. Look for opportunities outside your comfort zone but learn to recognize when the thrill of the new becomes stressful. In the early days, you might take on tasks that seems well beyond your competence because you're terrified of turning away work. As your career progresses, you can begin to say 'no' to work that lies outside your comfort zone.

Second, you want to feel autonomy: in control of your work and your life. Charge what you feel you're worth. Keep planting seeds for new projects. Work hard. But not too hard – there really is more to life than writing copy and your copy will benefit from a rich, enjoyable life.

And don't ignore your need for connectedness. Join professional networks. Get out of the house. Finding a co-working space might be good for your wellbeing and for the quality of your work. If you can't afford to pay for one, use your local library. Or a local café. Whatever works for you.

What's your attitude?

In Chapter 1, we looked at the core skills of creative writing. We explored the first-stage skills of curiosity and mental mobility and the second-stage skills of design thinking and objectivity. Surrounding those skills, and affecting our competence in all of them, are two others.

Inner motivation

What motivates you to do well? Some copywriters respond to tight deadlines or specific word counts; others find joy in a well-focused brief. You might enjoy the stability of employment; you might crave the dynamic environment of an agency; you might demand the autonomy of being your own boss.

WHAT MOTIVATES YOU?

Spend a few moments reflecting on what drives you as a copywriter.

- Is it the money?
- The recognition?
- Collaborating with other creative people?
- The joy of manipulating words?
- The satisfaction of seeing a piece of work come together?

What makes you feel happy when you're working? Why do some parts of your work make you feel happy and others don't?

If you're working on a piece of copy right now, ask the same questions about your reader.

- What would make *them* feel happy?
- What could *they* do to make themselves feel happier?
- How can your copy help to increase *their* stock of happiness?

How does thinking about your reader's motivation affect your own motivation?

Copywriters, like other creatives, tend to be deeply self-motivated. The technical term is 'autotelic'. We do an autotelic task for its own sake; external motivators – promotion, pay rises, industry awards – matter less than the work itself. Nothing beats the buzz. We seem to crave this mental high like a drug. Without it, our work turns to dust and ashes.

We might talk about being 'in the zone' or being 'totally immersed' in a project. The psychologist Mihály Csíkszentmihályi called it 'the flow state'. Csíkszentmihályi (pronounce his surname 'chicks send me high-ee') noticed that the flow state had three consistent features.

- We tend to ignore how others are observing us.
- We tend to live entirely in the present moment and ignore the passage of time.
- And we feel in control of the situation, even as it alters.

He also discovered that the flow state seemed to require an activity that stretches our capacities: a task that involved discovery or novelty. If the task was difficult or risky, all the better. Above all, the flow state appears when we *choose* to do the task.

Not every project will create the flow state. But you can find ways to create it for yourself.

FINDING THE FLOW STATE

- Care about the task at hand.
- Ensure the task is neither too easy nor too difficult.
- Choose tasks you're good at.
- Focus on the journey, not just the destination.
- Eliminate interruptions.

Managing risk

What's your attitude to risk? If you enjoy taking risks, you might have a 'Type T' personality ('T' for 'thrill'), putting you in the same category as hang gliders, mountain climbers and round-the-world balloonists, not to mention gamblers, daredevils and criminals.

Now, clearly, you should do – or write – nothing reckless or illegal. But you'll probably find yourself, on occasions, bridling at the risk-averse expectations of your client or colleagues, and wanting to try something more – well, off the wall. But think of the consequences. If your gamble succeeds, you'll be celebrated; if it fails, you might be out of a job. Then again, the danger of playing safe can often be greater than the risk of trying something new.

How could you manage the risk? You could run a pilot campaign, or A/B test different versions of a marketing email. You could manage your client's expectations by warning them that they might find your idea crazy; you might present the wild idea as one option among others.

Seasoned risk-takers embrace failure as part of the process. They cultivate an optimism bias: the belief that they're more likely to succeed than fail. Then, when they *do* fail, they're surprised: they say, 'Well, that wasn't supposed to happen', rather than 'That was bound to happen'. With the optimism bias in place, you'll learn from your mistakes and do better next time.

Being resilient

Resilience is possibly the most important survival skill of all. Embrace feedback. The scariest thing about creative work is being told that it's no good. And it can happen. Feedback is all part of the process. Be absolutely clear what you want from that feedback and demand it – especially if it's negative. Feedback gives you an opportunity to learn: about your own work and about your clients' expectations. Use it.

Stay informed. The more you know about industry trends, the more you'll be able to anticipate changes and adapt. Read industry blogs; join relevant forums; attend webinars. By keeping your finger on the pulse, you can pivot your approach whenever you need to.

Diversify your skills. Learn new writing styles; explore different niches; master one or two related skills like SEO or content strategy. You'll be shielding yourself from market fluctuations and opening up new opportunities.

Manage stress. Develop a routine that includes regular breaks, exercise and hobbies that take your mind off work. Mindfulness or meditation practices can also help you stay calm and focused. Some creative work benefits from moderate stress (the boffins call this 'eustress'); too much stress (which those same boffins label – guess what? – 'distress') is paralysing. Learn when eustress becomes distress for you – the borderline sits in different places for everyone.

Take time out to reflect. Assess what strategies have worked for you and which haven't. Self-awareness leads to continuous improvement.

STRATEGIES FOR BUILDING RESILIENCE

- Embrace change as an opportunity for growth.

- Stay informed about industry trends.

- Diversify your skills to shield against market fluctuations.

- Manage stress through regular breaks, exercise and hobbies.

- Reflect on your experiences to continuously improve.

Thriving as a copywriter requires a rare combination of skills. There are the core skills of the writer: curiosity, mental mobility, design thinking and objectivity. There are the skills of working productively in a team: empathy, collaboration, networking. You will need to adapt to the needs of different briefs and, sometimes, to ghostwrite for thought leaders. Above all, you'll need to be self-motivated – especially if you are a freelance – and you'll need to be able to manage risk.

No wonder copywriting requires a healthy dose of resilience.

Mastering all of these skills is truly a lifetime's challenge. But that's what makes copywriting such a rewarding craft. You are putting your creativity to work in a host of different ways; the opportunities to learn are almost endless.

It's a great way to earn a living.

SUMMARY

You can make money as a copywriter in three ways:

- You'll have a job with a salary.

- You'll work as a contractor to a business.

- You'll become a freelancer with your own business.

Some people combine these sources of income.
    Three essential survival skills are:

- **Time management:** so that you meet deadlines consistently.

- **Self-organization:** to keep on top of a varied workload.

- **Perseverance:** so that you can keep going, even when you're not inspired.

Copywriting is a collaborative craft. Cultivate your team-playing skills. You should be able to express your ideas effectively and you should be able to take feedback. You might even have to cultivate conflict management skills.

A talent for empathy will certainly make you more employable. Empathy also includes cultural sensitivity.

A strong professional network will give you support, advice and opportunities.

Try to start every job with a clear brief. At the very least, clarify the value proposition, the voice and the target audience. A detailed written brief, dated and counter-signed, is highly desirable.

When working with a thought leader, you become a ghostwriter. Your task is to create content that presents your client's ideas and authority and to write in *their* voice – as the best possible version of them.

Get buy-in. Agree parameters. Find their voice and use it.

Freelancing requires you to run a business as well as writing great copy.

Getting business might mean finding clients or becoming a contractor for an existing employer.

Grow your network.

To find potential clients, start where you are, with existing relationships. Cultivate potential clients and make a great impression by responding to their needs.

Working on a retainer offers regular work and a regular income, but don't become dependent on that one relationship. Scan for new opportunities.

Find a niche and become known as a prime player in that niche.

There are three ways of charging for your services:

- project pricing
- pricing by the hour or day
- pricing by the word

Project pricing is usually the best option.

Look after yourself:

- Stretch your competence.
- Stay in control of your life.
- Foster relationships.

Explore your attitude to 'flow'. Not every project will create the flow state. But you can find ways to create it for yourself.

Embrace risk and find ways to manage it. Cultivate an optimism bias.
Develop resilience.
Embrace feedback as an opportunity to learn:

- Stay informed.
- Diversify your skills.
- Manage stress.
- Take time out to reflect.

19

The copywriter's toolkit: Resources to support you

Throughout this book, I've been inspired by the work of other writers, thinkers and marketing professionals. You can take inspiration from them, too.

Chapter 1: Being a writer

On writing, a great place to start is *Creative Writing: A workbook with readings*, edited by Linda Anderson (Open University and Routledge, Abingdon, 2006). I took a lot of ideas from Ann Handley's book *Everybody Writes* (Wiley, Hoboken, NJ, 2014), and Beth Kempton's *The Way of the Fearless Writer* (Piatkus, London, 2022). Julia Cameron introduces Morning Pages in *The Artist's Way* (Pan Books, London, 1995). Louise Willder's *Blurb Your Enthusiasm* (Oneworld, London, 2022) offers entertaining insights about copywriting from a publisher's perspective.

The two stages of thinking and the concept of force-fitting are based on the work of Edward de Bono. Look at *Lateral Thinking in Management* (Penguin, London, 1982). The six competences of creativity – four in this chapter, together with inner motivation and risk-taking, discussed in Chapter 18 – are drawn from the snowflake model of creativity developed by David N Perkins.

On writing haiku, see Bruce Ross's *Writing Haiku* (Tuttle, Tokyo, 2022).

For a great selection of copywriting exercises, look no further than Wendy Ann Jones's *The Copywriter's Workout* (Wendy Ann Jones, Amazon, 2023).

Chapter 2: How copy works

David Abbott, Bob Levenson and many other brilliant copywriters discuss their craft in *The Copy Book* (Taschen, Cologne, 2021).

For more about the neuroscience of reading, see Yellowlees Douglas, *The Reader's Brain* (Cambridge University Press, Cambridge UK, 2015) and Maryanne Wolf's *Proust and the Squid* (Icon Books, Thriplow, Cambridge UK, 2008).

John Caples talks about headlines and much more in *Tested Advertising Methods* (5th edition, edited by Fred E Hahn, Prentice Hall, Paramus, NJ, 1997).

George Loewenstein's paper 'The Psychology of Curiosity' is available at www.contrib.andrew.cmu.edu/~gl20/GeorgeLoewenstein/Papers_files/pdf/PsychofCuriosity.pdf

Seth Godin's *Permission Marketing* (Pocket Books, New York, 2007) introduces this important concept.

Chapter 3: Profiling your reader

I've based my reader persona profiling tool on *Value Proposition Design* (Wiley, Hoboken, NJ) by Alexander Osterwalder and others.

Human Givens (HG Publishing, Chalvington, 2024), by Joe Griffin and Ivan Tyrell, includes an analysis of needs and resources. Their Emotional Needs Audit is a useful diagnostic questionnaire: www.hgi.org.uk/resources/emotional-needs-audit-ena

Andy Maslen explores the relationship with the reader in *Persuasive Copywriting* (Kogan Page, London, 2019).

Chapter 4: Finding your argument

Rosser Reeves discusses USPs in *Reality in Advertising* (Widener Classics, Cambridge Mass., 2015).

Lanning and Michaels' paper 'A business is a value delivery system' is available at www.dpvgroup.com/wp-content/uploads/2009/11/1988-A-Business-is-a-VDS-McK-Staff-Ppr.pdf

Chapter 5: Finding your voice

Joe Moran's book *First You Write a Sentence* (Penguin, London, 2018) has been a source of constant inspiration.

Edward de Bono develops his ideas on lateral thinking in *Lateral Thinking* (Penguin, London, 2016).

Nick Parker's Substack, *Tone Knob*, takes – in his own words – 'a nerd's-eye view of brands doing interesting things with their language and tone of voice'. Nick is worth following. https://toneofvoice.substack.com/

Chapter 6: Writing headlines and subject lines

David Ogilvy's most popular book is probably *Ogilvy on Advertising* (Welbeck Publishing, London, 2007). Ogilvy appears in a film, *The View from Touffou*, available on YouTube: www.youtube.com/watch?v=FcTB9goxSAg

Conductor's survey into headlines is discussed here: https://moz.com/blog/5-data-insights-into-the-headlines-readers-click

Interlude 2: Aristotle and the Three Musketeers

Aristotle talks about the three modes of appeal in *The Art of Rhetoric* (Penguin, London, 1991).

Chapter 7: Structures for browsing

Randy Olson talks with Tom Hollihan about the arouse and fulfil principle in a 2022 video: www.youtube.com/watch?v=4bZk51VHdhg

Steve Harrison tells the story of AIDCA in *How to Write Better Copy* (Bluebird Books, London, 2016).

Chapter 8: Storytelling and the uses of narrative

Walter Benjamin's essay 'The work of art in the age of mechanical reproduction' is available here: https://web.mit.edu/allanmc/www/benjamin.pdf

You can view the original Mini Adventure ad here: https://miniyregister.co.uk/blog/Press/yminiadventureadvert/

Donald Miller talks about case studies in *Building a StoryBrand* (HarperCollins Leadership, Nashville, 2017).

Randy Olson discusses *And, But, Therefore* in *Houston, We Have a Narrative* (University of Chicago Press, Chicago, 2015). He also appears on a Scicomm Academy lecture, 'Why science needs story': www.youtube.com/watch?v=2RDZiRMjM0U

Chapter 9: Building pyramids: Structures for searching

My image of a pyramid is based on Barbara Minto's pioneering book *The Pyramid Principle* (Pearson Education, Harlow, 2021). If you write B2B copy or technical copy, Minto's book is valuable.

Joseph M Williams explores the old-to-new sequencing technique in *Style: Lessons in clarity and grace* (Pearson, 2006). His book has been through many editions and is well worth seeking out.

Yellowlees Douglas discusses schemas in *The Reader's Brain* (Cambridge University Press, Cambridge UK, 2015).

Interlude 3: Six patterns of influence

Robert Cialdini explores the six patterns of influence in *Influence: The psychology of persuasion* (Harper Business, New York, 2021).

Chapter 10: Sentences: Putting your words in order

Gary Provost offers *100 Ways to Improve Your Writing* (Berkley, New York, 2019).

Joseph M Williams explores the 'characters in a story' technique in *Style* (mentioned under Chapter 9). Williams worked at the University of Chicago, which has an honourable tradition of studying and teaching the principles of good writing. One of the most recent teachers there is the brilliant Larry McEnerney. View him at work here: www.youtube.com/watch?v=3_lTELjWqdY

Then move on to these two, longer videos:

www.youtube.com/watch?v=vtIzMaLkCaM www.youtube.com/watch?v=aFwVf5a3pZM

On grammar, I've found David Crystal's books helpful: a good starting point is *Making Sense: The glamorous story of English grammar* (Profile Books, London, 2017). Roy Peter Clark's *Writing Tools: 50 essential strategies for every writer* (Little Brown and Company, New York, 2008) is packed with practical ideas.

Left- and right-branching sentences are discussed in Peter Elbow's *Vernacular Eloquence: What speech can bring to writing* (Oxford University Press, New York, 2012). The subtitle indicates that Elbow has much to teach copywriters.

The internet carries vast numbers of resources to help you develop your skills in grammar. Among the best is The OWL at Purdue: https://owl.purdue.edu/

For a list of transitional devices, go to: https://owl.purdue.edu/owl/general_writing/mechanics/transitions_and_transitional_devices/transitional_devices.html

Chapter 11: Doing and being: How verbs and nouns live together

Sam Hayakawa describes the Ladder of Abstraction in *Language in Thought and Action* (5th edition, Harvest Original, New York, 1991).

Interlude 4: A pocket guide to punctuation

David Crystal's *Making a Point: The Pernickety Story of English Punctuation* (Profile Books, London, 2016) is an entertaining guide.

Chapter 12: Creating a content strategy

AnswerThePublic is available in a free version. Paid upgrades are also available: https://answerthepublic.com/

HubSpot is an essential source of up-to-date information and ideas: www.hubspot.com

Nielsen Norman are world leaders in UX research: www.nngroup.com/

Susan Fournier and Lara Lee's article about Harley-Davidson is in the *Harvard Business Review*: https://hbr.org/2009/04/getting-brand-communities-right

Chapter 13: Writing website copy

Andy Maslen provides lots of practical advice in his *Copywriting Sourcebook* (Marshall Cavendish, London, 2010).

Google lays out its guidelines for quality raters here: https://developers.google.com/search/blog/2022/12/google-raters-guidelines-e-e-a-t

Chapter 14: Email marketing

Justin Kruger's research on email is documented in a paper in the *Journal of Personality and Social Psychology*: https://psycnet.apa.org/record/2005-16185-007

Kristin Byron's research on email is documented in 'Carrying too heavy a load? The communication and miscommunication of emotion by email', published in the *Academy of Management Review*: https://journals.aom.org/doi/10.5465/amr.2008.31193163

Chapter 15: Producing an email newsletter

Kim Arnold runs a great email newsletter. It's worth subscribing. www.kimarnold.co.uk

Chapter 17: Writing articles and blog posts

Alan Monroe explains his Motivated Sequence in *Monroe's Principles of Speech* (Forgotten Books, London, 2019).

Interlude 5: What about AI? As I was completing work on this book, the excellent Tom Albrighton published *AI Can't Write, But You Can.* It's probably the best review of this controversy at the end of 2024.

Chapter 18: Survival skills for copywriters

Mihály Csíkszentmihályi's book, *Flow: The psychology of happiness* (Rider, London, 2002), is a classic.

Eddy Shleyner runs a good resource called Very Good Copy: www.verygoodcopy.com/

The internet is full of support groups for copywriters. One of the best is ProCopywriters: www.procopywriters.co.uk

INDEX

Looking for another book?

Explore our award-winning
books from global business
experts in Skills and Careers

Scan the code to browse

www.koganpage.com/sce

Enhance your PR skills and knowledge

with our range of PR and communications books. Perfect for readers seeking to grasp effective communication and PR strategies in today's media-driven society.

From 4 December 2025 the EU Responsible Person (GPSR) is:
eucomply oÜ, Pärnu mnt. 139b – 14, 11317 Tallinn, Estonia
www.eucompliancepartner.com

www.ingramcontent.com/pod-product-compliance
Lightning Source LLC
Chambersburg PA
CBHW071541210326
41597CB00019B/3080

9 781398 613539